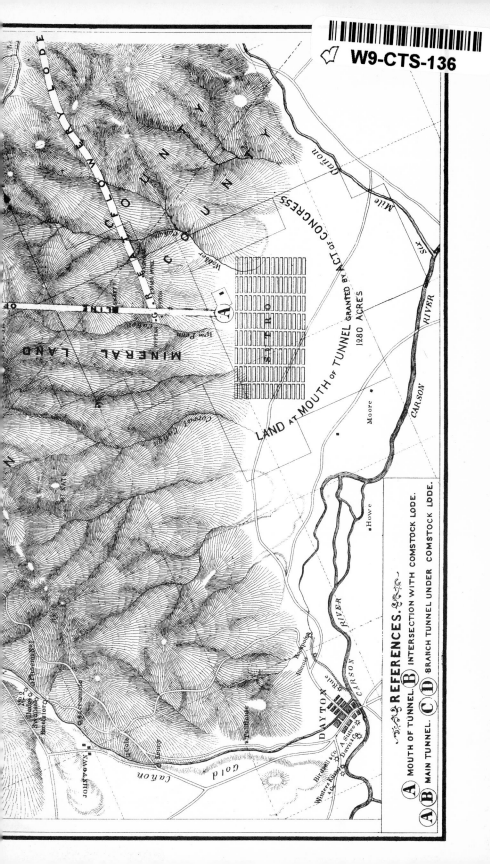

Adolph

SUTRO

A Biography

Adolph Sutro used this illustration of "the honest miner"
to decorate all the volumes he wrote on behalf of his tunnel.
It also appeared as part of the design for his bookplate.

Adolph

SUTRO

A Biography

by **ROBERT E. STEWART, Jr.**
and **MARY FRANCES STEWART**

Berkeley Howell-North *California*

1962

ADOLPH SUTRO, A Biography

Printed and bound in the United States of America.
Library of Congress Catalogue Card No. 62-16167

Published by Howell-North Books
1050 Parker Street, Berkeley 10, California

In memory of

Iola Doncyson Hudnall

THE LIFE of Adolph Sutro began in 1830 in the historic city of Aix-la-Chapelle, it influenced the development of the western United States, and in many ways it encompassed the world. Into Nevada Sutro brought the interest of the United States Congress and President U. S. Grant, and to the city of San Francisco he brought a multiplicity of benefactions, including a magnificent collection of books from all over the world. His four-mile tunnel to drain the mines of the Comstock Lode was not only an engineering feat, but the odds against which he labored seemed insurmountable. That he fought the organized opposition of the mineowners and banking interests is well known, but his great concern for his workingmen is seldom mentioned. Those things which are today called "fringe benefits" were, to Adolph Sutro, simply the decent, honest rights of his employees. He not only offered them such benefits but demanded that they accept.

Adolph Sutro has been mentioned, sometimes at length, in other books, but no single book has treated his whole life. No account so far has been able to explain how a man with so little formal education could become an engineer, construction superintendent, and financial wizard. This book has been written partly to fill a gap in Western biography and partly to satisfy our own curiosity. We started out to try and answer our own question: "How could he do it?" After nearly ten years we think that we have found some of the answers.

Sutro himself prepared the foundation for this biography and other books about him. He saved so many papers we sometimes wonder if he ever owned a waste basket. It would have grieved him to find that long after his death most of his papers had to be sold at public auction, but looking a little farther into the future he could have seen that the libraries and historical societies were well aware of the worth of his papers. They are still assiduously collecting them. As can be seen by reading our acknowledgments, the papers are scattered enough to make finding them all a treasure hunt, yet sufficiently localized in the states of California and Nevada that the task is far from insurmountable.

Adolph Sutro came to the West in search of riches. He was on the spot for two gold rushes and the great silver rush to western Nevada, yet he was never really a miner, never the owner of a fabulous mine, and only briefly the owner of a stamping mill. He found the riches he sought by utilizing his brilliant mind, by influencing others, and by investing in the future of San Francisco. He also sought to share his books and other collections, his ideas, and his concern for people. We have all been enriched by him.

Robert E. Stewart, Jr.
Mary Frances Stewart

Sacramento,
California
March, 1962

I F WE LISTED all of the people who have helped us gather the material for this book, the acknowledgments would require as many pages as the text. We have lived and loved this work for ten years, and nearly everyone who has come within hearing of our voices has been told about it. There have been countless chance acquaintances who have said, "As a kid I swam at Sutro Baths," or, "As a young man I worked in the Comstock mines," only to meet a torrent of questions as a result. We hope that we thanked them then; we wish to do so now.

In the state of Nevada we have been cordially received and aided by many people. Mrs. Clara Beatty, Director of the Nevada Historical Society, has not only welcomed us to the society's excellent library and museum, but she and her staff have answered many questions by correspondence. Mrs. Beatty also discussed our findings on the town of Sutro with her friend, Mrs. Clara R. Masterson, the former Clara Rammelkamp. Mrs. Emma Nevada Loftus of Dayton, Nevada, has been continuously acquainted with the town of Sutro since the early 1890's, and she has shared her memories and scrapbooks with us. Her son, Chester Barton, has also been very helpful. Mr. Peri, tunnel caretaker and for thirty years a resident of Sutro, has always made our camp-outs there enjoyable. In Virginia City we have been delighted to watch the restoration and care given by Mr. Abe Kendall to many of the things we first saw rotting away at Sutro. We are also grateful for the many courtesies extended by Dr. Effie Mona Mack of Reno and by Mr. Oliver F. Pratt, Clerk of the United States District Court, Carson City. We also appreciate the assistance of the Nevada State Library, the Nevada

State Museum, the Nevada State Park Commission, and the University of Nevada Library.

In Sacramento the California State Library has been especially helpful. Mr. Allan Ottley and his staff of the California Section have, through all these years, given us time, space, and aid. We have used not only their unique items relating to Sutro, but books and newspapers from 1850 to recent years. Also at the State Library we have come to know and appreciate the work of Mr. Arthur Desmangles of the Photo Services Section. He is not only a photographer of remarkable skill, but an artist who understands the historian's problems. He has taken the most weathered photographs and old maps and recaptured their beauty.

Who could write about California and not pay homage to the Bancroft Library? Both of us were once students at the University of California, Berkeley, and though only one is a trained historian, we have been equally welcome in "the Bancroft," whose treasures have been shared with us times without number. Hubert Howe Bancroft was puzzled by Sutro, and his own notes, plus those of his scribes, have been placed before us, not in copies but in their original form. The same has been true of all of their considerable and growing collection of Sutro materials. For this we are deeply grateful.

The collection of Sutro materials at the California Historical Society in San Francisco is large and is constantly growing. Both Mr. Donald C. Biggs, Director, who has himself written on Adolph Sutro, and Mr. James de T. Abajian, Librarian, have made the research we have done there most worthwhile. We especially appreciate Mr. Abajian's courtesy in notifying us each time new Sutro items have been acquired.

The Society of California Pioneers and its Director, Dr. Elliot Evans, have shared generously their maps, photographs, and library. Through their exhibits we believe that we have gained a better understanding of California during Sutro's era.

The Stanford University Library, the Huntington Library, and the Sutro Branch of the California State Library have all aided us. Mr. Richard H. Dillon, Librarian of the Sutro Library, and Father William J. Monihan, Librarian of the Gleeson Library, University of San Francisco, have both made us welcome and helped us to understand Sutro as a person and as a collector of books. We have also been made welcome at the Sacramento City College Library, the Sacramento City Library, the Sacramento State College Library, the St. Thomas Aquinas Library of Sacramento, and the Oakland Public Library.

Two valuable collections of Sutro materials were acquired too recently to be cited in the chapter notes. The Huntington Library has acquired over 3,000 manuscripts including many personal letters. The University of San Francisco now possesses a large collection of materials relative to the Sutro Baths including numerous photographs.

Our close friends, Hal and Lillian Altman, research historians, Union of American Hebrew Congregations, Western Region, have not only shared their great store of knowledge of the times about which we have written, but have encouraged us when we needed it most. Dr. Jacob Marcus, Director of the American Jewish Archives, Cincinnati, Ohio, has given us aid and direction in locating information about various congregations. Cantor Robert Harmon has contributed to our understanding of the history of the Sutro family.

The Sutro papers were sold at public auction, so we have been dependent on many booksellers. Some could remember to whom they sold materials, and they helped us locate the present owners. We wish especially to mention George Fields, David Magee, Warren Howell, and Glen Dawson. Our first Sutro autograph was obtained through Harold C. Holmes.

We have met some people who knew Adolph Sutro. Mr. Carlo S. Morbio is the son of the lovely Rosa Victoria Sutro Morbio, and hence a grandson of Adolph Sutro. Mr. Morbio has freely recounted boyhood memories of visits to his grandfather at Sutro Heights and shown us the magnificent volumes which his grandfather gave to him. We visited Miss Lilly McNulty at her home near the site of the Sutro property in Napa county and she generously told us her memories of Sutro and stories she heard him tell.

Oscar Lewis purchased a large box of letters, folders, and ephemera at some time after the Sutro auction. When we asked for permission to see the papers, Mr. Lewis not only invited us to his home in San Francisco to discuss Sutro but he generously gave us the whole lot. Mr. John H. Thies of Oakland kindly loaned us papers which he purchased at the auction. They included significant correspondence relative to Sutro's sale of tunnel stock and the printed auction catalog in which Mr. Thies noted the price for which each item was sold. Mr. Dudley Gordon of Los Angeles gave us access to all of his papers, many of which are now at the California Historical Society. Mrs. William Cavalier of Piedmont, California, opened her treasure chest of Sutro business papers and her son, William Cavalier, Jr., his collection of autographs. Dr. W. Turrentine Jackson of Davis, California, courteously loaned us the microfilms of the Price Papers, which he and Mrs. Jackson made in England.

We should also like to thank those who have given us permission to use photographs. Each illustration is acknowledged individually, but we should like to mention that in addition to the societies, libraries, and museums already mentioned we have obtained photographs from Father John B. McGloin, S. J., Archivist of the University of San Francisco; Roy D. Graves of San Francisco; James M. Stephens of Sacramento; and the late V. Covert Martin of Stockton.

We have also received assistance from the city government of Aachen, including Dr. Velz. We have benefited from the aid of Violet Ewart of Limpsfield, Surrey; Bernice Frankenheimer of Stockton, California; and numerous others. We are obliged to omit some names because of space and others, we fear, from error. All of our personal friends have been called upon for elucidation, specific knowledge, or inspiration. We should like especially to mention Albert J. Adams, Agnes Finch Lane, Peter W. Knoles, Dr. Herbert Copeland, Linda Harker Crane, Earl Bartell, and H. John Blossom.

We wish to thank Mr. and Mrs. Morgan North of Howell-North Books for numerous suggestions which have improved and strengthened the narrative and for aid in the search for suitable illustrations.

Professor Lawrence Kinnaird of the University of California, Berkeley, supervised the research done for the dissertation and after its completion he advised and helped both of us. Like thousands of other students we pay homage to him as a friend, guiding spirit, and true leader in learning.

Last, but far from least, we have sought to recognize a friend who through a long and painful illness read the manuscript, offered suggestions, revised, rebuked, and rekindled our enthusiasm for this work. In dedicating this book to her we acknowledge a great debt.

THE AUTHORS

~~~~~~~~~~ TABLE OF CONTENTS ~~~~~~~~~~

Preface vii

Acknowledgements ix

Illustrations xvii

Chapter I   Ho for Washoe! 1

Chapter II   From Prussia to California 9

Chapter III   First Year in the New World 20

Chapter IV   The Tobacconist-Engineer 30

Chapter V   The High Road to Success 41

Chapter VI   "But Now Commenced the Tug of War" 59

Chapter VII   Rally at Piper's Opera House 70

Chapter VIII   The "First Pick" 81

Chapter IX   Congress Creates a Tunnel Commission 89

Chapter X   He *Was* the Company 103

Chapter XI   Superintendent In Absentia 116

Chapter XII   The General Superintendent
Keeps Informed 130

Chapter XIII   The Great Work is Finished 145

Chapter XIV   Exit the General Superintendent . . . 161

Chapter XV   A Man in Search of a Cause 170

Chapter XVI   A Tunnel to the Sea 180

Chapter XVII   Labor Conquers All 202

Notes 215

Bibliography 229

Index 235

Group I, the early days . . . . facing page 46

San Francisco in 1860
Long Wharf, San Francisco
Virginia City in 1859
Wood on the Carson River
Virginia City in 1864
Miners descending a shaft
Miners and ice water barrel
Water being discharged from a mine
The Gould and Curry Works, 1862
Miners coming off shift
Vertical section of the
    Comstock Lode

Cross-sections of the Sutro Tunnel
Gold Hill Miners Union Hall
Placard announcing Sutro's speech
A group of Yellow Jacket miners
Virginia City and Maguire's
    Opera House
Father Patrick Manogue
Shaft No. 2 of the Sutro Tunnel
Portal of tunnel and theodolite
Underground scene in Sutro Tunnel
Court house at Dayton, Nevada
V&T train on a trestle

Group II, the town of Sutro, Nevada . . . . facing page 78

Plan of the town of Sutro
Enlarged view of the plan of the
    town
Photograph of the town of Sutro
Leah Harris Sutro
Adolph Sutro swinging a pick
Adolph Sutro and party in a mine
Tunnel entrance circa 1880
Tunnel facade erected 1888
Stock certificate of the
    Sutro Tunnel Co.

Office of the Sutro Tunnel Co.
Virginia City in 1878
General Grant and party, 1879
The Sutro mansion, two views
Mrs. Allen
C Street, Virginia City
Methods of lowering ore
Shaft No. 4 of the Sutro Tunnel
Hoisting works of the Savage Mine
Melting bullion on the Comstock

Group III, Sutro returns to San Francisco . . facing page 174

Inside property
Outside property
Sand dunes, San Francisco
San Francisco map showing
    Sutro Heights
Telegraph Hill Cable Railroad

First Cliff House
Second Cliff House
Seal Rocks
Entrance to Sutro Heights
Plan of Sutro Heights
Sutro Heights — the Main Drive

Group III *continued*

Sutro Heights — the Conservatory
Floral tapestry, Sutro Heights
The parapet, Sutro Heights
Interior view of Sutro's home
Exterior view of Sutro's home

Statuary on the rocks
Sutro on the rocks
"Arcadia"
Employees at Sutro Heights

Group IV, Sutro in active retirement . . . . facing page 190

Sutro in London as a book collector
Sutro Baths nearing completion
Interior of Sutro Baths
Aerial view of Sutro Baths
The scenic route, showing the
  Golden Gate
Sutro Railroad electric car

Ferries and Cliff House Railroad,
  1905
Third Cliff House, built by Sutro
Triumph of Light
Adolph Sutro, a portrait
Book plate of the Sutro Library
Sutro in his home library

CHAPTER I

HO FOR WASHOE!

A T THREE O'CLOCK in the morning on March 20, 1860, a husky man of impressive mien climbed into a stage-coach in Placerville, California, bound for Virginia City, Utah Territory. He was five feet, ten inches tall, weighed 225 pounds and was nearing his thirtieth birthday. The side whiskers which he wore of necessity and his luxurious head of hair were a crisp, coal black. His eyes were opalescent and his face had a faint Semitic overlay. This was Adolph Sutro.

Agile of body, he was ready to follow the driver's com-mands, shifting weight as directed and getting out to walk when necessary. Such inconveniences were cheerfully met for, in the slang of the day, he was on his way "to see the elephant." But a fifty-mile ride of fifteen hours was a long stretch for a city man, and he later wrote that he arrived at Strawberry "almost worn out."

For the next part of the journey the Pioneer Stage Com-pany provided mules and it took ten hours for the travelers to cover the twenty-three miles to Woodford's. Eventually Sutro reached Carson City and then continued to the little mining camp of Virginia City. To the west he saw Sun Mountain, which contained gold and silver ores of great promise.

Adolph Sutro was not a miner. He was a tobacco mer-chant with three retail stores in downtown San Francisco, two of them on Montgomery Street. He was also a whole-sale supplier to stores in mining towns as far north as Marys-ville. This was the second time he had left his wife and children in San Francisco to go and look for gold, but he did not hanker to don the red shirt of a miner and wade into icy water with a gold pan or take a pick and work underground. Gold he wanted, but in the form of minted coins, not dust and nuggets.

The *Alta*, the *Evening Bulletin,* and the *Herald* had been printing gloomy news on page 3 about Washoe. Reason is hardly a part of a man's thinking when his brain is stirred by gold, but his earlier sad experience in seeking a fortune — the Fraser River fiasco — had been disconcerting to both Adolph and the San Francisco newspaper editors. Better look before you leap, cautioned the *Daily Alta California.* The editor added that if you must leave our state, the Rogue River in Oregon was more worthy of a rush than was that "Washoe Country" just east of California. Why search for uncertainties when the mines of California were doing so well? Adolph decided he would at least take a look at the prospects over in Utah Territory, but he would not go encumbered with preconceived ideas. He would do as the editor suggested and look before he leaped.

When the road over the Sierra was sufficiently free of snow to allow coaches to make part of the trip, it took about five days from San Francisco to Virginia City. For a man of Sutro's vigor and temperament it could be delightful. The route to Washoe was fairly well defined, consisting of a boat ride from San Francisco to Sacramento, a rail trip to Folsom, and then stage company service across the mountains.

The river was full of boats but the most popular were the *New World* and the *Antelope* of the People's Line, handsome little side-wheelers of over 500 tons burthen. The steamers left at 4 p.m. and the trip took at least seven hours and thirty-five minutes. While the captain looked after social and administrative details with an elegance befitting the appointments of his steamer, the pilot (who was more highly paid than the master) steered with neither charts nor records of soundings to help him. The engineer had to be a combina-

[2]

tion ballet dancer and laboratory technician to start, stop, and reverse the massive crank which transferred the power of a single cylinder to the paddle wheels. While the ship burned about a cord of wood per hour the passengers sat down to a meal which took several hours to eat. This dinner, which cost a dollar, usually included fish, fresh game, oysters, roasts, fine vegetables, and rich desserts. A man of Sutro's inclinations could eat such a dinner with gusto.

After reaching Sacramento there was a twenty-two mile ride to Folsom on "the cars," or Sacramento Valley Railroad. This was California's first steam railroad, having begun service in 1856. The flat-roofed coaches were forty feet long and although the seats were uncushioned and the windows tiny, the huge brass candle lamps were ornate and the wood-burning engines a delight to the eye.

Luxury travel ended at Folsom, where a seat in a stage-coach would have to be purchased. Only a distinguished personage such as a senator or judge could hope to ride beside the driver, but with luck the traveler might secure one of the eight "comfortable" seats inside. The coach accommodated nine in its interior, and about a dozen could sprawl on the top, but the least comfortable of all was the hapless "space creature" who had to sit on the jump seat in the very middle of the inside. He had nothing to hang on to but a strap suspended from the roof.

The Concord coach was a magnificent vehicle weighing at least a ton. It derived its name from its place of man-ufacture — Concord, New Hampshire, where the Abbott-Downing Company had developed the finest stagecoach available. When one of their coaches was driven at the speed of a well organized royal procession over a good road the carriage would sway majestically, cradled on twin leather thorough braces.

These two heavy leather straps slung between the front and rear axles were not designed, however, with the idea of royal comfort. Although these wonderful stagecoaches were pulled by handsome horses and often driven by men who were geniuses in their line, the passengers were also a vital force in the successful completion of a run. The coach was so engineered that if a front wheel struck a big stone, the weight of the body and passengers combined would add the extra thrust necessary to propel the vehicle over the obstruction.

Sutro knew that all winter long men had been walking over the Sierra in order to get to Washoe. Placer miners had been scraping the surface of Sun Mountain for gold with modest success for years, but that was not what attracted these eager newcomers. They were interested in the heavy bluish sand which had formerly been roundly cursed by miners because it interfered with their every effort to free the gold. In June, 1859, a curious visitor sent some of this refuse to Grass Valley, California, for assay. The value per ton figured out at $3,000 in silver and $876 in gold. A small stream of adventurers began crossing the Sierra Nevada eastbound, but the exodus from California was not a general one.

To really make money the mines would have to go deep and this would take a lot of capital. That was one reason the newspapers had been urging miners not to go to Washoe, at least not until the weather was decent. Even when the weather was good and there was water in the streams one man alone could not make much more than a bare living. When everything was frozen, when the "Washoe Zephyrs" blew, when the streams were dry, in fact, for most of the year, the Comstock Ledge offered a rare panoramic view and little else that was good.

The rising mining camp was named in honor of a bibulous but well liked early locator known as "Old Virginia" and "Virginia" it was called despite "Old Pancake" Comstock's letters of protest to the editor of the *Alta*. And Virginia it is still called by those who know the listener understands and will not get his mind switched from the pine nut mountains to the Blue Ridge. Whereas the State of Virginia was once

[4]

a Crown Colony and named for a virgin queen, Virginia City was once in Utah Territory, then Nevada Territory, and then the State of Nevada and named for a hilarious alcoholic.

In March of 1860 Virginia had half a dozen stone houses, several hundred tents and if a man could not find room to sleep in any of these he joined those sleeping in wagons. There were three streets, A, B, and C, but no cross streets. After a hundred years there are now cross streets, but no one has ever taken time away from thinking about the next strike to indulge in the stupidity of changing the names of the streets.

Sutro roamed the streets and hills of Virginia mingling with the people. He never hesitated to ask questions despite his thick German accent. He was a good listener, had a versatile background, and was interested in nearly everything. He was able, therefore, to move about the environs of Virginia and in ten days to gather a remarkably large amount of information. He purchased a quitclaim for some ground in the Virginia district but still had enough of a sense of humor (not one of his stronger characteristics) to poke fun at the behavior of speculators.

It was typical of this man that at the end of his brief stay he was able to draw up a concise summary of conditions and to make a series of suggestions involving complex engineering problems. On his return to San Francisco he wrote in the *Daily Alta:*

> The mine-working is done without any system as yet. Most of the companies commence without an eye to future success; instead of running a tunnel low down on the bed, and thus sinking a shaft to meet it, which at once insures drainage, ventilation and facilitates the work, by going upwards, the claims are mostly entered from above, large openings made which require considerable timbering, and which expose the mine to wind and weather.

[5]

It was also typical of Sutro that he would toss off a proposal for a costly project and feel sure the expense would be small. He continued:

A railroad from Virginia City to Carson River, some seven miles distant, could be built at a very small expense, the country sloping gently down towards it. The cars loaded with ore could be made to pull up the empty train, and ore once at the river, can easily be worked.

As Sutro prepared to leave, Virginia was completing three weeks of fine weather and now snow was found only on the hilltops and in deep ravines. On April 3 Sutro started home. He had made his analysis of the situation and was glad to quit the inferior lodgings, poor food, and vile water. He contemplated a pleasant trip to San Francisco.

The next morning at Woodford's he was one of a party of eight which mounted mules and started for Strawberry. Before they had traveled a mile the wind commenced to blow a gale. Then snow and hail blew into their faces with such force as to sting like needles and to nearly blind the men, who were all feeling venturesome or they would have turned back. The mules sensed the danger and hurried on as if fleeing before a terrible enemy. "The lofty pine trees swung to and fro, and the noise of the wind breaking through their branches, creaking and howling, was truly fearful." At last the party reached Strawberry Valley House at three o'clock in the afternoon. Sutro added:

On the very summit, we met a lonely rider dashing along at a tremendous rate. We wondered what could possibly induce him to go on through that gale, and thought it must be some very important business. It was the Pony Express.

In the next year and a half travelers would easily recognize the fast and determined young riders of the Pony Express, but this eastbound horseman carried the first Pony Express mail across the Sierra.

The next day travel for Sutro and his companions was even worse. This part was supposed to be done by stage and the men piled in, but soon they came to a hill and had to walk. The pine trees were loaded with snow and the slightest breeze would shake snow from the top, which falling to the next limb would start an avalanche. Eventually the coach stuck in the snow and had to be abandoned, so the driver unhitched the horses from his $1,000 vehicle. He and his passengers shouldered sacks and bags and pushed off for Perrine's where they spent the night.

The snow continued to fall and the next morning the travelers found that although there were no coaches or wagons available there were animals for rent because there was no fodder left in the mountains and anyone who had an animal was trying to reach Placerville where hay could be purchased.

The little party rented several wagon horses and the rest had to be content with pack mules. Those on horses had no saddles at all, while the men on mules found that the pack saddles were so wide they could not bend their knees. In his report to the *Alta*, Sutro said that the sight was ludicrous, but he did not say whether it fell to his lot to ride bareback or with his legs horizontal. Other travelers joined them until at least a hundred men and their hungry beasts started westward. The mountain road was two to four feet deep with snow and when the animals floundered the riders often went head-over-heels into snow. Yet many of the men could re-member worse trips. Sutro had crossed Panama through heat, mosquitoes, and tropical rains. Crocodiles, bandits, and the threat of yellow fever were but a few of the risks he ran. Compared to the Isthmus this was good clean fun, and Placerville waited below with hay for the horses and good food, even oysters, for the men. After a night at this most welcome stop the journey became very pleasant, as reflected clearly in Sutro's words:

[7]

Coming down from Placerville to Folsom next morning, we commenced to breathe free again. The beautiful green hills; the fields covered with flowers; the balmy air, told us that we had reached a different climate. The contrast between the icy, cold, stormy mountains and the lovely scene before us was affecting. Many travelers have described the wonderful effects on the human heart, on entering Italy from the snowy Alps, but I dare say it cannot be more impressive than the descent from the Sierra Nevada Mountains into California.

Adolph traveled home without further incident. He had been "to see the elephant."

CHAPTER II

FROM PRUSSIA TO CALIFORNIA

H OME TO SAN FRANCISCO. What a wonderful place to call home! Then as now San Francisco had residents whose greatest love affair was with "the city," as well as those who merely lived within its boundaries as a matter of expediency. Adolph Sutro was one of the latter, and many years and many troubles would engulf him before he would be in a position to select a place to live without reference to business opportunities. Eventually he would take San Francisco to his heart, mold it, endow it forever, and add one more word portrait to its ever-growing gallery of characters.

In San Francisco, as in Paris, many people find a sense of proportion coupled with a sense of freedom. They expand their potentials and develop their heretofore hidden talents. So far, Sutro had lived in or near San Francisco for ten years and had used but a portion of his talents. Although he had worked hard, he had gained little, and had had a dull time. A near-genius at twenty, he was now merely a successful tobacco merchant. In terms of what he had done prior to his arrival in 1850 and in terms of his future careers, this was but small accomplishment.

Adolph Heinrich Joseph Sutro had been born in Aachen (Aix-la-Chapelle), Prussia, April 29, 1830. He was the third child of Rosa Warendorf Sutro and her husband, Emanuel Sutro. Rosa Warendorf had been born and raised a few miles away at Düren — and because of her beauty of face and character had been called "the Rose of Düren." Emanuel was from Bruck, Bavaria, and had recently come to the Rhineland to join his elder brother, Simon, in the establishment of a woolen cloth factory to be known as "S. and E. Sutro."

The Sutro home was a beautiful, twenty-room mansion with a clock tower and lovely garden, located at No. 48 Bergdrisch. Harmony was the key word of the household, although by 1848 there were eleven children, of whom only darling Laura was entirely docile.

Sometimes the children tested the patience of their parents almost beyond endurance, and this was especially true of the second son, Adolph. He entered the "Bürgerschule" when he was eight and excelled in its practical curriculum of science and mathematics. He was an energetic learner, he wrote a good hand, and he led his class in his ability to sharpen a quill. There were times, however, when Adolph caused grave concern in the family. Once when he committed an infraction of the family rules his father started to whip him and Adolph ran upstairs to his bedroom. Finding his father in hot pursuit, Adolph jumped from the window. He landed safely below but his father was so shocked at the thought of what might have happened that he vowed never again to flog one of his children. Probably no other child of the family would have dared the jump, but the elder Sutro demonstrated his absolute fairness in foreswearing corporal punishment for all, since that mischief-making Adolph had made it impossible for one. At the age of sixteen Adolph was wild to go to Poland to join a rebellion, but he listened to his parents' reasons against it and submitted to their judgment.

Since the parents had both insight into their children's needs and money to encourage their interests, Adolph acquired a two-and-one-half-inch telescope. It was set up in the turret of the house, and night after night Adolph went up there to study the heavens. He found that the clock had been removed from the turret and discarded because some parts had been broken. To the astonishment of his family he fitted new parts and soon had the clock running and striking again.

Adolph also had a small chemical laboratory of his own and the usual boyish propensity for risking explosions.

He spent much time in the forests near his natal city and was often accompanied by a botany teacher on his walks. The teacher used to say, "My son, live ever near to Nature's heart, for to depart from Nature is to depart from happiness. Choose companions among such as love trees and little children. The man who loves these can never commit a crime."

Of all his interests, however, the most compulsive were books and machinery. As for books, he recalled later that when a public book sale occurred his parents could not keep him from it. He started to buy books when seven or eight years of age. He would get permission from his father to buy $2 or $3 worth and then he would spend four or five times that amount. He would be in trouble when he got home for exceeding the limit, but rebukes did not bother him. He had the books and that was what he wanted.

Adolph also showed great interest in his father's factory (the uncle seems to have dropped out of the business). Adolph studied the machinery there and built a little steam engine. The factory employees took delight in initiating the master's son into the mysteries of their craft and Adolph became skillful in detecting flaws in the cloth and acquired a remarkable knowledge of wools. He learned to sing *Der Wissqueist* to the rhythm of the work, and in the lull he chatted with the workers while drinking a glass of beer or a cup of coffee.

Adolph's younger brother, Otto, also gave much promise. He was now eleven years old and was so talented in music that his parents decided to find out just how much they should encourage him. His father was successful in persuading Felix Mendelssohn to see the boy and hear him play the piano. Otto played well and Mendelssohn recommended that he be sent to the conservatory in Brussels. If only he would study hard he might become a great musician; he might even

[11]

be invited to stay on at the conservatory and become a Herr Professor.

Emanuel had to leave home on a business trip and he started off as usual. He traveled in his own carriage, drawn by his handsome horses, and he was well armed. On his return, perhaps thinking of the hazard of loaded pistols in a household of eleven children, Emanuel decided to arrive home with them empty and in a burst of ill-considered bravado he discharged them into the air. The carriage horses took fright and ran away. Emanuel was thrown into the ditch and when he was found his spine was broken and he was paralyzed. Although he was a hopeless invalid, his strong body managed to hold out for nearly a year and on December 11, 1848, he died at the age of forty-eight. During the period of Emanuel's illness and after his death the management of the mill was shared by his eldest sons, Sali and Adolph.

Adolph was sixteen when he was obliged to leave school, much to his disappointment. In languages he had his native German and was proficient in both French and English. His mechanical and scientific hobbies were a great asset to him and much useful knowledge had been gained by his constant visits to the mill. He was conversant with the looms, shrinking vats, shearing machines, rinsing bowls and engine room. In addition he had established friendships with the workmen which were of inestimable value. If there had been peace in Europe, the widowed Rosa might have lived out her many remaining years in much the same kind of security she had known during her happy married life. Without peace, it is doubtful if even Emanuel could have continued with the mill.

The year 1848 was punctuated by one revolution or rebellion after another. In February barricades appeared in the streets of Paris, King Louis Philippe prudently fled to England, and the Second French Republic was born. In March revolutions occurred in Italy, in the German states including

Prussia, and in Austria. In June Paris had three days of bloody street fighting and in September Austrian forces began a reconquest of Hungary.

These were only a few of the major events of a year of European tumult, and their effect on business was disastrous. Normal channels of trade were cut off for months at a time, and it is easy to understand why the two young Sutro brothers decided that their best hope was to close the factory and liquidate their assets.

Like so many Europeans of that period, Mrs. Sutro turned her thoughts to America. Emanuel had some nephews named Frankenheimer who had emigrated and were now in Birmingham, Alabama. In due course they invited Sali to come over and join their business as a salesman and he accepted. There was enough money after debts were paid for Rosa to remain in her home and rear the remaining children.

The various talents of Adolph came to the attention of Mr. O. G. Kaapche of Memel, whose own interests were not unlike those of the young Adolph. Kaapche had started out in Memel with nothing, and by 1849 he owned iron foundries, ships, warehouses and flour mills. He was Memel's richest man. Ever eager to expand, he had noted that the one thing Memel did not have was a cloth manufacturing plant. He had bought a vacant public bathhouse which he proposed to remodel as a factory and then he went to Aachen to purchase machinery from the Sutro mill. While he was there he became impressed with Adolph's abilities and offered him the opportunity of coming to Memel to take charge of the remodeling, establish the factory, hire the workers, and run the mill. Eventually Adolph would be given an interest in the business, but at the start he would have a good salary and a suite of rooms in which to live rent free. Since Adolph was eager to accept such a wonderful opportunity and to help support his mother, it looked as if Rosa's future was assured.

[13]

Adolph left Aachen with its memories of Charlemagne and its glorious past when it had been the center of Western culture; deep within him he stored the knowledge of his home town. Here he had learned about hot water coming from the earth at 171 degrees Fahrenheit; here he had seen the pilgrims come to view the Four Great Relics in the cathedral which were exposed to view only every seven years; the last viewing had been in 1846. Adolph was of Jewish lineage but his parents were not orthodox and raised their children according to their own ethical beliefs. There is no record that Adolph ever joined the Catholic pilgrims to see The Cloak of the Blessed Virgin, The Swaddling Clothes of the Infant Jesus, The Loin Cloth worn by Our Lord on the Cross, or The Cloth on which the head of John the Baptist lay after the beheading, but his later behavior would indicate that he began to brood on the idea of keeping treasures under lock and key. Eventually he would become so devoted to the idea of art for everybody that the public would sometimes grow weary of his efforts; many of his offerings were destined to be vandalized.

Now nineteen years old, Adolph turned his attention to Memel, the ice-free port on the Baltic Sea. Adolph enjoyed the four-hundred-hour trip to Memel. It was his first long trip and he went by train, ship, and stage coach. Before he arrived at Memel he had caught glimpses of Berlin, Königsberg and Tilsit. The night he was on the Baltic Sea he spent on deck, looking at the stars. He was familiar with the heavens, as he had often studied them from the turret of his home with the aid of his own telescope, and he had also read some about the lives of great astronomers. Now he clearly saw the stars of this northern latitude for the first time, stars he had seen before only on charts.

His opal eyes were even more impressed by the city of Memel and its main street lined with linden trees. Adolph was pleased to find that Kaapche's bathhouse was not only located on The Linden, but it was surrounded by arcades and a lovely garden.

Fifty masons and carpenters awaited the coming of the young Sutro. He would be in charge of renovating the building so that it could be used both for the manufacture of cloth and for building mountings for the ships Kaapche was building for the Peruvian trade.

The first thing Sutro had to do was to choose his own living space. He selected a part of the basement close to the spinning machinery. Kaapche provided a bed, but Adolph had to buy a table, chairs, a dresser, mirror, and dishes. He knew his mother had plenty of linens and he was eager to husband his resources so he wrote and asked her to send half a dozen sheets, a bedspread, a bureau cover and materials for a down cover except the feathers, which were very cheap in Memel. He would also appreciate some silver spoons and any other items she might feel necessary.

Adolph found delight in establishing this first home of his own. True, it was in the basement of an erstwhile public bathhouse, and his furnishings were meager, but it was his own. He had no idea that eventually another home of his, surrounded by even more magnificent gardens than those of the Memel establishment, would overlook another bathhouse, owned by himself and served by his own street railroad as well. He could not see that far in the future, but he could manage to provide himself with silver spoons and a tea pot.

Adolph was not cut off from familiar faces by his change of residence, for his first official action in Memel was to send for two of his former employees. The first to come at Adolph's bidding was Ahn, who was to be master of the forge. The second man was a helper at the forge named Holnartz. The latter, being only a helper, must have lived in town, but eventually five of the foremen shared the basement with Adolph. Prumm, foreman of weavers, and Ahn were on one side of Adolph's apartment. The three foremen on the other side included Spruck and Leister, spinning foremen from Aix-la-Chapelle.

Mr. Kaapche knew nothing about the manufacture of cloth and had complete confidence in Adolph, so the young man had a free hand to plan and set up the plant. Adolph bought machinery and directed its installation as well as that of the steam engines. When Mr. Kaapche had envisioned this business he had overlooked one essential item. No matter how magnificently his building might be located or how commodious and well equipped it might be, without a source of clear, soft water the wool could not be processed. Only with the proper water could the wool be rinsed so that it could emerge soft and white as snow. The little boy who had roamed the forests of Aix with his botany teacher had been developing a keen sense of observation, one that would lead him some day to his greatest enterprise, but now he used it to solve the problem of water.

Adolph went out into the country seeking to buy top grade wool from the farmers. While near Tilsit he found a small brook whose water was ideal for his purpose. Adolph was able to make a favorable arrangement for its use with the government, and he had a pipe laid to bring the water to the factory. The government made only the modest charge of $12 per year for the water, and also granted Adolph the honor of being addressed as "Herr Engineer."

Talk of the factory was on every tongue and occupied much space in the newspapers. As soon as the process of manufacture began people stood for long periods at a time in the freezing cold to peer through the windows of the spinning rooms. Adolph allowed only a few visitors inside, he was appalled by their foolish questions, and he wanted to spend his time forcing the work along. He calculated that if they could finish a dozen pieces of cloth by the first of the new year the factory could hit its stride and produce three hundred pieces during the year ahead.

If ever there was a person whose attitude was that money was made to be spent it was Adolph Sutro. Whether it was his father's, Kaapche's, or his own, and so long as the end product was worthy, it never occurred to Adolph to be frugal. He was not a wastrel, he was even very conservative about his own clothes and managed to look well dressed because of spotless linen and good grooming rather than expensive clothes. But when machinery was concerned, only the very best would do. If a steam engine was needed, it must be the finest. Adolph never compromised on machinery, and he preferred to leave a position rather than live within a budget that did not allow for those things which he deemed necessary. Adolph knew that his contract would terminate on January first, and even if it were renewed there would again be a clause to the effect that Kaapche could sell or close the factory at any time within the first five years. Adolph went ahead, hired a total of seventy-five men, and kept his mind on the production of cloth.

With Sali in America Adolph felt responsible for his family in Aix. He assumed a very domineering attitude and wrote his mother advice about everything. Emil should stay in agricultural school a year and a half. Otto should continue studying music at least a year. Adolph would take charge of Ludwig later and teach him factory work.

Every Sunday Adolph would push his little table up near the fire and write his long letters to his family full of news and advice and he constantly prodded his sisters to write him in French or English. Laura, always to be the most devoted of sisters and the idol of the entire family, did as her brother requested. No doubt, Adolph started his voluminous correspondence because at first he was lonely. Then as Sali started to write from America proposing plans for the family, Adolph found his position in the family challenged, and he tried to become his mother's chief adviser. Sali wanted to move to Baltimore and open a retail store. His mother and all the children should come and all of them work in the store. The idea that his sisters would become salesladies appalled Adolph. He took every opportunity to oppose his brother and to speak his mind freely. If he was capable at this point in his life of exercising diplomacy, he failed utterly to use that talent. Of course, Adolph wrote those letters out of the love he felt for them all and out of the sure conviction that he, better than Sali or anyone else, knew what was good for the family.

On New Year's Day, 1850, Adolph was supremely happy. The twelve pieces of cloth were finished, his mother had turned down Sali's proposal, and the new contract with Kaapche was far better than he could possibly have expected. Not only was Adolph to receive a raise in salary of 15 per cent, but he was also to receive 25 per cent of the profits. Mr. Kaapche said nothing about the fact that Adolph had already spent more than the amount of money he had expected to put into the factory and Adolph estimated that he needed twice as much more to continue with improvements. Mr. Kaapche did not remain silent for long, however, and when he did speak to Adolph he had a plan to propose. He would be glad to sell out to Adolph and would not only loan the youth money, but also help him secure credit at the bank.

Memel was full of opportunities, but Adolph didn't feel that buying the cloth factory was one of them. War was in the air again, capital was timid, and rather than take on so large an undertaking, Sutro and Kaapche agreed to close the factory. Adolph remained in Memel and started negotiating for a position as manager of a business in Moscow.

At home in Aix, Mrs. Sutro had problems of her own. Although she had rejected Sali's plan to come to America, the door was still open as far as Sali was concerned. Adolph was out of employment, but worst of all, the young sons at home were in jeopardy. Prussia and Austria were bitter rivals and were arming. The leadership for any new German nation which might develop out of the present revolutionary unrest was at stake, and both sides were demanding conscripts. Aix-la-Chapelle was in the unique position of always being the first and longest to feel the effects of war; the military commission had already started conscripting unusually large numbers of young men.

"Herr Engineer" received a letter from his mother which must have made him feel younger and less able to manage his affairs than he did the day he jumped out of the window. He was to buy some things in Memel for Sali's store, and to return home at once, by way of Antwerp. There, he was to purchase passage from the Atlantic Line on a steamer sailing in August for himself, his mother, and all of the children excluding Otto, who would continue his musical education. Rosa Warendorf Sutro did not suggest this; she demanded it. Adolph complied.

In the lives of all of us there are traits which mold all the days of our years. Adolph Sutro had one such trait that few people share, and that was the ability to let go of a fact, a habit, an opportunity, or a behavior pattern and never again try to resume it. At this point in his life he resigned from his self-appointed position as his mother's adviser. He had failed in his attempt to direct her thinking, and even in his ability to choose his own country. He would go to America with her, but never again would he tell *her* what to do. Secondly, he was through with the cloth business. Never again would his eyes check a bolt of cloth for flaws, never again would he be concerned with warp and woof except as a purchaser of material for his own use or for resale.

CHAPTER III

FIRST YEAR IN THE NEW WORLD

T HE STREETS AND HOTELS of New York City swarmed with young men from every nation eagerly preparing for life in the land of gold. They strutted about in rough woolen trousers tucked in high boots; knives and pistols hung from their belts. Hardly any store was without its quota of these colorful figures, but their especial haunts were those selling guns and ammunition, rubber goods, and provisions. The bakeries were operating day and night to meet the prodigious demand for ships' loaves. On every wall, and in every newspaper, one saw announcements of ships sailing for the new Promised Land — some by way of Cape Horn and some by way of the Isthmus.

Adolph succumbed to this pleasant contagion and decided that he must go to California. With some difficulty he talked his mother into allowing him to take the goods he had purchased in Memel which were intended for the projected store in Baltimore. There were two bales of German cloth and two trunks of fancy articles (notions) which would bring wonderful prices in California, Adolph was certain. Within a few years Adolph would make his fortune whereupon he would return to the east and share it with his mother.

Amid such rosy hopes Adolph arranged for passage on the wooden steamship *Cherokee*. At three o'clock on Saturday afternoon, October 12, the *Cherokee* left the New York docks amid the hurrahs and hand-waving of those on the shore. Adolph Sutro had stationed himself aft to get a good look at the colorful city where he had remained less than two weeks. He could also see Brooklyn, with its new houses of red brick, and farther down he enjoyed the view of Staten Island. The Narrows, with its fortifications on each side, reminded him of the Porta Westfalica in Germany.

Before long Adolph learned that the most illustrious party aboard the *Cherokee* was that of Colonel John C. Frémont, who was traveling with his wife, daughter, and maid. The famous explorer was now returning from his first session in Washington as United States Senator from California. Luck favored this sea voyage, for the eight days needed to get to Chagres were clear and sunny with the water smooth as glass.

On arrival at the Isthmus Adolph hired a canoe for a hundred dollars. It was to take Sutro and his luggage and three fellow passengers the sixty-five miles to Cruces. Thence they were to go by mule trail the twenty-four miles to Panama. The road by Gorgona was shorter but this was the rainy season and that road was impassable.

The canoe was made from the bark of a tree and its design afforded no protection from the piercing rays of the tropical sun. The river had many twists and turns, its currents were swift and strong, and it abounded in alligators. The passengers were in constant fear of overturn or collision. Recently four Frenchmen in a canoe had capsized but had been rescued. Fourteen Americans the previous week had been less fortunate.

Gatun was the first overnight stop and Adolph immediately found out what problems he could expect to face each night on the Isthmus. Few hammocks or huts were available and in far fewer number than could supply the demand. Even ladies could be seen wandering around, groping in the dirt and darkness wondering where they would sleep. Adolph came upon the Frémont party and saw that the colonel had only a miserable hut for himself and his three ladies. It was open on all sides and most inadequate shelter from both weather and mosquitoes.

The mosquitoes were so thick that they seemed to fill the whole air. An additional annoyance was the heavy tropical rain, certain to fall at this time of year. A night in the open carried some risk of contracting a fever which might ruin one's health for life. Adolph had purchased a supply of quinine from the ship's physician before leaving the *Cherokee* and he dosed himself daily in hope of avoiding such a fever.

The first night Sutro decided to sleep in the canoe. Although cramped it was clean, and he would feel better about the safety of his luggage. He wrapped his face against the countless mosquitoes and placed pistols by his side. The night rain wet him to the skin.

In the morning Adolph found two or three hundred men had spent the night on the ground in the open. Some were late arrivals and some were travelers and boatmen who had spent their first hours after arrival at the busy roulette tables. Adolph resumed the difficult journey and found he was obliged to spend three more nights in the crowded canoe.

Sutro and his party bade their canoe good-bye at Cruces where the mule trail began. Adolph hired a riding mule and three pack animals, at a cost of seventy dollars. The pack mules were necessary to carry his four bales and two trunks.

Although the road from Cruces to Panama had been improved by the Spaniards in the sixteenth century it had since fallen into decay. Any traveler now going over it confidently pronounced it the worst in the world.

There were numerous ways one could suffer loss or bodily harm. Besides the hazards of the road, the lawless character of some of the muleteers, and the danger of disease, Adolph had his own fears, based on news of an occurrence the night before. A young American by the name of Robinson had been murdered by his muleteers and his trunks rifled of nine thousand dollars.

As dusk gathered Sutro's friends from the *Cherokee* decided to push on to Panama that night. Since Adolph had so much baggage he had to spend the night on the trail. This was probably the worst night he ever spent, and the one exception he always had to make when later he would boast that whatever the worries of the day he could always be sound asleep within five minutes of going to bed. Perhaps it was one of the few nights of his life when he went to bed soaking wet and hungry. The one slice of bread he had been able to buy for a shilling from a fellow traveler could not have satisfied the stomach of a man of twenty years. He must have done some sleeping because he was well armed and if awake he might have been able to prevent the loss of his riding mule, which was stolen during the night. Perhaps it was taken by one of the 150 Californians who had been sleeping in the same clearing as Sutro.

Bad as walking might be, at least Adolph still had his three pack animals and he started to walk the seven miles to Panama. Luck was still with him, however, for he was able to get a lift part of the way for a couple of dollars.

Adolph was filled with joy when he first saw Panama City and the Pacific Ocean. After obtaining the best possible lodgings he set out to question as many people as he could find relative to conditions in California. What he learned confirmed his earlier ideas about the advisability of being a merchant rather than a miner. The mines were very rich, but the number of men trying to work them was fantastic. These hordes of men needed many things, wanted still more, and were willing to pay enormous prices to the merchant who could anticipate their wants. Just why Adolph thought that with his background in manufacturing he could meet the needs of these men is hard to explain, but the "gold fever" worked in mysterious ways.

Adolph was busy shuttling between the steamship office, the American Hotel where he was stopping, and the haunts of the Californians who were returning to the states and whose knowledge he wanted to mine. He dug deep into the experiences they had had and does not seem to have been discouraged by these men who had turned their backs on California.

[23]

Of course, Adolph was eager to be on his way, for Panama had a reputation as a death trap. If you escaped small pox, cholera, and Panama fever you might still arrive at death's door by the slower route of scurvy. Supplies were always short (ships' captains preferred to sell their provisions for high prices in California), the meat smelled, and much of the food was full of flies and maggots. It would be many a year before Adolph would become a gourmet, import his wine from Germany, and set one of the best tables anywhere, but he was always scrupulously clean. It was bad enough to be obliged to stand the foul smells of Panama night and day; he could not and would not stand the food even of the American Hotel. He courted scurvy but avoided worse by living on bread and tea.

By the time Sutro appeared in Panama City eight steamships were operating between that port and San Francisco, but they fell far short of conveying all of the gold-seekers awaiting passage. Many California-bound emigrants reluctantly left Panama aboard sailing vessels, even though northwest voyages were certain to be plagued with contrary winds.

Sutro was fortunate and was able to board the wooden side-wheeler *California* after a wait of only six days. Imagine his emotional depression when he learned that the *California* could not carry his bales of cloth! Fifteen hundred tons of freight lay there in Panama and almost an equal amount was at Chagres awaiting transportation across the Isthmus. No wonder prices were high in California when tons of goods lay rotting at the Isthmus. Adolph put his trunks and himself on board the *California* and steamed out of Panama on November 1, 1850.

Nearly forty years later Sutro summed up his reaction to the days he spent on the Isthmus of Panama when he declared that he would not live in that country if he were made sole proprietor over all of it. Considering the length of time many people had to spend in Panama before boarding ship for California it would seem that Adolph was specially favored by the gods. Certainly he was fortunate to be alive and well. He not only got his trunks on board but managed to borrow enough money to travel first class and thereby escape the horrors of steerage. The gentleman who offered the loan was the Swedish consul. Sutro repaid him a few weeks after he got to California.

On November 13 the *California* stopped at Mazatlan and her passengers learned just how lucky they were to be aboard a ship powered by steam. Also in Mazatlan was the American brig *Gulnare,* carrying 140 passengers bound for San Francisco. She had required 115 days to get from Panama City to Mazatlan!

The *California* steamed out of Mazatlan and it made a call at San Diego. At this port they picked up six wild-looking men, a few of the survivors of the Parker H. French expedition. This unfortunate group of 250 men had left New York trusting in a "guarantee" that they would be guided to San Francisco in two months. Their route was to be by sea to New Orleans and on to the obscure Texas port of Lavacca. From that point they were to go overland via "express wagon train." The group suffered horribly and some of the survivors reached San Diego six months or more after leaving New York.

The *California* then proceeded to Santa Barbara. Some of the passengers were ill and soon many were stricken with the fever. They lay all around with no one to attend them. An acquaintance of Adolph's, a Mr. P. Bloomingdale, leaped from his berth in delirium. Adolph watched aghast as the fever ran its course. Within an hour Bloomingdale was dead, and within another hour he was buried at sea.

Adolph was deeply touched by this event. Three months before they had both been in Germany; now the life of one of them had ended without his ever reaching the Promised Land. For once Adolph grew homesick. No doubt the terrors of the Isthmus and the bad food had made him less valiant than he later remembered. In later years he chose only to remember his fellow passenger John Randohr. Randohr had been raised in the Hartz mountains and later he and Sutro conducted experiments with silver ore.

At about 8:00 a.m. on Friday, November 21, 1850, the *California* steamed through the Golden Gate with Adolph Sutro aboard and well. The visibility was limited and Sutro and other eager passengers were unable to see the hills guarding the famous passageway.

San Francisco paid no attention to the man who was to have so much to do with helping her grow from an awkward town into a gracious city. The San Francisco *Picayune* (November 21-23) had no reference to the *California* in its marine news, but the S. F. *Pacific News* on November 22 published a passenger list. It no doubt meant Sutro when it listed "Adolphe Lubio"; the S. F. *California Courier* of the same date listed "Adolph Sutio." But in later years all San Francisco papers were to learn to spell the name correctly and they would spell it often.

Adolph had to find a place for his trunks and himself — no easy task since he was out of money. He delivered a letter to August Helbing, who had fled the Rhine with Carl Schurz, the liberal leader, and found that Mr. Helbing could offer a place to sleep. Meyer, Helbing and Company were importers of crockery, glass, and china, and their store was located at California and Sansome Streets. The store lacked a fire watcher at nights and the owners were delighted to allow Adolph to store his goods and sleep under the counter free of charge. Adolph's job was to be alert to fires either in the store or neighboring stores. If one broke out he would be responsible for saving the goods from fire and looting. Fortunately for him no such emergency arose.

As soon as his trunks were delivered Adolph had to try to sell things in order to have money to eat. Before the sun went down on his first day in San Francisco he had good reason to learn that the city was in a period of financial depression. Six months before, in May, business had boomed.

[26]

A great many Mexicans had done well in the mines, come to San Francisco and spent prodigiously, and gone back to Mexico. Then other miners came and in as lavish a manner as their dust allowed they stocked up for the winter. By November, five and six ships a day made port from all over the world and they carried full cargoes. There were few purchasers and warehouses were bulging. Adolph could hardly have contrived a worse time to arrive and be dependent on selling his goods.

But when Adolph made up his mind to do something, nothing stopped him. He not only sold his goods but he went into the commission business, buying and selling goods for others at 5 to 10 per cent commission. He slept in the store, he sold anything he could find to sell, and he wrote letters. He wrote at once to his first cousin Bernard Frankenheimer who was now at Stockton.

Adolph was soon settled at Stockton in a store which he described six months later as "a little hole of a store at the end of the levee." He was in partnership with his cousin under the firm name of Sutro and Frankenheimer, with each receiving half of the profits. The store handled clothing, boots, shoes, cloth by the piece, notions, etc. In March the partners rented a nice store on the levee just opposite the bridge and Adolph was so pleased he described it as "about the finest store on the levee."

The levee presented a very active scene, for Stockton was the terminus for ocean-going ships which ascended the San Joaquin River and steamships plied regularly between Stockton and San Francisco. Thus Stockton was the distributing center for all of the southern mines, and hundreds of wagons were constantly being loaded at Stockton for journeys inland.

On May 6, 1851, fire broke out in Stockton, which was primarily a tent city. The fire chief and many of his firemen were absent, however, for they were at San Francisco viewing the ruins of a large fire of a few days previous. Inexperienced persons tried to operate the lone engine but the fire overtook them, destroying the hose and badly damaging the engine.

The store of Sutro and Frankenheimer luckily escaped the fire and business promptly improved. The admittedly dull trade previous to the fire had netted each partner about one hundred dollars a month. In May the share of each shot up to about three hundred dollars.

Like many young merchants, Adolph and his cousin were single and could live in their store at minimum expense. Although one or two meals a day were taken at restaurants, breakfast and snacks revolved around an alcohol stove, tea, sugar, and bread. For beds they used the floor of the store and Adolph claimed that they slept like tops. He did caution, however, that one should go to sleep quickly; otherwise the fleas would bother you too much.

Adolph did not regard the store as a complete existence and he welcomed occasional change of activity. From time to time he would make a business trip to San Francisco. On Sunday he and Bernard would generally borrow some horses and go out driving in a cart or take a ride to the farm of some friend. On some Sundays they went hunting and broiled what they shot. Adolph usually restricted himself to pigeons, snipe, partridges, and sometimes ducks.

Although a young bachelor beginning to prosper, Adolph was ever mindful of his family in the East. He wrote Sali in February applauding him for going to Baltimore and staying there for a time to assist their mother. A few months later Adolph had evolved a plan for his family, excluding his mother. It was nothing less than a scheme for all of the grown sons to come to California as soon as possible. Sali could get a position possibly at $150 a month or else open a store. Adolph was sure he could get positions for Emil and Otto paying $100 a month. Hugo and Ludwig were still boys but boys were employed in California in stores, as markers at billiards, and for many other things. They could get fifty dollars a month and board.

If Emil and Otto should fail to get positions, Sutro and Frankenheimer could open branch stores for them at such places as San Francisco, Sacramento, and possibly Sonora. Adolph painted in rosy colors the advantages of operating several stores. Summing up his proposal, Adolph felt sure that if all five brothers came out most of them could return East at the end of a year with total savings "at the worst" of 3,000 to 5,000 dollars.

Three of the brothers responded to this glowing invitation. Emil and Otto joined Adolph late in 1851, when he was abandoning Stockton for San Francisco. Emil became a salesman for Hamberger Brothers at 93 California Street while Otto played the organ in churches. Hugo came in '53 and worked for Dubor's Brothers, jewelers, at 129 Montgomery Street. After a time all three returned to their mother in Baltimore. Whether one or more of the brothers returned home with the large savings Adolph had promised is unrecorded but unlikely.

Adolph happened to be present in San Francisco when one of the year's most dramatic events occurred. He was sleeping at Meyer Helbing's on the night of Tuesday, August 19. At 2:00 a.m. he heard the ringing of the Monumental Fire Company bell. He sprang from his blanket "frightened to death," but soon determined that it was ringing for a hanging rather than for a fire.

Adolph did not go back to sleep but dressed, took his revolver, and followed the other people to the offices of the Committee of Vigilance on Battery Street.

The Committee considered taking the jail by force to retake the alleged murderers, two "Sydney ducks" named Mackenzie and Whitacker. More sober counsels prevailed, however, and the matter was postponed a few days until the victims might be captured by more subtle means. On the following Sunday the jailer was tricked and the victims seized. They were taken directly to the offices of the Committee of Vigilance and hanged.

[29]

CHAPTER IV

THE TOBACCONIST-ENGINEER

I T WAS TRUE that San Francisco was still a city where men
went about "heeled" with bowie knife and pistol and
where an unauthorized committee could conduct hangings.
It was also a city heavily in debt and almost in a commercial
panic. Yet permanent buildings were arising from the ruins
of the last fire and the men of San Francisco felt a greater
sense of security. They began sending for their wives and
children and many refinements were appearing. The flannel
shirt was fast disappearing for the frilled shirt and social
life was soon embellished with concerts, balls, operas, dra-
mas, and parties.

Before his first year as a California resident was over,
Sutro returned to San Francisco and opened a store on Long
Wharf. He planned to stay three years and then go East to
live. In the meantime he sold anything a person wanted to
buy, from turpentine to lager beer. What he didn't stock,
he sold on commission and his orders ranged from "$5 worth
of classic music" to a dozen soup plates.

By 1854 he had two stores. At 103 Clay Street he imported cigars and tobacco and at 110 Sacramento Street he
imported variety goods. From this latter store he routed
goods to the southern mines by way of Stockton and to the
northern mines via Sacramento, sometimes to as far north as
Trinity Bay. Adolph invested in real estate and built a house
at Camptonville, close to the mining towns of Grass Valley
and Downieville. This venture brought in a rental of twenty-
five dollars a month.

The precise fate of Sutro's stores on Clay and Sacramento
Streets is unrecorded, but before long Adolph was connected
with two stores on Montgomery Street and a third on Wash-

ington Street. At Barry and Patten's, 116 Montgomery Street, Adolph had a retail store for the buying and selling of cigars, meerschaum pipes, and tobacco. Here he was joined by his cousin Gustav Sutro, but apparently the store bore Adolph's name. The managers of this store were aggressive in their merchandising methods if we may judge by certain details which are still available. The store invested in newspaper advertising from time to time, stressing a Turkish tobacco, which was put up in skins resembling sausages. They were the sole agent in California.

The Turkish tobacco gained additional attention by the erection of a smoking automaton in front of the store. A wooden Turk about five feet high was painted in gaudy colors. The figure held a huge tobacco pipe between his lips and at certain hours of the day he would smoke the tobacco. The sucking and puffing were accomplished by use of a pump actuated by a string and weight.

Adolph and cousin Gustav had a second store in the Armory Hall Building on Montgomery Street. This was a wholesale and retail importing business also interested in cigars, pipes, and tobacco. Gustav's brother, Charles, also came to San Francisco and he served as an accountant for Barry and Patten. In 1858 Charles and Gustav became stock brokers, founding the firm of Sutro and Company which is still flourishing.

Adolph had a third store at Peter Job's on Washington Street. This was a retail tobacco store similar to the one at Barry and Patten's. In this third store Adolph had a partner named Moses Wasserman.

During these years in San Francisco Adolph was the victim of a knifing by an irate broker by the name of A. J. King. In March of 1855 the broker lost a package of scrip which was found by Adolph's cousin, Charles Sutro, and returned after a delay of two or three days. King was angry at the delay and that led later to name-calling and a knife attack on Charles which nearly severed his lower lip.

Later the same day King and Adolph Sutro met at the entrance to the City Hall. Adolph said later: "Mr. King passed me and then sprang around and said, 'You call me a scoundrel?' He then cut me with a knife a ghastly wound from the ear down to the mouth. There were fifty persons standing about, but it was done so suddenly that I doubt if any person witnessed it."

It is easy to understand why Adolph wore flowing side whiskers the rest of his life.

At about this time there were two changes in his status. He became a United States citizen, and voted for his old acquaintance from his passage to Chagres — John C. Frémont who was running for President. This was the start of a long procession of unsuccessful candidates for whom Sutro would vote.

In either 1855 or 1856 Sutro married Leah Harris in a Hebrew ceremony, probably at Leah's request for she was far more religious than her liberal-minded husband. Leah was of English ancestry with simple tastes and a good heart. She had no dreams of grandeur, and would have been most happy to see her life revolve around home, husband, children, synagogue, and the charities of the congregation. Whenever she could, these were the things she did, but as her husband's life expanded she assumed the roles he forced upon her with dignity and charm. Had she found it a little more possible to be his companion rather than his hostess she might have saved them both considerable heartache.

In 1858 San Francisco was in the throes of a new mining "excitement." Gold had been discovered in the Fraser River in British Columbia. The mad rush which followed seemed to be depopulating San Francisco and scores of mining camps.

The chief distributing point for the Fraser River country was Victoria, where a frantic real estate boom was under way. Among the hopeful gold seekers were Adolph and Gustav Sutro, bent upon setting up a cigar store at Victoria.

As their boat approached the dock at Victoria it came dangerously close to dumping its entire load of passengers into the seething waters of the harbor.

The Fraser River did have gold but the number of prospectors was hopelessly out of proportion to the amount of metal readily available. The story of most of the gold-hungry pilgrims was one of untold hardships, meager returns or none, disillusionment, and in some cases, death. Adolph Sutro returned from British Columbia minus his travel expenses and also out of pocket the investment in his Victoria store. His one new asset was a town lot of dubious value in Victoria.

In spite of its bad results, the trip to British Columbia left its lasting memorial in his family. Adolph was already a father, for a daughter named "Emma Laura" had arrived in November of 1856. Mrs. Sutro was expectant when Adolph left for British Columbia, and the second child, a girl, was born on July 1, 1858, the very day of the almost fatal landing at Victoria. Very appropriately, the new baby was named "Rosa Victoria."

News of a gold and silver strike east of the Sierra Nevada reached San Francisco in July 1859, but no great interest was aroused in view of disillusionment over collapse of the recent Fraser River bubble and the fact that the new deposits (if verified) were highly inaccessible. Indication of the great richness of these new mines did reach the city by late autumn, but a winter of great severity prevented travel to the new El Dorado. In the early spring one of the first persons to travel to the "Washoe country" was Adolph Sutro, as already related.

Hundreds of men and women were finding San Francisco the most exciting, charming, demanding place in the world. Considering the fact that Sutro had grown up in an extremely old and refined city which Charlemagne had made a crossroads of the world one might expect him to prefer a city, however young, to the absolute rawness of Washoe. On the other hand, if he stayed in the tobacco business the former Herr Engineer would never get a chance to engineer anything more complicated than a dummy with weights and strings. Washoe lured most men with her gold, but she must have lured Adolph Sutro with her problems.

Upon his return to San Francisco, Sutro wrote the report for the *Alta* already cited, which was printed in three installments. In the articles he described his trip and gave his evaluation of the mining situation in Washoe. He then set his own house in order. Leah remained at home and took care of her growing family, for tiny Gussie Emanuel had arrived in the fall of 1859. Leah also aided Adolph in the age-old manner of wives and widows who need to augment the family income. She opened two lodging houses and operated them for at least two years. The one at the northwest corner of Sansome and Washington Streets was called "Government House" and the second, on the southwest corner of Montgomery and California was called "Sutro House." These were no mean lodgings for the humble, and the Sutros paid $400 a month rent for Sutro House, $500 a month for the other. They were elegantly furnished and no meals were served. Mrs. Sutro took care of this new business while her husband liquidated his tobacco shops and made another trip to Washoe during the middle of May.

The San Francisco *Bulletin* published his next articles. In them he told a little about mining, but it was hard to think of gold when Indians were on the warpath. A band of Paiutes had massacred seven whites at the Williams' Ranch and a Pony Express rider brought the news to Virginia while Sutro was visiting there. A public meeting was held and he sent this report to San Francisco:

> Everybody seemed ready to go. Whether the darkness and bad news had any influence in getting up the spirits of so many individuals I really don't know; but this morning, when it came to turning out, there were but precious few on hand, and the persons who

said they didn't want any horse either, if they couldn't get one — nor any weapons, if they were not handy, but would just go and slay so many thousands with their fists, like Sampson of old — were nowhere to be seen today.

But others, who had but little to say, quietly organized some cavalry companies, and will in all probability start out before evening, and do effective service.

An expedition of 105 armed men did leave to chastise the Indians, and they made contact with the savages near Pyramid Lake. After a preliminary skirmish the inexperienced whites followed the enemy into a ravine which proved to be a trap; the white force was cut to ribbons.

In reporting the outcome of this ill-fated expedition Sutro followed a remarkable practice for that day. He took great care to verify his facts, he gave the names of those he interviewed, he qualified his statements, and he also pointed out the possible bias of those interviewed. Sutro interviewed Captain Archibald McDonald, Joe Baldwin and others. Then he wrote his account and read it to six men who had been in the battle. He cautioned the reader that an eye-witness might err, then wrote:

Only forty-eight have returned. A few stragglers will likely come in yet, but it is feared that all the others have been butchered by the savages. A gloom hangs over our young city — some of its best citizens are no more. Amongst the killed are Major Ormsby of Carson City, who fought nobly to the last; Henry Meredith of Nevada, esteemed and honored by all who knew him — he was too proud to retreat, and he was cut to pieces; Edward Spear of Downieville, said to have borne himself like a hero — he was left dead on the battlefield. . . . Many more could be named who have acted nobly in the engagement.

Although Adolph promised further reports, either he did not write any, he used a pseudonym, or the papers rejected his efforts. The idea of A. Sutro letting any brain child of his appear with any other name is most improbable. The chances are that he was too involved in other things to take time out for newspaper dispatches. Although the papers printed hundreds of such unsolicited news reports and did not edit them for English grammar or usage, it must have given the German immigrant some satisfaction to come off so well in his new language. At any rate, he had found his pen and he had been able to gain the full cooperation of the Pyramid Lake veterans when writing his story. He was a sober intellectual with little ability to mingle as an equal with men of different backgrounds, and he may have been concerned about possible discrimination because of his Jewish ancestry, but after his trips to Washoe he was convinced that he could get along there.

Sutro now felt confident that he could develop a more efficient process for extracting gold and silver from the quartz ores and was sure that the chance of making a lot of money was worth his time and effort regardless of temporary sacrifices on the part of his wife and children. Upon his return to San Francisco he looked up John Randohr, the German chemist whom he met aboard the steamship *California* between Panama City and San Francisco in 1850. They found a little place on Market Street and together they experimented in trying to perfect a process for refining quartz ore. Some of the Comstock ore yielded readily to quicksilver, but some of it resisted all known methods. What they hoped to do was to develop a way in which not only the new ore coming out of the mines could be processed more efficiently, but the refuse or tailings generally thrown away could be reworked to advantage.

By April 20, 1861, the men were sufficiently confident of their process that they signed an agreement as to division of any profits. Originally the agreement called for five-sixths to Sutro and one-sixth to Randohr but two words were crossed out to change the division of profits to four-sixths and two-sixths. Randohr was to keep secret, under penalties of perjury, the Randohr-Sutro process of extracting gold and silver from ores, tailings, etc. On July 15, 1861, Sutro gave permission to Randohr to use the process in the Esmeralda District, Mono County, and in San Francisco, but still under pledge of secrecy.

When the invention was nearly completed Sutro went again to Washoe to look for a place to establish a reducing mill. As on his previous trips, he found four bustling camps on or near the Comstock Lode. Dayton lay in the Carson River valley east of Sun Mountain and at the foot of Gold Canyon. It had promise mainly as a center of commerce and milling. Three miles up the canyon Sutro found Silver City, the smallest of the mining camps. He then passed through a narrow defile known as Devil's Gate and a climb of three more miles brought him to Gold Hill. He was now approaching the heart of the Comstock Lode. A mile and a half more and he was at Virginia City, already the largest of the Comstock mining camps.

Sutro found a fine mill site at Dayton and started in a small way, but by 1863 he had a substantial establishment with eight stamps and twenty amalgamating pans and an assay office attached. The works also had two roasting furnaces twelve feet in diameter, each capable of roasting one ton at a time. Steam power was used to drive the machinery and the entire works was surrounded by a neat fence. Wood for the furnaces was plentiful and cheap. Sutro started out working the tailings and sometimes got out more value than had been taken out when the rock had first been processed by inferior methods. Many years later he recalled a contract with the Gould and Curry Co. which was a bonanza. He got $75 a ton for working the better class ores and could work six tons a day. He remembered a net profit of almost $10,000 a month.

Adolph's brother Hugo came West and ran the mill for a time and Adolph spent much of his time on horseback, riding up to Virginia City to report on assays and work on contracts for ore. He kept a little leather-bound notebook in which he recorded the assays, but as he rode over the hills and up the steep grade to Virginia he was prospecting for something other than metal. He still had a tunnel in mind. He had proposed a different method of removing ore in his first report from Washoe; he was now more convinced than ever that what was needed was a tunnel "which at once insures drainage, ventilation, and facilitates the work." Adolph spent countless hours searching for the best place to start a common tunnel to go from the edge of the valley straight into the Comstock Lode.

Sutro would leave the cottonwoods along the Carson and go through the sagebrush and occasional pine trees towards the top of Mt. Davidson, as Sun Mountain had been prosaically renamed. There is many a hill and narrow pass in the short distance between Dayton and Virginia, and the land rises 1,600 feet in the less than six miles a crow would need to fly between the two towns. As Adolph neared Virginia City he must have loved to turn back to admire the view. In the fall the gray of the sagebrush on the hills ends in the vibrant yellow of the cottonwoods along the river, but in all seasons of the year the mystery and immensity of the desert pervades the valley of the Carson River.

During the time Sutro lived in Dayton but worked in Virginia he became acquainted with a young journalist on the staff of the *Territorial Enterprise* who was developing a style of writing for which he would become famous. He was not alone in using this style, nor in applying it to the region. J. Ross Browne had gone on foot to Washoe in the fall of '59 and *Harper's Magazine* had printed his humorous articles and lively pen and ink drawings. Browne was a man of many talents; Samuel Clemens concentrated on one. During his two-year stay on the Comstock Clemens had to strain for an effect he was later to produce with apparent ease. His later jibes at Sutro were superior to his first, both in real humor and in giving a truer picture of the man whom he said had no sense of humor. It is interesting, however, to read one early effort of Mark Twain which concerns Sutro:

Eight left Virginia yesterday and came down to Dayton with Mr. Sutro. Time 30 minutes — distance 8 or 9 miles. There is nothing very slow about that kind of travel. We found Dayton the same old place but taking up a good deal more room than it did the last time I saw it, and looking more brisk and lively with its increase of business, and more handsome on account of the beautiful dressed stone buildings with which it is being embellished of late.

Just as we got fairly under way, and were approaching Ball Robert's bridge, Sutro's dog, "Carlo," got to skirmishing around in the extravagant exuberance of his breakfast, and shipped up a fight with six or seven other dogs whom he was entirely unacquainted with, had never met before and probably has no desire to meet again. He waltzed into them right gallantly and right gallantly waltzed out again.

We also left at about this time and trotted briskly across Ball Robert's bridge. I remarked that Ball Robert's bridge was a good one and a credit to that bald gentleman. I said it in a fine burst of humor and more on account of the joke than anything else, but Sutro is insensible to the more delicate touches of American wit, and the effort was entirely lost on him. I don't think Sutro minds a joke of mild character any more than a dead man would. However, I repeated it once or twice without producing any visible effect, and finally derived what comfort I could by laughing at it myself.

Mr. Sutro being a confirmed business man, replied in a practical and businesslike way. He said the bridge was a good one, and so were all public blessings of a similar nature when entrusted to the hands of private individuals. He said if the county had built the bridge it would have cost an extravagant sum of money, and would have been eternally out of repair. He also said the only way to get public work well and properly done was to let it out by contract.

"For instance," says he, "they have fooled away two or three years trying to capture Richmond, whereas if they had let the job by contract to some sensible business man, the thing would have been accomplished and forgotten long ago." It was a novel and original idea and I forgot my joke for the next half hour in speculating upon its feasibility.

Clemens spent only two years on the Comstock but he enriched the area with his pranks and humor and took away a golconda of memories.

At about this time an event occurred which was entirely lacking in humor. The Sutro Mill burned late in 1863 and a man sleeping on the premises perished in the flames. The mill was insured for a large sum and the usual rumor went the rounds that the fire had been arranged by the owner. The fact that the mill was not rebuilt no doubt strengthened the rumor, and certainly it was an excellent time to liquidate. But Sutro was not a violent man and he maintained excellent relations with employees from the first time he entered his father's mill as a child, and would do so until his death. He may possibly have been capable of destroying a thing by fire, but certainly not an employee, and probably not a thing bearing the name "Sutro." On occasion this voluble man could keep silent, for he twice cleared out of a situation and offered no explanation. This was the first time; he would wait sixteen years for the next.

CHAPTER V

THE HIGH ROAD TO SUCCESS

A LTHOUGH A "MILLING CRAZE" had resulted in too many stamp mills, the Comstock mines were still booming. Adolph Sutro was a member of the Washoe Stock and Exchange Board and he actively bought and sold stock for others. He also loaned money and he offered stock for sale in his own mine known (of course) as the Sutro mine. Now instead of constantly roaming the hills on horseback he occasionally sat in the exchange hall, which was richly furnished and had a skylight of stained glass. Still he could not stop thinking about a tunnel.

The Comstock Lode became well known for its many bonanzas but it had its times of borrasca too. If you looked down C Street, Virginia City, late in 1864 you could watch miners walk by, heavy of foot and heavy of heart. Many of them were wondering whether to stay with the declining mines or get out, as some of their fellow miners had already done. Time was when you could get a job in almost any mill or mine, and at good wages. Sometimes a few spare dollars invested in "feet" (shares) in a mine would bring rich rewards, but now the market price of all stock was low. If you still owned stock you were more likely to get an assessment than a dividend. In spite of depressed conditions hundreds of men were still at work in the Gould and Curry and in other mines. Bullion worth $12,400,000 had been taken out of the entire Comstock Lode in 1863 and production for 1864 would at least equal that year. If a man was working he might as well hang on and wait for the upturn promised by the more hopeful.

[41]

If you listened as you walked along C Street you would be conscious of an over-all throbbing sound. The heavy tread of oxen, the crack of a teamster's whip, and the clunk of money on a bar were irregular compared to the monotony of the pumping of the mines. The Ophir Mine was having real trouble with the floods of hot water trapped deep within Sun Mountain. Last year a miner had driven his pick through a clay seam at a point 313 feet below the surface. He released a spout of water which soon created a lake 21 feet deep, 30 feet wide, and 100 feet long. Fortunately no lives were lost and by using suction pumps and a bailing tank in the adjacent Mexican Mine the water was finally held in check. This reservoir was not fully pumped out until eleven months later, but almost immediately another water pocket was tapped which flooded the shaft to a depth of 160 feet.

Virginia City, Nevada Territory, was now five years old. If all went well, Nevada would soon be a state and the boys could vote for Lincoln in the November election. They could then whoop it up and keep their thoughts off of the troubles in the mines. When they celebrated in Virginia it was likely to last for days, whether it was for a funeral, a visit from a celebrity, or any other convenient pretext.

No one knew just how much ore there was beneath the surface of the mountain on which Virginia hung so precipitously, but one thing was sure — the remaining ore was not to be mined easily. The mines were going deeper and deeper and old Sun Mountain demanded an increasing toll. Machinery was becoming costlier than ever before, wood for timbering was coming from ever greater distances, and mining claims were so snarled that litigation was a major industry. Sober estimates indicate that in those first five years about twenty per cent of the product of the mines was spent on law suits.

In spite of over six months of depression, Virginia City was still one of the outstanding cities of the Far West. She boasted twenty-seven quartz mills and hoisting works, of which the Gould and Curry was the largest in the territory, perhaps in the world. The Savage Mine had 800 feet on the Lode and a fifty horsepower engine, although many felt that it was too small. The Chollar had one rated at one hundred horsepower.

The fear of being a man who was careless with his pick, or of working near such a man, obsessed some of the miners. If you did not look carefully you might hit clay which was serving as a natural bulkhead for the hot, nasty, smelly water. Then out would pour thousands of gallons, everyone would drop his pick, rush for the shaft, sound the alarm, and get pulled to the surface. Then there would be delay, perhaps the loss of work for weeks or months, all because you did not exercise more care.

A man could find places in Virginia to forget his fears. There were excellent performances at Maguire's Opera House (later named "Piper's"), dozens of saloons and gambling halls, and a row of cribs on D Street. Water for drinking was scarce, but other beverages were plentiful thanks to six local breweries and a river of imported whiskey. But a man could not live forever on what he saved from his wages of four dollars a day. He could not spend all his time in one of Louis Bach's three bathing establishments or in the saloons and gambling houses. He could not read Virginia's four newspapers forever and unless the mineowners solved the problems of excess water and foul air, he might as well take the next stage for Summit City, or Idaho, or Montana.

Mine accidents must be an anticipated part of underground mining. The men who panned gold in California might die from pneumonia brought on by exposure — or from bullets. Gunfire was just as frequent in Nevada, but medical care for illness or wounds was much better on the Comstock than it had been at Whiskey Gulch or Iowa Hill. In 1864 Virginia had a city hospital, seldom used since the city doctor, J. C. Tucker, M.D., made home visits instead. But the county hospital located in Virginia had two buildings three stories high, with beds for sixty men and fourteen women. Dr. Thomas H. Pinkerton was visiting physician and superintendent. Anyone wanting a private room could have it for five dollars a day. Less pretentious quarters were available at two dollars a day for "patients who have money," and free to those who did not. There was an insane department located in the basement and the kitchens were designed to serve for disasters, with cooking ranges capable of preparing food for 200 persons.

The city had just organized its accommodations for the dead. Twenty-seven acres had been purchased on Flowery Hill for $2,500, the Catholics were about to erect a cross forty feet high on Mount St. Mary's, and the Eureka Society was opening a Hebrew cemetery on Cedar Hill.

Virginia City was a man's town, but there were women there and children as well. The Sisters of Mercy and the Sisters of Charity ran schools, there were numerous other private schools including those of the Misses Heggens and Dr. H. M. Bien, and the public schools taught 129 boys and 140 girls. There was a Storey County Bible Society organized "to circulate the Bible without note or comment." Also there were churches: two Roman Catholic, one Episcopal, a First Methodist Episcopal, a First Presbyterian, and an African Methodist Episcopal.

The Comstock had its full share of political activity. The early settlers pleaded a distaste for Mormon rule and won political separation as Nevada Territory. Now the territory was making ridiculous statements about her population. She claimed that the 6,857 of 1860 had risen to 100,000 and she was demanding statehood. If the United States had not been engaged in a civil war, Nevada's claims would surely have been subject to closer scrutiny. Corrupt politicians and a system of law based on bribery are hardly good recommendations for statehood, let alone false estimates of population. President Lincoln had problems of the present and was

[44]

planning for a restored Union which would have a Congress with many Southern members. Lincoln was eager to welcome a free state which would provide two senators and at least one representative who could all be counted on to vote for the anti-slavery amendment in Congress. This same new state could also be counted on to ratify the proposed amendment, helping to obtain the necessary and difficult approval of three-fourths of the states. Lincoln also thought that he might need Nevada's three electoral votes in the presidential election of 1864.

Nevada had already drawn up one state constitution but made the mistake of combining the vote on the constitution with the first election of state officers. The many would-be public servants who failed of nomination tended to oppose the constitution, none more vigorously than William M. Stewart. This colorful and dictatorial lawyer, who dominated the Comstock bar, found that the new state could tax the shafts and drifts of new mines which had never produced. Stewart carried on a whirlwind campaign against this iniquitous constitution on behalf of the "poor honest miner," and the voters sustained him by a four-to-one ratio in January of 1864.

A second constitution was drafted leaving out all taxation clauses and the fatal concurrent state election, and Stewart backed it with all of his considerable ability. The election was held in early September and the constitution overwhelmingly approved. In the grand manner of a community resting on a mountain of gold and silver, all 15,000 words of the constitution were sent to Washington by telegraph, dot and dash, at a cost to Nevada taxpayers of $3,416.77. On October 31 came word that the President had signed the act of admission earlier that day, and all Nevada went wild.

The city directory for Virginia and adjacent towns for 1864-65 opened with a statement well designed to please Comstock merchants. It read: "Virginia owes the proud position that she now occupies, more to the indefatigable go-aheaditiveness of her business men than to any natural cause (other than the mines)." While it contained a grain of truth, the excepting of the mines inflated the role of the business men beyond all reason. So long as there was ore in Sun Mountain men would flock there. Let the ore peter out, the mines flood, or the mine management be inefficient, then what would be left? With no money coming in all the "go-aheaditiveness" in the world could not function.

It was in 1864 that Virginia City experienced its first major depression, and it was also the year in which a new factor appeared upon the scene. The Bank of California opened a branch in Virginia City and sent William Sharon as manager. He was a small man with a tall plug hat and cold gray eyes. He had recently lost his fortune in a crooked mining stock deal and was consumed with a desire for revenge. Behind him was William C. Ralston, driving force of the bank in spite of his modest title of "cashier." The bank's first move in Nevada was to offer loans on good security at two per cent per month, a reduction of from one to three per cent over prevailing rates at the local banks. Since mills were considered good security, and since the mines were not producing enough high-paying ore to keep the large number of mills busy, it was not long before many mills were in debt to the bank. Eventually the bank organized a corporation, the Union Mill and Mining Company, to manage the mills they had assumed due to defaults on loans. And, of course, if a mill was good security a mine could be even better.

While the Bank of California made its early bids for power Sutro approached the first legislature of the State of Nevada. He wanted a franchise for his proposed tunnel. Many of the legislators considered him somewhat crazy, a man with but one idea and that not a very good one. There had been some tunnels, none very long nor very efficient, and here was this dreamer talking about a tunnel four miles long! Some men, or as Sutro said, "a few thinking men,"

San Francisco in 1860, when Sutro left the city for "Washoe." *(California State Library)*

Long Wharf, San Francisco, where Sutro had one of his first retail stores. *(California State Library)*

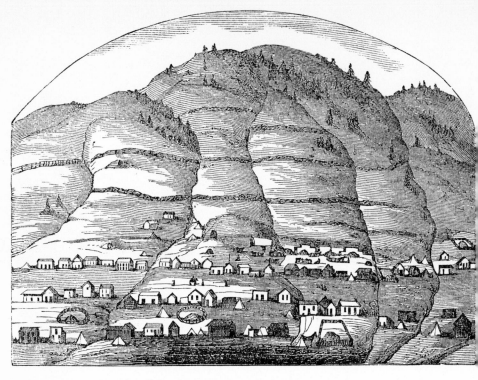

Virginia City in 1859. One of the earliest known pictures, it appeared in *Hutchings' California Magazine. At right:* Some idea of the city's rapid growth may be obtained by an artist's fanciful sketch made in 1864 (both pictures: *Bancroft Library*). *Below:* Wood being floated down the Carson River for use as firewood. The Sutro Mill at Dayton was powered by steam and used large chunks of wood such as these for fuel. (*Nevada Historical Society*)

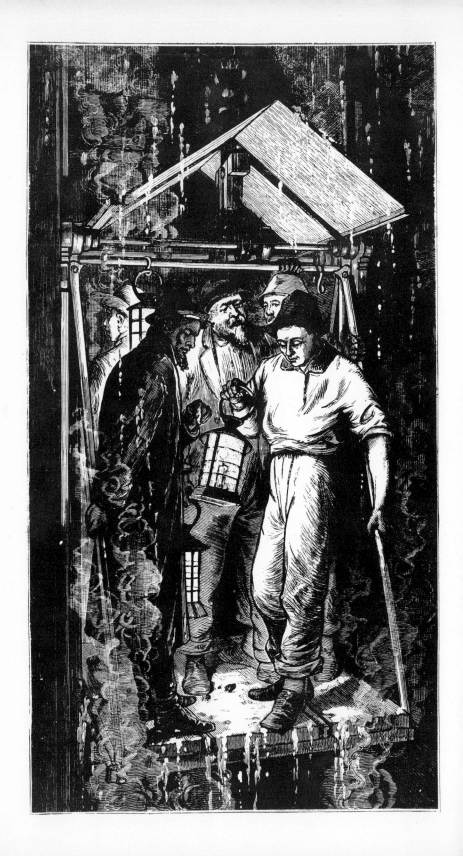

Heat was always a problem on the Comstock. Long after the advent of Sutro's tunnel, it was the cause for cessation of deep mining. Good ore was left in the deeper levels when live steam and boiling water forced the miners away. Here are shown near naked miners at the ever present ice water barrel. Lower woodcut depicts visitors watching steam rising from the water at the pump discharge on the surface. *Page left:* Miners descending one of the shafts with the steam ascending with the updraft as they go by. This was evidently after the tunnel as its completion did at least cause more draft and a slight cooling of the upper areas was accomplished.

The Gould and Curry Silver Mining Company's Reduction Works near Virginia City, about 1862. Eliot Lord called it "the most conspicuous monument of inexperience and extravagance ever erected in a mining district." (*Nevada Historical Society*)

Miners coming off shift in one of the deep mines. They are coming up a manway in one of the very heavy square-set stopes common to Comstock ore bodies. These mines were worked 'round the clock so the men composing the next shift are standing by to descend as soon as the ladders are cleared.

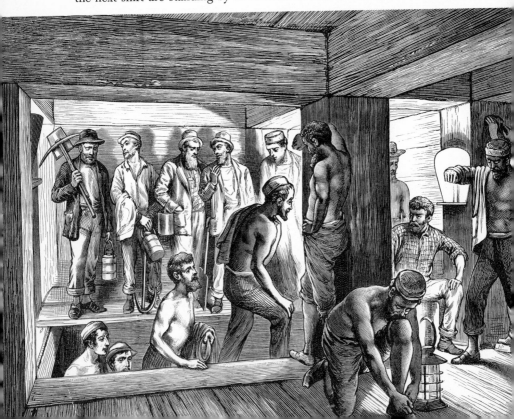

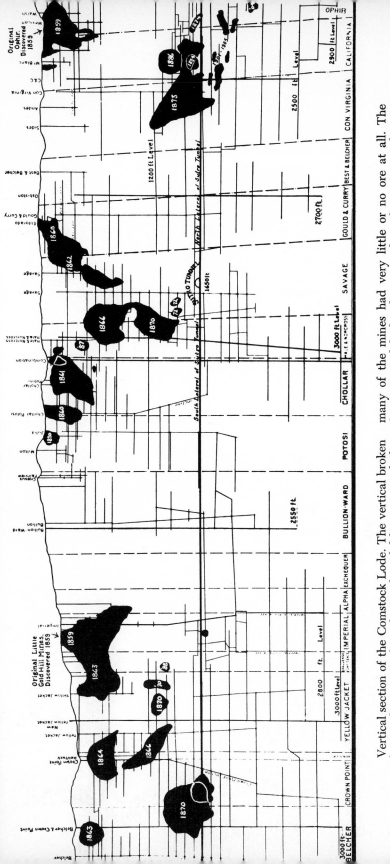

Vertical section of the Comstock Lode. The vertical broken lines indicate mine boundaries, the solid lines major shafts. Black areas are the stopes or bodies of ore removed. The large stope to the right at the Sutro Tunnel level is the Big Bonanza. This is a graphic illustration of the fact that many of the mines had very little or no ore at all. The Sutro Tunnel had value as a drain but was too late to collect royalties on significant quantities of ore. *(Bancroft Library)*

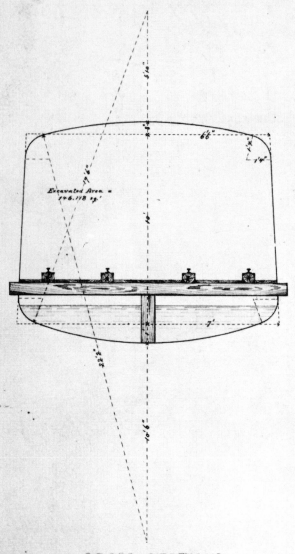

Excavated Area =
146.118 sq'

6'6"

1'4"

7'

Excavated Area
247.968 sq'

Excavated Area
222.968 sq'

Timber regd in Main Tun
550 Feet.

CROSS-SECTIONS
OF
SUTRO TUNNEL
1874.

Scale. ¼ inch = 1 foot.

Carl O. Wederkinch. C.E.

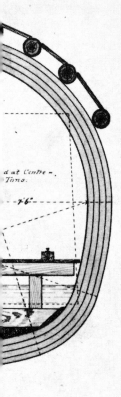

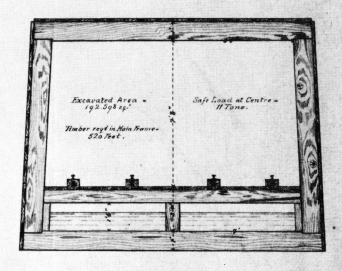

Excavated Area =
192.598 sq.'

Safe Load at Centre =
11 Tons.

Timber reqd in Main Frame =
520 Feet.

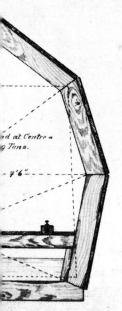

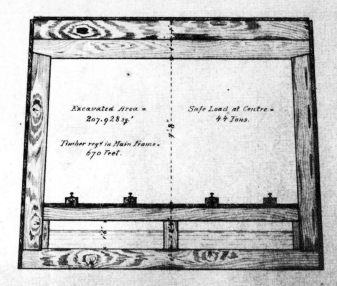

Excavated Area =
207.928 sq.'

Safe Load at Centre =
44 Tons.

Timber reqd in Main Frame =
670 Feet.

Gold Hill Miners Union. A view of the building many years after the heyday of its activity. *(James M. Stephens)*

MINERS! LABORING MEN!

MECHANICS! RALLY!

GREAT MASS MEETING

AT

PIPERS-OPERA HOUSE

ADOLPH SUTRO

Will address the Citizens of

Virginia City — Sept 20th 8 o'clock P.M.

SUBJECT: "The Sutro Tunnel and the Bank of California." Admission

FREE. Seats reserved for Ladies. Come one! Come all!

A group of miners at the Yellow Jacket mine at Gold Hill. The fire which originated at the 800 foot level of this mine on April 7, 1869, helped to turn public sentiment in favor of Sutro's tunnel. *(Nevada Historical Society)*

Virginia City in 1867 or earlier, with Maguire's Opera House in the background. It was in this building, renamed "Piper's Opera House," that Sutro held his mass meeting on September 20, 1869. *(Nevada Historical Society)*

Father Patrick Manogue, beloved priest, during his years at Virginia City. While working as a gold miner in California, Patrick Manogue was inspired to devote his life to religious service. Immediately after being ordained he was assigned a parish in the Comstock area. After twenty years as "the perfect parish priest" he was consecrated bishop of the diocese. He later became the first Bishop of Sacramento and built the Cathedral of the Blessed Sacrament. *(Rev. John B. McGloin, S.J.)*

Shaft No. 2. Four shafts were started along the line of the tunnel with the intention of digging both ways from the bottom of each, thus with each end as well, the work would be in progress at ten places and greatly speed up the work. So much bad ground and water was encountered that only the first two were completed and these were too late to use as working places. They did serve good purpose for ventilation.

Portal of tunnel during early construction. Theodolite mounted on block at left was used to keep the work in perfect alignment. *(California Historical Society)*

Rare underground view. Pilot tunnel was driven ahead at maximum speed by one crew while the enlargement and timbering were carried on by another. Candles attached along the wall in pilot bore must have been duplicated in greater number behind camera. This exposure must have taken a long time as no men or mules can be seen. Fancy sprung inspection car must have been used to transport photographer. Economy of operation is indicated by the wooden rails with thin strap iron on the running edges of the track. This was a method used in many of the "depression" gold mines just a few years ago. (*Louis L. Stein, Jr.*)

Lyon County court house, Dayton. When rain fell on the "first pick," everyone adjourned to this building for additional speeches and the barbecue. This photograph was taken about thirty years later. *(Nevada Historical Society)*

A train of the Virginia and Truckee Railroad on its trestle at the Crown Point mine hauling freight Sutro had counted on for his projected tunnel. *(Nevada Historical Society)*

were convinced and somehow he managed to get a unanimous vote for the franchise.

The Nevada act was approved February 4, 1865. It gave a right of way, as far as it lay in the power of the state to grant it. The question of payments to be made by the mines for the advantages provided by the tunnel was left to such agreements as Sutro might be able to make with the mining companies. He was required to begin construction within one year and to complete the tunnel within eight years.

With this grant as a basis he now proceeded to have the land surveyed. He pointed out the exact spot which he believed to be the ideal place for the tunnel mouth. The surveyor came back with a report that Sutro had been off on his calculations by a few feet, and no doubt complimented Sutro on his ability to come so close to the spot without the aid of instruments. Sutro, however, sent the man back to check his figures. The schoolboy in Aachen had been proficient in mathematics and the surveyor had spoken too soon. The proper place to start a tunnel had already been chosen and the surveyor admitted he had made a mistake in his calculations.

That problem settled, it was high time to get to work on the mining companies and other potential investors. Sutro started another of his leather-bound notebooks. First he entered the names of the directors of each mine and in the back of the book he began drafting a proposed pamphlet. He scratched out and crossed over but only succeeded in producing a choppy, dull article which became the first part of a pamphlet he soon published. In the pamphlet he quoted a letter from a geologist, Baron Ferdinand Richthofen, Dr. Phil. The baron was of the opinion that "the future of Washoe, indeed, depends on the execution of this magnificent enterprise." Endorsements from businessmen were also included. One letter which "cheerfully" recommended Mr. Sutro's proposition was signed by three bankers, of whom

[47]

one was William C. Ralston, and another endorsement was signed by William Sharon.

By July 24 Sutro was sufficiently encouraged to enter into the formation of the Sutro Tunnel Company, organized as an association of individuals under the laws of the state of Nevada. The first trustees were: William M. Stewart, Louis Janin, Jr., Henry K. Mitchell, D. E. Avery, and Adolph Sutro. The President of the new company was Stewart, Senator from the newborn state of Nevada and already noted as great leader of the Nevada bar.

Although Sutro seemed to have impressive support, it was an uphill struggle. He found a vast indifference on the part of the mine superintendents, even though many of the mines were in the midst of a baffling and apparently insoluble water problem. Many of the best mines were flooded and efforts at pumping were making but precarious gains. The tunnel offered drainage not now but in a seemingly far-off future. Sutro stated later that it required eight months of the hardest sort of work to win over the mine superintendents.

During this same period, months were spent in working out a contract to be signed by the tunnel company and the mining companies. Both parties employed lawyers to make sure that they had a thoroughly adequate instrument. Once satisfied, these agreements were executed on parchment, and, as Sutro noted, "the care with which they were gotten up will indicate at a glance that they were intended to last a great many years, and probably for a century."

Parchment was nice, but the importance of the contract lay in its terms. Each mining company that signed agreed to pay a royalty of two dollars on every ton of ore extracted after the Sutro Tunnel reached its mine. This fee was strictly for the service of drainage and ventilation. A schedule of additional fees was agreed to for removal of ore through the tunnel (twenty-five cents per mile per ton) or for bringing wood or other material from the mouth of the tunnel to the mines. Persons would be transported the length of the tun-

[48]

nel for twenty-five cents each. There was nothing in the contract to compel a company to use the tunnel for anything but ventilation and drainage — in fact, so long as they paid the two dollars per ton on all ore removed they could drain or ventilate in any way they wished.

These contracts assuring royalties were essential, but the millions of dollars needed for construction were equally necessary. The task of educating the public as to the character of the Comstock vein and the necessity for a deep-drain tunnel or adit must go forward. The board of trustees of the Sutro Tunnel Company asked Baron Richthofen to expand his earlier observations into a thorough study of the future of the Comstock Lode with special emphasis on the proposed Sutro Tunnel.

Baron Richthofen seemed ideally suited for such an assignment. He was of German birth and had been educated at Breslau and Berlin. He had carried out geological investigations in the Tyrol and Transylvania. Subsequently he served as geologist on a Prussian diplomatic mission to the Far East in which he visited many lands. He was now in California and was willing to undertake the investigation proposed.

The baron studied the Comstock mining district carefully and composed a full-length report stating his views. Completed on November 22, 1865, the report was published by the tunnel company in 1866 as an eighty-three page booklet. The majority of these pages dealt with the geological structure of the Comstock Lode and he proved to his own satisfaction — and probably to everyone's — that this was a true fissure vein. The writing was lucid and convincing. As to the continuity of the Comstock vein in depth he said:

> It was proved in the foregoing pages that the Comstock lode presents in all respects the character of a true fissure vein, and these in such perfect degree as but few veins of this class exhibit. It was furthermore proved that the mode of its formation can only

be explained in one way, namely, by solfataric action connected with the outbursts of trachyte. No theory but this is able to explain the origin of the vast quantities of vein-matter, the profuse diffusion of ore through it, the abnormal quantitative proportion of the metals in the ore, the thorough decomposition of the eastern country for miles in width, the mode of distribution of the ore in the vein, and the formation of the "horses" which obstruct it in many parts. As the creative forces acted from below, they must have found an open way for the communication of the laboratory below with the place of deposition in the upper portion of the vein. No sound mind can therefore doubt the continuance of the fissure, and therefore of the vein, in depth.

Baron Richthofen pointed out with great clarity that the chances for discovering rich bonanzas of the type already found, and exhausted, near the surface would never be duplicated in depth and that ore found would "not materially differ at any depth from what it is at the present lower levels."

In concluding his remarks on the mode of continuance of the vein, he said:

In winding up these considerations, we come to the positive conclusion, that the amount of nearly fifty million dollars which has been extracted from the Comstock lode, is but a small proportion of the amount of silver awaiting future extraction, in the virgin portions of the vein, from the lowest levels explored down to indefinite depth; but that, from analogy with other argentiferous veins, as well as from facts observed on the Comstock lode, the diffusion of the silver through extensive deposits of middle and low grade ores is far more probable than its accumulation in bodies of rich ore.

At this point it may be well to consider the emotional impact of the term, "true fissure vein." In the minds of many this seems to have been nearly synonymous with "mother lode," and represented to many people in 1866 — as it does to many today — an inexhaustible supply of riches. California and Nevada were crowded with men and women trying to amass fortunes by buying and selling mining stock. People of the West were swayed by the term "true fissure vein." They were, in fact, hypnotized by it and the baron was telling them exactly what they wanted to hear. *They should have paid much closer attention to his prophecies of middle and low-grade ores in the lower depths.*

Richthofen also spoke of the increasing costs as the mining struck lower and lower levels, but on this point he felt that a deep-drain tunnel offered great hope. In fact, he concluded his report by giving seven reasons why such a tunnel should be dug. Briefly they were:

1. Drainage of the mines, "the greatest benefit."
2. Permit work to be economically done at "the unusual depth of at least twenty-four hundred feet."
3. Removal of the ore more economically than at present.
4. Giving vent to a "perpetual flow of water."
5. A thorough ventilation of the mines.
6. The thorough exploration of parts of the Comstock vein so far unproductive.
7. Exploration of the country from the mouth of the proposed tunnel to the Comstock vein.

This was an excellent study and stands today as the answer to the question: "What did a real mining expert know about the Comstock Lode after six years of mining?" Nearly $48,000,000 worth of gold and silver had been removed between January, 1862 and December, 1865. It was good to know that the mines could be expected to continue to be lucrative even though a tunnel must be bored. Richthofen was uncanny in the accuracy of most of his prophecies; in his evaluation of the proposed tunnel, however, he was assuming it would be built in a short period, such as two years. He made one miscalculation and that concerned the difficulty of the physical job of construction. He wrote: "Construction of the work would be comparatively easy."

Adolph Sutro was well aware that many obstacles must be overcome if his tunnel were to be constructed. Among the major problems would be the financial and legal ones. He would begin his search for capital in New York and Europe where interest rates were far lower than on the Pacific Coast. In order to assist in this quest he obtained a letter of introduction from the powerful Bank of California. Signed by William C. Ralston, it was addressed to the Oriental Bank Corporation of London. After outlining the nature of the tunnel project, Ralston wrote: "Too much cannot be said of the great importance of this work, if practicable upon any remunerative basis." Ralston stated that he had learned that certain scientific men had endorsed the project without reserve and he hoped that this letter would gain Mr. Sutro an opportunity to present his enterprise to the public fairly and upon its merits.

Sutro was also aware of a major legal problem. He knew that the United States government held title to the land in the Comstock district and that technically the mining companies were mere "squatters." By the same token, only the United States could grant clear title to a right of way for the Sutro Tunnel. As soon as the royalty contracts were signed, Sutro would go to Washington, D. C., and on to New York and Europe.

Leah would stay behind in San Francisco and care for her growing family. Kate had been born in 1862 and Charles in 1863. The happiness of the birth of a third son, Edgar, in 1865 was followed by tragedy within less than two months. Little Gussie, the first-born son, died on Christmas day. Emma, the eldest child, was not quite nine when the sixth child was born, and Leah was also destined to suffer two stillbirths. Finances had been hard for the Sutros and would become much worse, but such problems were as naught to Leah compared to the loss of her two babies and five-year-old Gussie. When the sorrow of the loss of a child enters a woman's heart, it leaves only with the last beat.

Adolph steamed out of the Golden Gate on May 10, 1866. In Panama he was undoubtedly impressed by the ease of crossing that neck of land in comparison with his hardships of 1850. The opening of the Panama Railroad in 1855 had turned the Isthmus into the favored route for passenger travel between California and the East, and Sutro used it on this and numerous later occasions. On this first journey via steamships and jungle railroad he reached the national capital in four weeks, arriving early in June.

He found no opposition in Congress and on July 25, 1866, President Johnson signed an act often referred to later as the Sutro Tunnel Act. The same session of Congress passed the first general mining law since the organization of the Federal government, a law under which actual occupants on mining lands could apply for legal title to their claims. Interestingly enough, the general law was passed one day *after* the Sutro Tunnel Act was passed.

The Sutro Tunnel Act granted the right of way for a tunnel and certain other rights not to the existing tunnel company but "to A. Sutro, his heirs and assigns." Sutro was also given the right to buy as much as two sections of non-mineral land near the mouth of the proposed tunnel for $1.25 an acre. Sutro could buy any mineral lands within two thousand feet of the tunnel on either side at $5.00 an acre. The Comstock Lode was specifically excepted from this right, however, and so were mining claims already filed and occupied.

Last, but far from the least of the rights, was the provision that the mines on the Comstock must pay royalties to the owners of the tunnel. No specific rate of pay was set but it would be determined by negotiation between the mineowners and the owners of the tunnel. But every mine benefited must pay whether it had signed a contract or not, and its title from the government would be subject to that condition.

Along with all these rights, Sutro accomplished the remarkable feat of keeping his obligations and penalties down to a minimum. There was no forfeiture clause, no time limit on the life of the grant, and no time limit set for completion of the tunnel. Since Federal lands were concerned this grant from Congress no doubt superseded the year-old Nevada act with its troublesome time limits. But with or without a time limit Sutro would build the tunnel promptly.

Full of confidence he went to New York to raise the necessary million or so of capital. He wrote a pamphlet about the tunnel enterprise and turned it over to a printer. Published under date of September 1, 1866, it is no doubt an accurate reflection of the oral arguments used by Sutro in his many meetings with New York capitalists. He was elated with the ease and extent of his triumph in Washington. He assured his hearers in New York that the tunnel was going to be immensely profitable. The minor services made possible by the tunnel and town lot sales would be as lucrative as the royalty itself.

Sutro predicted a great shift of the Comstock population from Virginia City and Gold Hill to the tunnel company land at the mouth of Sutro Tunnel. He admitted that this would result in considerable loss to individuals and others, since these two towns had an assessed valuation of over $6,800,000 exclusive of mining property. He asserted that such a loss was inevitable, since with present methods the mining costs would soon exceed the value of bullion produced. In other words, the Sutro Tunnel would do nothing to save the doomed towns of Virginia City and Gold Hill but it would assure the continuance of successful operation of the mines themselves.

He foresaw the growth of a new and large town at the mouth of the tunnel. Miners would ride to work through the tunnel instead of being lowered in little cages. Ore would be removed through the tunnel, and the cars going into the mine would haul timber, powder and other supplies. Waste rock could be economically removed and low-grade ores now of no value could be profitably worked after the advent of the tunnel. This assumed the rise of large stamp mills at the mouth of the tunnel which could utilize the great flow of water from the tunnel for power. Of the present reduction mills at Gold Hill and Virginia City he said bluntly: "The only course left to them is to remove to the tunnel company land."

Had Sutro written in a milder tone he might have infuriated people less, but Congress had given him so much so easily he now wrote with unseemly authority. He gave the impression that everything good and prosperous on the Comstock Lode would drain into the tunnel company land (and treasury) just as the tunnel would drain the mines.

Financially, Sutro's imagination soared. Royalties at present levels of ore extraction would be $3,000 a day. Waste rock would bring $1,000 per day. Transportation of the 3,000 miners now employed at twenty-five cents a trip would bring another $1,500 a day. (The careful historian Grant H. Smith says that in 1866 an average of 1500 men were employed underground.) Sale of town lots he figured at a total of $3,000,000. On one item Sutro was very cautious — he said that the revenue arising from discovery and development of ore bodies on the tunnel route could not be estimated. Actually, he had high hopes for real riches from this source.

Summing it up, Sutro anticipated an annual revenue of between $2,300,000 and $6,000,000 on a tunnel which would cost slightly less than $2,000,000 to dig. Since he estimated revenue from various sources during construction of the main tunnel would amount to $500,000, he was of the opinion that capital of only $1,500,000 would be required for his enterprise.

In addition to oral arguments he had letters of introduction to leading New York figures. He had at least two letters from Senator Stewart, one of them addressed to Collis P. Huntington, important member of the group behind the Central Pacific Railroad. The railroad was under construction and Huntington was the partner stationed in the East to take care of purchasing and financial problems. A second letter was to James Gordon Bennett, prominent editor of the New York *Herald*.

Sutro visited as many financial houses and wealthy individuals as he could reach. The New Yorkers were well impressed with the idea of building a deep-drain tunnel to make the wealth of the Comstock more easily available. To them only one thing seemed odd. Why, if this tunnel was so needed in Nevada, didn't the people there put up any money to build it? How could Sutro expect to raise money in New York if he had no showing of good will from Nevada and California?

Sutro used his great persuasive powers on these men urging them to write a letter stating this objection and promising him Eastern capital if he obtained an adequate "home endorsement." Sutro returned to the Pacific Coast in August and such a letter was written under date of October 5, 1866.

After describing the lack of Pacific Coast money in the enterprise as a "fatal objection," the letter said that if a portion of the requisite capital, "say $400,000 or $500,000," were subscribed in California and Nevada and if work on the tunnel were actually commenced, "we think you will find it comparatively an easy task to obtain the balance of the funds here." The letter continued:

Let some of the leading men on your coast, who are known here for their commercial standing and their integrity, form a preliminary board of directors, and you may then, while the tunnel is daily progressing, return to New York, we think, with confidence of success, and we shall use our best effort to assist you in accomplishing your object.

The letter was signed by forty individuals or companies who, in Sutro's opinion, represented "probably $100,000,000." Names of interest to the modern reader were: Peter Cooper; August Belmont; J. & Wm. Seligman & Co.; Eugene Kelly (former partner of Wm. C. Ralston); R. C. Fergusson; Wm. T. Coleman; J. C. Frémont; and C. P. Huntington. The names of two important men whom Sutro had approached were lacking — Commodore Vanderbilt and William B. Astor.

Sutro promptly set to work on the task of getting stock subscriptions from mining companies, individuals, and other sources. He was concerned, however, about the time limit in his royalty contracts. He had agreed to raise three millions in stock subscriptions, with at least 10 per cent paid in cash, by August 1, 1867, and he had also agreed to begin construction on that day at the latest. Sutro went to the mining companies and obtained a written extension of time of one year.

While busy attempting to get stock subscriptions he took the trouble to obtain further legislative favors. In January, 1867, the Nevada legislature passed two resolutions at his behest. The first one expressed the legislature's thanks to Adolph Sutro for originating and pushing his plan for a tunnel. The legislature also expressed "entire confidence in the ability of Mr. Sutro to present to Congressmen and capitalists" the claims of the enterprise; knowing that he will prepare with skill, and clearly exhibit the arguments "without overlooking or exaggerating any of its merits."

A second resolution presented a new idea. It asked for Federal aid for the tunnel project. It advanced the argument repeatedly urged by Sutro that the doubling of the value of the taxable property of the United States within the last eighteen years "has mainly resulted from the vast addition of the precious metals within this time." The resolution went on to predict that the tunnel would make possible an ultimate production of bullion from the Comstock Lode of one

[57]

thousand millions, which "would be an increase to that extent of the public resources, and virtually, a reduction to a considerable extent of the public debt."

These resolutions had obvious value as part of Sutro's publicity campaign, but he did not rest content. He prevailed upon the Mechanics' Institute of San Francisco to evaluate the Sutro Tunnel project. The Institute was a major social and literary organization of that period. A special committee was appointed on March 7, 1867, which four weeks later reported on the proposed tunnel in glowing terms. At a regular meeting on April 4 the Institute unanimously accepted these favorable findings, which were so lengthy that they occupied twenty-six printed pages.

Sutro continued his efforts to raise money. He went to the mining companies with the idea that tunnel stock would be an enormously profitable investment. By owning some they would get back as much as they paid in royalties. Best of all, income from tunnel stock would be based on all Comstock production and would be steady, thus providing welcome income when a mine was not itself producing ore.

Through the early part of the year 1867 he concentrated on the mining companies in his efforts to raise money. He planned to go to San Francisco in about June to obtain money from private sources. On April 26 the trustees of the Savage Mining Co. signed an agreement to invest $150,000. By May Sutro had $600,000 subscribed, partly by mining companies and partly from individuals. In his own words: "I had a fair prospect of raising $1,000,000 in San Francisco, and the whole amount required, perhaps, in California." He saw the end of his struggles in sight. He did not relax, but no doubt he began to think in terms of tunneling equipment rather than this endless round of financial conferences. For seven years he had dreamed of a great tunnel and now, at last, he could begin construction.

CHAPTER VI

"BUT NOW COMMENCED THE TUG OF WAR"

A DOLPH THOUGHT he could forget the time when he had been called "crazy Sutro." He had friends now, and backers. He was greeted cordially as he walked down C Street in Virginia City. He counted Ralston and Sharon as friendly associates. He knew the mine operators were not overly enthusiastic about a tunnel, but they were pledging money toward construction and that was what counted. He knew (as did everyone else) that the Bank of California was dominated by Ralston in San Francisco and by Sharon in the Virginia City office, and that they in turn controlled most of the mines and mills on the Comstock. Since Ralston and Sharon endorsed the tunnel project the mine superintendents were endorsing it too.

In fact, it was growing increasingly difficult to make any major decision in this area just east of Mt. Davidson without having it dictated by the Bank of California. By mortgages and stock manipulation the bank contrived to gain more and more power, and its greed has been well expressed by Grant H. Smith, author of the study titled *History of the Comstock Lode, 1850-1920*. He wrote: "It was wormwood to Sharon to see a prosperous mine and mill that he did not control." Sutro had been wise not to rebuild his mill, but not so wise in some of his investments. Forty thousand dollars invested in a mine claim in Dayton was gone and he needed ready cash for propaganda materials such as the scale model of the tunnel done in plaster which he had ordered.

The Crown Point Mining Company was scheduled to hold its annual meeting on June 7, 1867. It was generally understood that the stockholders would ratify the $75,000

[59]

pledge the trustees had made to the tunnel company. Sutro considered himself, as he said later, "on the full road to success" and the ratification of the Crown Point pledge would just be another milestone along that road. Actually the road was ending and Sutro would face an uncharted wilderness.

A secret meeting was called by the bank the day before (on June 6) and the decision was made not to ratify the Crown Point subscription of $75,000 for tunnel stock. In addition, the President and Superintendent of Crown Point were to be discharged and replaced by men under the full control of the Bank of California. The annual meeting the following day carried out these orders and the bank showed the full force of its control.

Sutro knew immediately how this change in policy of the "bank ring," as he later called it, would affect his project. Other annual meetings would fail to ratify, agreements already ratified would be repudiated outright, and the $600,000 pledged would soon be only a memory. There is little positive evidence which proves the motives behind this change in position of the Bank of California. It is not too difficult, however, to analyze this change with a high degree of probability.

Sutro had begun his active promotion of the tunnel at a time when the Comstock mines were in a period of depression. Faith in the future of the Lode had been badly shaken, and one of the biggest factors in this depressing situation was enormous quantities of hot water underground. Pumping was costly and making only halting progress. Sutro came along and proposed a deep-drain tunnel. He would require a fee or royalty for this service, but only *after* the tunnel was in operation. Capitalists from the East or from Europe would be allowed to provide the millions needed for construction and Nevada would reap the benefits. Although it took considerable effort on Sutro's part, the leaders of the Comstock district, including Ralston, were convinced that the tunnel might help and that there was little harm in letting Sutro raise the capital so as to try out his scheme.

When Sutro's quest for Eastern capital failed, his plan appeared in a considerably altered perspective. Pacific Coast money would be necessary after all and in considerable amount. This was a much more difficult proposition to accept, but Sutro's great powers of persuasion proved equal to the task. It is quite probable, however, that this "home endorsement" which involved risking money was made more reluctantly than the purely verbal one which preceded it.

Sutro later believed that his Nevada resolution requesting Federal aid was very displeasing to the bank. One cannot prove that this was the turning point, as Sutro stoutly maintained, but it certainly did little to increase his popularity with Ralston and Sharon. An Adolph Sutro responsible to the stockholders such as the bank-controlled Comstock mines and to distant capitalists was one thing. A Sutro who was largely financed by a complaisant or friendly Congress would be much more difficult to control. Domination of the Comstock and monopolization of most of its profits were absolutely essential to Ralston's far-flung, and expensive, program of expansion of bank investments.

It is quite possible that these apprehensions were intensified by reading Sutro's New York pamphlet. We do not know that it circulated on the Pacific Coast, but we do know that in that pamphlet Sutro made detailed estimates of tunnel income for the first time. He predicted income between three and six million dollars annually at a time when the bullion production of the entire state of Nevada was $16,500,000 a year. In addition, Sutro boldly predicted in his pamphlet that the great bulk of the people would abandon Virginia and Gold Hill and settle near the mouth of the tunnel. Great stamping mills would be erected there and existing mills must either move or go out of business. Such a costly transformation could be justified only if necessary, and was it really necessary? Giant pumps had proved themselves in the mines during the past year; the water problem was under control.

Sutro now appeared as an interloper, bent upon performing a service of doubtful utility. He was not only an interloper, but also of alien race; in addition he had revealed himself to be very domineering, a man impossible to bend to the wills of others. Sutro must go! The Bank of California would write "finis" to the tunnel drama.

The men of the Bank of California had had a close call. They had foolishly encouraged a situation which could easily have ruined their kingdom. They were late in seeing their mistake, but once they saw it they had a devastating plan of action. Eastern capital had demanded local endorsement. Prohibiting any local endorsement would doom Sutro and his tunnel.

Sutro on the one hand, and Sharon and Ralston on the other, each underestimated his opponent's strength. In 1867 Sharon was forty-six years old, Ralston forty-one, and Sutro thirty-seven. In the end, only Sutro would enjoy his Comstock earnings. Sutro would take out the smallest amount of money, enjoy it the longest, and not let it lead him into serious trouble, let alone death. Sharon and Ralston had confederates in San Francisco and puppets in Virginia City. What did Sutro have? He had very little except his indomitable will.

Sutro was deeply hurt by the way his former associates now treated him. He also found that nearly all the people who had stood by him deserted him now. Old friends crossed the street rather than shake his hand. Once the bank had rejected him he was avoided as if he had an infectious disease by everyone who courted the favor of the bank. Thanks to the web Sharon had spun on the Comstock, this meant nearly everybody in western Nevada.

Sutro was mortified. Nothing in his past history had been like this, not even his mother's packing him off to America. Then he had had the security of her love even when she rejected his plans. Friends had counseled him against the expansion of his tobacco business in California, but had not deserted him when he failed to take their advice. He had made some dreadful mistakes, like the Fraser River fiasco, and he had blundered in some investments. He had never had many real friends outside his relatives and close business associates, and had even been called "crazy," but he had written that off to the ignorance of those who could not think in large terms. This new experience of being shunned by nearly everyone who knew him seared his soul. He made what he called a sacred vow to devote the remainder of his life to carrying out the tunnel project. He would defend his rights as long as there was breath in his body.

While engaged in the tobacco business in San Francisco Sutro had met Joseph Aron, who was connected with the wholesale firm of Weil and Company. Aron had prospered and recently had become a partner in the business. On one of his many business trips to San Francisco Sutro had seen Aron and of course talked about the tunnel. Aron was so impressed with the scope and logic of the project that he offered any assistance he could give. Sutro needed none at the time, but went to Aron when the bank withdrew its support.

Aron refused to buy tunnel stock, according to his testimony, but he offered Sutro his personal support. He gave Sutro $3,000 for his personal expenses and promised to send Leah $200 a month for the support of her and the children. There were now five children — Kate, Charles, and Edgar having been born since their father became interested in Nevada. A sixth child was on the way who was born in October and named Clara. The mother and six children were dependent for their support on Joseph Aron for a period of several years. Adolph had made his vow never to forsake his tunnel. Judging by his actions, it was more sacred to him than his marriage vows and he left San Francisco by steamer in July of 1867 with hopes of raising money in New York.

[63]

These new hopes soon received a dash of cold water. The Bank of California had not only telegraphed news of its new attitude, but the bank's New York agents, Messrs. Leese and Waller, had posted a notice in their office. In large print it read that the stockholders of the Savage Company, at their annual meeting had refused to ratify the subscription made by their trustees of $150,000 to the stock of the Sutro Tunnel Company, and that the same was utterly null and void. Sutro felt that he was being treated as if he were "an absconding bank clerk, a forger, or criminal."

Thus under a grave handicap in New York, Sutro decided that his main hope lay in Congress. There, surely, the weight of honest facts would prevail over the opposition of a self-seeking bank. Sutro still had the friendly resolutions of the Nevada legislature and he also had a petition signed by a thousand miners and other residents of Nevada and California. The petition recited the familiar arguments for construction of the tunnel and went on to request that Congress extend financial aid to insure speedy completion of the work.

But Congress had just recessed on July 20 and would not meet again until late in November, so Sutro decided to carry out the European portion of his plan first. As always, one of his first steps was to collect letters of introduction. He needed replacements for some he already had, of course, such as the one from Ralston to the Oriental Bank Corporation of London. In Washington James W. Nye, Senator from Nevada, had not heard about the bank's change in position, or was willing to defy its will. At any rate, on July 18 he wrote a friendly letter endorsing the tunnel, and he also entertained "no doubt" that the government would grant aid "at no distant day." In Baltimore Sutro gathered more letters, probably through the good offices of his brothers and their business associates there.

With what must have been an enormous supply of these introductions and endorsements he left for Europe. His purpose in going was two-fold: he wanted to find out the chances

[64]

for gaining financial aid abroad and he wanted to become better informed about the engineering job he proposed to do. Sutro had read many of the great works on mining written by European scientists. Now he hoped to meet these men, visit mines and tunnels and eventually return to Congress and present the facts.

He traveled in Ireland, England, France, Belgium, Holland, Prussia, Austria, Poland, Hungary, Bavaria, Switzerland, and Italy. He entered into correspondence with Europe's greatest scientists and in many cases secured letters from them endorsing the tunnel. These letters were to serve him well in Congress. Occasionally he was rebuffed, however. He tried to see Bismarck, the great Prussian statesman, and received a note saying Count von Bismarck was very busy but a legation official would be available at certain hours.

The money situation in Europe was troubled. Sutro had no home endorsements and he left Europe about December without money, but with some feeling that after he obtained a loan from the United States government he would not need any from Europe, or if he did need more money he would at least have a home endorsement of the finest kind.

When Sutro returned Congress was in session. His funds were low but his reception in Europe had cheered him, and he was always a man to enjoy the company of great scientific minds. He did not say so, but if anything could have healed the wound caused by his rejection on the Comstock it would be a trip to Europe. A visit to his birthplace, good food, good drink, exploring mines, and most of all, corresponding with and meeting men such as Von Cotta, Weissbach, Chevalier, Burkhardt, and Koch was certainly a soul-restoring experience for Adolph Sutro.

One of the first greetings upon his return to America was from Mark Twain, one-time acquaintance in the Comstock area. Under date of December 14, 1867, Mark wrote a lengthy Washington letter to the San Francisco *Daily Alta California:*

Mr. A. Sutro of the great Sutro Tunnel scheme arrived yesterday from Europe on the *Russia*. He brought his tunnel back with him. He failed to sell it to the Europeans. They said it was a good tunnel, but that they would look around a little before purchasing; if they could not find a tunnel to suit them nearer home they would call again. Many capitalists were fascinated with the idea of owning a tunnel, but none wanted such a long tunnel, or one that was so far away that they could not walk out afternoons and enjoy it.

But after his ironical opening Mark turned serious and reported that the Europeans said they were afraid of American stocks. Sutro was in Washington to try to get Federal aid and Mark expressed his great admiration for Sutro's "industry and tenacity."

Sutro had previously cultivated members of both houses of Congress. He now gathered together the most gratifying of his letters from Europe, the report by Richthofen, the report of the Mechanics' Institute, and assorted pronouncements of his own and prepared them for publication as a book.

Before this volume could be printed, bound, and distributed, however, Ralston and Sharon heard that Sutro was back in Washington, D.C., full of vigor and intent on getting a loan from Congress. They addressed a telegram to Senators Stewart and Nye as well as many others; Stewart had been the first president of the tunnel company and Nye had written a favorable letter six months before. The telegram was dated January 15, 1868, and read: "We are opposed to the Sutro Tunnel project, and desire it defeated if possible." The name "William Sharon" headed the list of signers; the other eight names were those of superintendents or presidents of major Comstock mines. Other similar messages were sent, including one to John Conness, Senator from California. Sutro was kindly in his judgment of the company officials who signed such missives, pointing out that they had no effective choice in the matter.

He wrote Aron about the telegrams and also about the strategy he used in getting his message before the lawmakers. Most documents of that type, he said, were unattractive and went to the wastebasket immediately. He had his book printed on large paper and very handsomely bound. It could be used as a decorative object and he surmised that it would be placed on many a center table. Then while the friends of Senators and Representatives waited around for Federal appointments they would pick up the book and casually flip through its pages. Since such waiting often demanded many hours the person would eventually become interested in the contents and read the book. Ultimately he would see the member of Congress for whom he had been waiting and perhaps call the tunnel project to his attention. Although some of the writing was ponderous, Sutro aimed to attract the casual reader by inserting a page in the presentation copies which was done in a facsimile of his own handwriting and included a few choice oversimplifications such as: "We have a vast mining interest; we also have a large national debt. The development of the former will secure the easy payment of the latter."

Even the title of the book was designed to ensnare rather than inform the potential reader. Sutro called it *The Mineral Resources of the United States*. Actually the book should have been called, *How the Sutro Tunnel Will Solve All the Financial Problems of the United States*. At this time Sutro seemed to think that the United States had no problems other than financial ones.

But Sutro did not distribute the books immediately; he kept them under wraps. He wanted to wait until a bill recommending a government loan for the tunnel was placed before Congress. The bill reached the Committee on Mines and Mining of the House of Representatives in May and its action was very gratifying. The committee recommended a bill loaning the tunnel company five million dollars in exchange for a first mortgage on the property. The bill was accompanied by a thirteen-page printed report strongly urging the House to adopt the measure.

Two weeks later the chairman of the committee, Mr. D. R. Ashley, had two additional documents printed to reinforce the recommendations of the committee. One was a letter from the Secretary of the Treasury which was brief and only mildly favorable. A second letter, however, was strongly favorable and was from the Commissioner of the General Land Office. It was so long that it occupied more than five printed pages.

Sutro was confident of a three-fourths or five-sixths majority in the House, according to a statement made by him four years later. At the time, however, he wrote Aron in more restrained language. "I can count to-day votes enough to pass my bill in the House, and after that nothing will hinder its passage in the Senate."

Sutro had built up his cause with large numbers of Congressmen and he also had the warm support of the most powerful single member of the House, Thaddeus Stevens. Although sick and in bed, Stevens had Sutro's book and he kept reading it. Sutro sat by him many times in his sickroom explaining the great project. But after the impeachment trial of President Johnson began in the Senate, the House could think of little else. Congress recessed in July with much business unfinished, including the Sutro Tunnel aid bill. Thaddeus Stevens died two weeks later.

Sutro returned to New York and California but when Congress met again Sutro was there. U. S. Grant had been elected President and Congress was in one of those miserable periods when the shadow of a president-elect rendered it impotent, and Sutro was impatient. Obviously he had never before witnessed the spectacle of a "lame duck" Congress. A naturalized citizen, he had had neither time nor reason to observe this phenomenon before, and he was unprepared for the stalemate.

He did have one suggestion, however, and one which was characteristic. Sutro was devoted to the propagation of learning and he had applauded Senator Stewart's bill of two years previous proposing a National School of Mines in Nevada. The bill failed but Sutro went further and in January, 1869, two tunnel subsidy bills provided that in return for government assistance, 10 per cent of income from operations of the completed tunnel would go to the government "to endow a National School of Mines."

Congress, however, continued in an unhurried mood and the bill did not even reach the Committee on Mines. In explaining the slow progress of his bill, Sutro wrote Aron that the example of a Federal loan for the Union Pacific-Central Pacific railroad had inspired a flood of similar railroad bills. Public opinion became aroused and President-elect Grant counseled against any law tending to increase the national debt. This deepened the normal do-nothing attitude of a lame duck session.

Sutro saw the President-elect personally on February 19, but apparently got no direct promise. He did accomplish the remarkable feat, however, of getting a veiled reference to the Sutro Tunnel into Grant's rather short inaugural address. It was a hollow victory, however, for Grant also said clearly that government aid to such a project should not precede resumption of specie payments, an event then lying in the indefinite future. After the inauguration, the new Congress met in special session but sat only five weeks and little could be accomplished. Once more Sutro left for the Pacific Coast.

While little of interest to the people of Nevada happened in Washington during that five-week session of Congress, Nevada had drama enough at home.

CHAPTER VII

RALLY AT PIPER'S OPERA HOUSE

A s APRIL 7, 1869, dawned at Virginia City it seemed like any other day. The night shift had left the mines as usual at 4 a.m. and only the carmen were left below until 7 a.m. when the day crew started work. The mines were all heavily timbered, foul smelling and hot. Miners had grown careful about those things which were unique to Comstock mining and, although the fear of being flooded with hot water remained, the men were vigilant to avoid it.

Perhaps it was an overawareness of the unusual aspects of the mines which had caused a man on the night shift of the Yellow Jacket Mine to grow careless of more common hazards, and endanger not only his fellow Yellow Jacket miners, but the men in the connecting mines. Perhaps some form of internal combustion took place, but it seems more likely that a man simply left a candle sticking against a timber on the 800 foot level and forgot to blow it out when he left work.

When miners of the day shift entered that level, almost immediately they were engulfed in smoke and suffocating gases. The alarm was sounded and the cages of the Yellow Jacket and the adjoining Crown Point and Kentuck mines all descended to begin the work of rescuing the men trapped below. Smoke and gas belched forth from the entrances to all three mines while the wives and children of the men below gathered to wait and pray for rescue.

The Gold Hill and Virginia City fire departments came, and of course the Reverend Father Manogue was there. Men fought for the chance to go below and try to rescue their mates, but for two hours the smoke was so dense that no one could go. About 9 o'clock the smoke drew away from the shaft of the Kentuck and two dead bodies were recovered. At noon it was possible to get into the Yellow Jacket as far as the 800 foot level and several more bodies of asphyxiated miners were brought up.

By the morning of the tenth there was absolutely no hope of recovering anyone alive and the shafts of the three contiguous mines were sealed off and steam from the boilers was forced through the air pipes. On the twelfth the mines were opened for rescue work but after a few bodies were recovered the mines had to be sealed again. The men who went down to fight the fire and recover the bodies were often overcome by the gases and had to be returned to the surface for resuscitation. All but three bodies were recovered. Those three men had been in the area of the original fire and were probably the first to die.

Forty-five men had died, most of them from asphyxiation. One young man told how he was running for the shaft in hopes of reaching a cage and being pulled to safety when he realized that if the cage was not there he might fall down the shaft into the sump two hundred feet below. He therefore dropped to his hands and knees and crawled forward. When he reached the shaft he lay and waited but was unable to warn two or three men who came running for safety and plunged to their deaths below. Several men actually reached the cage, only to die on the trip to the surface. They were so nearly overcome with asphyxiation they were unable to remain upright and were crushed between the sides of the cage and the timbers of the shaft. Only three men were burned, and they probably died before the fire reached them. No man was rescued alive after the first two hours of the fire.

The disaster affected many men in many walks of life. First of all, it took the lives of forty-five men. A few others, like John P. Jones, acted heroically and were highly acclaimed. Sharon and Ralston were accused of being negligent of the miners' welfare, and Sutro became the man who could, with his tunnel, provide escape should such a fire ever happen again. Fire smoldered in the mines, but in the hearts of the miners and those close to them a bitter hatred also smoldered. The men grew increasingly resentful of the monopoly which flourished on their labor, yet gave them no protection for their lives.

Sutro himself was not averse to dominating the lives of others but it was the role of benevolent monarch and not tyrant that he used as his pattern. He was concerned about the plight of the working man in general, and of the miners of Washoe in particular. He pictured to himself, and afterwards to others, how easy escape from a burning mine would be if only there were a Sutro Tunnel.

Right at this time Sutro needed a dynamic cause for his tunnel because the bank ring had obviated one need for it. Recognizing the wisdom of a proposal Sutro made on his first visit to Washoe, Sharon and Ralston were building a railroad from the valley of the Carson River to the heights of Virginia City. Now the ore taken out of the mines could be hauled cheaply down to the river to be processed by cheap water power and wood could be hauled inexpensively up to the mines. Sutro had counted on doing this business through his tunnel — but the ring beat him to it. Sharon estimated that this would save the mines about one million dollars a year based on their present freight rates.

Sharon hired a surveyor who figured out a way to build a railroad from Virginia to Carson City, a distance of twenty-one miles with a descent of 1,575 feet. Thirteen and one-half miles of it had an average grade of more than 2 per cent and the equivalent of seventeen complete circles. The railroad's supremacy as a feat of engineering was only challenged by its even more remarkable financing.

The Virginia and Truckee, as Sharon's new railroad was called, was able to get outright gifts from two counties —

$200,000 from Ormsby County and $300,000 from Storey County. Mining companies dependent on the Bank of California for credit were induced to subscribe $387,383.53 to the new venture. Much of this was money originally pledged to the Sutro Tunnel Company. It is asserted that Sharon, Ralston and Darius Ogden Mills did put up $1,500,000 of their own money to finish the project and maintain tight control of what promised to be a very lucrative investment. (Mills was the wealthy banker from Sacramento who had been induced to serve as President of the Bank of California. He had agreed so long as Ralston took the main responsibility for running the bank.)

It must have been a great source of frustration to Sutro to see a railroad planned in January well on its way to completion by fall. The Virginia and Truckee was formally opened to Gold Hill on November 12, 1869, eight months after Sharon had obtained a charter from the legislature. Virginia City had its first train on January 29, 1870.

Sutro could no longer anticipate a yearly revenue for the tunnel company of from $710,000 to $2,190,000 for hauling wood, waste rock, and ore. He could not even talk about how the mills must locate at the mouth of the tunnel, but he could emphasize the human element. Here was a way to save lives. Sharon and Ralston might consider the human element unworthy of concern, but the miners were concerned and would listen eagerly. The Yellow Jacket fire had greatly increased consciousness of the problem of safety and if Sutro had a way to save miners from death on the job he was their man.

The ability to fraternize with working men while still maintaining the position of leader came easily to Adolph Sutro. Probably no man on the mountain had had as much experience in participating in such a dual role, and Sutro played it to the hilt.

Sutro did not cast his lot solely with the miners; he still thought that his main hope lay with the United States gov-

[73]

ernment. He heard that the Ways and Means Committee of the House of Representatives was on its way west to investigate the newly completed Pacific railroad. Sutro telegraphed the committee invitations to visit the Washoe district on the way west but they declined. In San Francisco their principal hosts were the men of the Bank of California but Sutro gave them no peace until they promised to visit Virginia City on their eastbound trip. After their arrival in Virginia City, however, Sharon tried to maneuver the committee into situations which excluded Sutro. Sharon was bold enough to tell one of the committee members, former Governor Blair of Michigan, that the bank wanted to drive Sutro out of the country.

The committee members went into the mines and "came near fainting." Sutro showed them the lay of the land and attempted to convince them of the need for a tunnel; he was sure that he succeeded. One thing is evident; the committee was convinced that Sharon did not want the tunnel built and would do almost anything to stop Sutro.

Sharon was, in fact, becoming absolutely worn out with Sutro's persistence. First the bank had taken away its financial support of the tunnel, then they had built a railroad which cut down the anticipated revenue of the tunnel. Now all that was left was hot water and hot air. Sutro's interminable talking was adding enough hot air to warm the high winds called "Washoe Zephyrs" by at least ten degrees. Now, however, it was just the miners who were paying any attention to this local phenomenon with a German accent. The miners were all talking over the Yellow Jacket fire, just like old soldiers re-fighting a battle. What did it matter if they drew diagrams in the dust and deployed imaginary soldiers or long lost miners — it was the same. Surely Sutro would soon fade away.

Sutro, however, was not fading; he was gathering strength for his ego. He now had an audience, something he had missed during his days of humiliation. It was so gratifying to him that later he embellished the story. When he had a chance to tell a Congressional committee about how the miners had listened to him, he became so concerned with his story that he ignored some of the facts.

Sutro told the committee that he had had no chance to explain himself to the public. The bank ring owned all the newspapers and they would not print anything about the tunnel, even in paid advertisements, so Sutro decided to make a speech in Virginia City. He made a speech and aroused great enthusiasm and "the Miners' Union subscribed $50,000 then," thus leaving the impression that the Union action followed the speech.

For a man who seldom if ever threw away a scrap of paper, who saved originals, copies, and copies of copies, all duly labeled and carefully filed, it seems strange that Sutro should have presented such an inaccurate account of the circumstances of his opera house speech. Not only would his own papers contradict his narrative, but he surely knew that the files of newspapers like the Virginia City *Territorial Enterprise* and the Carson *Daily Appeal* would challenge his dangling "then" and other inaccuracies.

The fact is that on August 20 the *Enterprise* had a news item about the tunnel and then a long advertisement appeared daily. In due course additional news items as well as advertisements were published heralding a speech which was finally set for September 20.

Meanwhile Sutro spent considerable time talking to miners and he found them willing to listen. He found that at this time they were greatly concerned about the possibility of another fire similar to that in the Yellow Jacket mine. Although they were interested in the better working conditions represented by diminished heat and improved ventilation, their chief interest at that time was in a means of escape in case of fire.

Sutro became well acquainted with the leaders of miners' unions as well as with individual miners. It was at his request that a joint meeting of the Virginia and Gold Hill Miners' Unions was called for August 25. Sutro presented reasons why the miners and their unions should support the tunnel financially, and he had the gratification of getting a subscription of $50,000 from the unions by a unanimous vote.

The close relationship between Sutro and the miners' unions which facilitated this enthusiastic endorsement is illustrated by an incident which occurred a few days before the joint union meeting. Representative George W. Julian, a Congressman from Indiana, was planning to visit Virginia City. The Comstock miners were looking forward to his visit, for he was widely hailed as a true friend of the workingman. Carriages were to meet Julian at Reno and large numbers of workmen would meet him at a given point on the Geiger Grade, near Virginia, and escort him the rest of the way. Representative Julian was seriously ill, however, and telegraphed his deep regrets. He addressed his telegram not to the two unions concerned but to Adolph Sutro. This gives us some hint of the very close relations existing at that time between Sutro and the unions. It was no secret, either, for the telegram was published in the *Enterprise*.

The joint union meeting was a triumph for Sutro and he was so confident he opened a stock-subscription office at 76 C Street, Virginia City, on September 1. He promptly began a large-scale advertising campaign. The text of the unions' resolution pledging $50,000 was published in the *Territorial Enterprise*. The second day of publication the unions' resolution was joined with a long appeal for stock subscriptions. Both advertisements were printed daily for two months.

By now Sutro was undoubtedly planning his public speech to try to get additional subscribers and to cement his relations with the miners even further. If his speech should be successful, the unions' support plus substantial popular backing would provide the "home endorsement" so necessary to bankers. One advertisement read: "It is not so much the amount of money which can be raised in Nevada; it is the home endorsement which is required."

Piper's Opera House was a busy place, and Sutro may have had difficulty getting a free night, but the speech was finally set for September 20. On September 16 his advertisements announcing the speech began to appear in the *Enterprise*. Two days later a news item in the *Enterprise* also informed readers of the forthcoming event.

Sutro had gained greater self-confidence. He not only had a little money, but he also had a moral victory. The very men who earned a living in the bank-controlled mines had given proof of their friendship with the bank's enemy through the stock subscriptions of their unions.

When Sutro took his place on the platform he was unaccustomed to such a large audience, but not to speaking. He knew his audience well and as to his subject — it was his life. He had pleaded his cause in America and Europe; many had listened and nearly all who did were convinced. Here were no chiefs of state, eminent engineers, authors, legislators, or committee members. Here before him sat the miners, for whom he had deep respect. Like most of them he had led a bachelor life in Washoe, cooking his own food. In fact, one witness remembers Sutro telling how he would repeatedly burn the pot of rice he meant to have for dinner.

Sutro, like the miners, had watched the bank ring grow its tentacles, but unlike them he could find no refuge in establishing a union to combat the ring. He had of necessity fought the bank single-handed, and now he would tell his proven friends exactly what the fight had been like.

When a man speaks from the heart, when he is convinced that his cause is right, when utter sincerity is his only motivation, it does not matter whether he has an accent, or is unaccustomed to the public platform. He has a power over his listeners that can never be matched by mere polish. Sutro did overestimate the use and the revenue of the tunnel, but he presented honest convictions. That he was devoted to his cause was well known to his listeners, and now he spoke like a zealot.

Fortunately the speech is preserved. Sutro had it reprinted many times and he sent it to the Sutro Tunnel Commissioners, who printed it as an appendix to their report. The speech occupied over seventeen pages of fine print in the report; Sutro required "about two hours" to deliver it at the opera house.

Sutro began by saying he would explain what his tunnel would accomplish, and to do so he would have to "expose some of the doings of an institution called the California Bank. I shall tell the truth, without fear or reservation, for I have come here to 'fight it out on this line,' and I intend to do so, 'though the heavens fall.' "

Sutro seemed to know exactly how much he could say of a mineralogical or historical nature, and then how to turn the subject and catch any interest that might lag. He quoted Sharon and Ralston and he quoted himself at length (from *Mineral Resources of the U. S.*). After a long exposé of the bank ring he drew a pathetic picture of himself when they had nearly crushed him. He said:

Fellow-citizens: Have you ever been in a position where your friends shunned you? If you have you know how mortifying it is on meeting an old acquaintance to have him pass by pretending not to see you, instead of shaking you by the hand and welcoming you. Have you noticed them cross over on the other side of the street when they saw you at a distance? Have you seen their nervous hurry, trying to get off, when you happen to engage them in conversation? You may possibly have made similar experiences if you were ever broke and your good friends were afraid you might ask them for a loan.

Sutro had truly suffered from this humiliation, but now he turned it into profit. The miners knew exactly how he had felt; he was able to elicit empathy as well as sympathy.

[78]

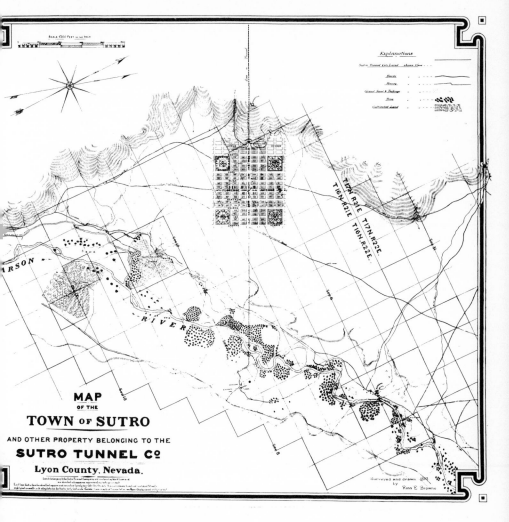

Plan of the town of Sutro drawn by Ross E. Browne, 1873. [Borders of the original map measure 19½″ x 18⅜″.]

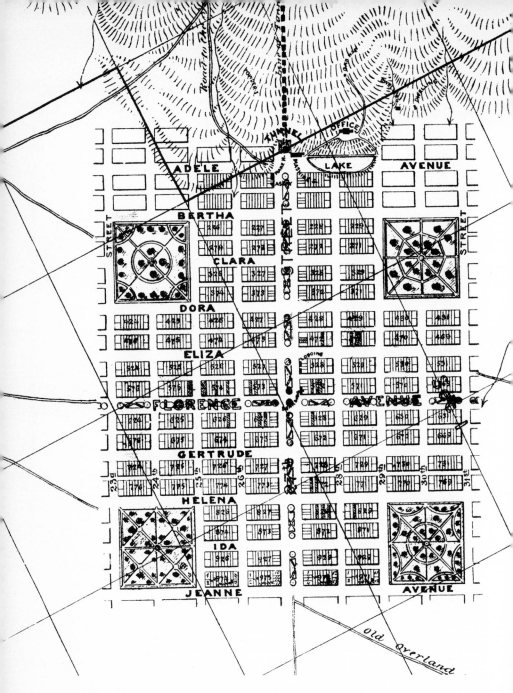

Enlarged view of plan of the town of Sutro drawn by Ross E. Browne, 1873. Note alphabetical sequence of feminine street names.

At right: The town of Sutro from a photograph by James H. Crockwell, 1890. To the left is the mansion overlooking the town with one of the squares outlined by trees in the middle distance. Tunnel Avenue is still bordered by trees, although some are dying out down by Florence Avenue. Entrance to tunnel between buildings at extreme right. *(Nevada State Museum)*

Leah Harris Sutro was devoted to her home and family, but her letters indicate long and profound frustration caused by her husband's nomadic life. *(Nevada Historical Society)*

Adolph Sutro in London in 1869. The faulty backdrop and polished shoes detract from the fact that here we see Sutro as he really was: strong, stocky, and at thirty-nine already beginning to turn gray. (*Nevada Historical Society*)

Adolph Sutro and Party at Sutro Tunnell.

Adolph Sutro (top center) and party assembled on one of the cages of the Savage Mine. This shaft connected with the main tunnel 1700 feet below. *(Nevada State Museum)*

Tunnel entrance circa 1880. Although the mansion was imposing and many of the mines and mills had elaborate buildings, Adolph Sutro spent little money on the adornment of his shops or the tunnel entrance. *(Nevada State Museum)*

Tunnel facade erected 1888, eight years after Sutro left. This more elaborate facing still marks the portal of the historic tunnel. *(Nevada Historical Society)*

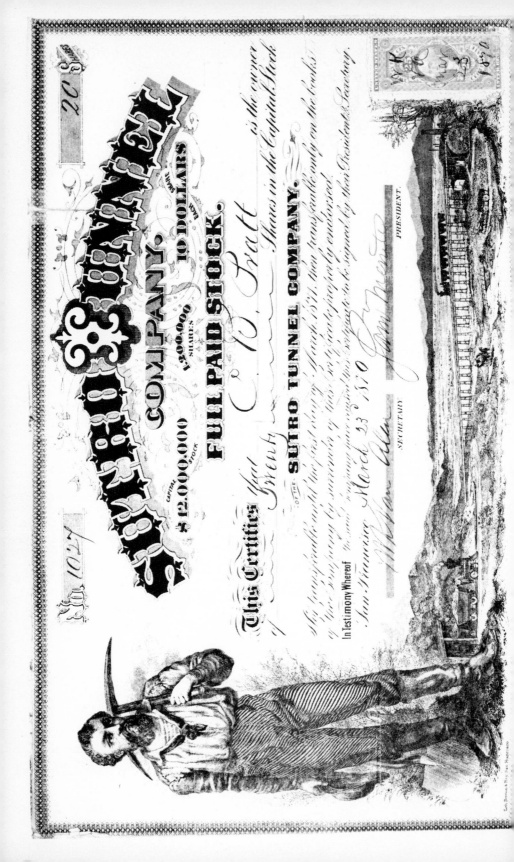

Office of the Sutro Tunnel Co. in San Francisco. *(Bancroft Library)*

At left: Stock certificate of the Sutro Tunnel Company, 1870. The beard and receding hairline resemble Sutro's but the eyebrows in full flight, turned-down mouth, and poetic hands, as well as the general lean and hungry look could have belonged to almost anyone but Sutro. The landscape, including steam locomotives, is pure whimsy. *(Nevada Historical Society)*

Virginia City in 1878. Six Mile Canyon in background is roughly along the line of the Sutro tunnel. *(Grahame Hardy Collection)*

The next day General Grant, U. S. Grant, Jr., Col. J. G. Fair, and Gov. J. H. Kinkead went to the town of Sutro and breakfasted with Mrs. Sutro at the mansion. They returned to Virginia City by way of the Sutro tunnel. *(Nevada Historical Society)*

Mr. J. W. Mackay.   Mrs. M. G. Gillette.   Mr. U. S. Grant, Jr.   Mrs. U. S. Grant.   GEN. U. S. GRANT   S. Yanada.   Mrs. J. G. Fair.   Gov. J. H. Kinkead.   Col. J. G.

EN. GRANT AND PARTY, AFTER COMING OUT OF THE BONANZA MINES.   OCT

Two views of the Sutro mansion at Sutro, Nevada. *Above*, an early one before landscaping and *below*, decades later when cables were added to brace the house against "Washoe zephyrs." It was from this porch that General Grant spoke to the insistent crowd. *(Roy D. Graves Collection)*

VIRGINIA CITY'S $90,000 DIAMOND WIDOW.

When the late Adolph Sutro became acquainted with Mrs. George Allen in Virginia City, Nev., she was known as "the $90,000 diamond widow." Nobody knew why she was so called, but her sobriquet was attributed to the richness of her apparel. It was in the International Hotel, Virginia City, that Mrs. Sutro charged her husband with undue intimacy with Mrs. Allen. A rupture in the Sutro family followed, and Mrs. Allen was severely criticised. In the Sutro will there is a legacy of $50,000 for Mrs. Allen, given, as testator states, in reparation.

The "$90,000 diamond widow." *(San Francisco Examiner)*

Looking North on C Street towards the International Hotel. It was here Mrs. Allen had her apartment. *(Grahame Hardy Collection)*

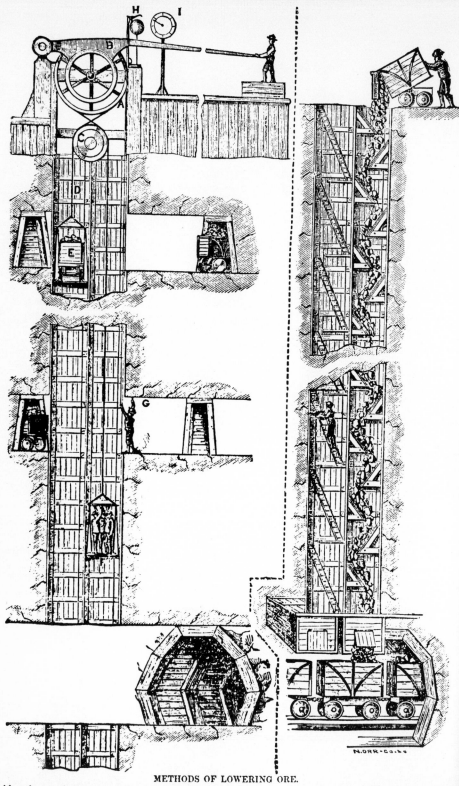

METHODS OF LOWERING ORE.

After the completion of the Sutro Tunnel the ore may be sent down to the tunnel level into bins and cars by means of shutes as shown in the right-hand illustration; or it may be lowered in cars, E, placed on a cage with rope D, attached, reaching to the *surface*, which is regulated by a brake, B, controlled by one man, as shown on the left hand. The ore lowered from above in one compartment may be made to hoist men or timbers to any level above in another compartment of the shaft, and also from below the tunnel to its level.

No. 4 shaft of the Sutro tunnel. This was one of the two that did not reach the intended depth due to too much water. Had it been successful, it would have reached the tunnel level at a point 17,500 feet from the portal.

Hoisting works of the Savage Mine. It was directly below here the tunnel made its connection with the Comstock Lode. *(Wells Fargo)*

Melting the bullion at one of the Comstock mines. Scenes such as this must have hurt Sutro for had his tunnel been completed earlier, he would have enjoyed a royalty from every bar of precious metal cast.

He told the whole story of his efforts, his travels to Europe, his work in Washington. He came back time and again to blast the bank and the mismanagement of the mines. He said that the Lode was yielding $16,000,000 a year, but that almost the entire amount was absorbed in production expense. He asserted that if the tunnel were in existence, $40-$50,000,000 a year could be "poured out in a silver stream" and the "nation would be enriched beyond all expectation, and the benefits to the Government and the people would be incalculable."

Sutro's last thousand words were spent in urging his listeners to buy stock in the tunnel, not only to help the great work but at the same time to strike a blow at "the vampires that have nearly sucked you dry." This was probably the first formal exposure of the policies of the Bank of California, and Sutro dared to utter it in the heart of the Comstock — the bank's most cherished principality.

Sutro concluded his address with a moving appeal:

> Miners and laboring men, what is the price of your health, your liberty, your independence? Are they not worth more than all the filthy lucre you could possess? Who is there among you so avaricious as to refuse to give and donate outright a few paltry dollars per month to a cause . . . which will insure to you liberal wages . . . a cause which will make you the power of this land, make powerless your oppressors, and break up your arch enemy, the California Bank. . . .

> Let a noble rivalry spring up among you who shall come in first; drop all prejudice; let all trifling objections fall to the ground; let one excel the other in magnanimity; let all make one joint, grand, unanimous effort, and victory will be ours.

The miners were enthusiastic in their approval. The excitement was so intense that there was talk of hanging the leaders of the bank party, but Sutro went among the miners and pacified them, according to a statement of his made five years later. At any rate, Sutro always deprecated violence and the *Enterprise* said the next day that "the speech was very calm throughout."

Nevertheless, Sutro's speech was a sensation. The *Enterprise* published an editorial the following morning briefly mentioning his main points and promising a full text of the speech the following day. The text was delayed one day, which is understandable, for it occupied the entire front page and two columns on the last page. It was accompanied by a lengthy editorial discussing Sutro's arguments.

Sutro had brought his case before the public. Strengthened by the knowledge that individual miners were behind him and that their unions had pledged him money, he had been able to stand before them and give an outstanding speech. Sutro's self-confidence had been restored, and if during his time of humiliation people had treated him as if he had a loathsome disease, now they caught the contagion of his enthusiasm. Only the "bank crowd" remained grim. Only the people with large quantities of money remained unmoved. If a tunnel could be dug with words, Sutro and the miners would have it finished before the winter snows could fall.

THE "FIRST PICK"

S UTRO HAD a sense of history. Who else would have saved
such trivia as this?

Western Union Telegraph Co.
Dayton, Nev.
Oct. 18, 1869

A. Sutro
International Hotel
Virginia City

Bring down a flag there is none here.   Bethel

John D. Bethel was completing preparations at the tunnel site for the great public celebration in which Sutro
would officially begin construction of the long-heralded Sutro
Tunnel. Meanwhile the tunnel's projector was bending every
effort toward a maximum sale of tunnel stock. On the appointed day he would swing a purely symbolic "first pick,"
since a gang of workmen under Bethel had spent days cutting an approach to the site of the ceremony. They had also
built an exceedingly tall flagpole, so we can visualize Bethel
cursing at the lack of a flag just one day before the festivities.

Adolph Sutro, the master hand at publicity, used newspaper advertisements and other means to invite the entire
population of Nevada and California to witness the historic
act. There would then be a giant barbecue followed by a
ball. Somehow Bethel had found tables and chairs for the
barbecue and he had erected a shed and a speaker's stand.
He had also directed the building of an oven which would
roast eight pigs and the digging of a pit fourteen feet long
and five feet wide for roasting beeves. By the time Bethel

[81]

wired for the flag two cords of wood had been used to heat the pit and a load of charcoal was ready to be used at the discretion of the boss cook. Two assistant cooks were on hand to turn the cranks for the spit on which hung two beeves.

Obviously Sutro regarded his invitation as a gesture; otherwise he would have ordered more meat and more than 200 loaves of bread. Never a man to rely on prayer or to believe in miracles, he must have felt that fewer than one per cent of his 200,000 "invited guests" would attend. Still, the stables in Virginia City had numerous reservations for carriages for the morning of the nineteenth, and it was hard to say how many Indians might come out for the free food.

The nineteenth of October was a day which would cheer only the most vindictive of the bank ring. The first snow of the season had fallen in Virginia City during the night. By morning a rainstorm was pouring on Sun Mountain and men of little courage canceled their orders at the livery stables. At 9:00 a.m. Adolph Sutro set out from Virginia City with a small group. The wind lashed the rain with such force that even those riding in the back seat of a closed carriage were drenched.

Upon arriving at Dayton they found the streets presented a sorry sight. At the agreed assembly point in front of I. D. Cross's hotel not a person could be seen except the eleven-man Gold Hill Miners Brass Band, which had been hired for the occasion. Sutro would not give up. He had the band take their positions in front of the hotel and play their most inspiring music. This brought many people out and at 1:00 p.m. the band mounted a two-horse express wagon and played a pied-piper's tune. Two hundred people in carriages and on horseback fell in line and the procession paraded through Dayton and then proceeded three miles north to the site of the tunnel approach.

After a flag was raised and the *Star-Spangled Banner* played by the band, Sutro stood in shirt sleeves with a pick

[82]

over his right shoulder. Without even mounting the specially constructed platform he made a short speech about the significance of the act he was about to perform. This was probably the shortest speech he ever made. Then he struck the blow, and passed the pick to Dan De Quille of the *Territorial Enterprise*. Then came a swing by James Phelan, President of the Workingmen's Association. All others in attendance who so desired were then given turns, ending with J. H. Jaqua, proprietor of the Golden Eagle Hotel, who shoveled the earth into a barrow. George P. Howe, a grocery and hardware merchant of Dayton who had subscribed $1,000 worth of supplies to the tunnel company, had the honor of wheeling the first barrow of earth to the dump.

Cheers, guns, anvils, and giant powder (dynamite) were loud in their acclaim. Sutro had determined that work would start on the tunnel and nothing had stopped him. Not even Mother Nature had been able to stop the swing of that first pick, although she had done her utmost in the way of foul weather to postpone the start of the new work. Apparently she relented momentarily, for the sun burst forth and a rainbow of perfect dimensions hung low in the sky and seemed to start less than two hundred yards from the tunnel opening. The crowd shouted anew. Nature had a lot in store for Sutro, but at least she cooperated for that brief moment.

The tables and chairs were wet and the weather too formidable for outdoor eating. The people and the food all went back to Dayton. A meal was spread out in the Court House and there amid speeches and music from the band it was discovered that the boss cook had made a sad miscalculation. He had presumed that twenty-four hours of roasting would be sufficient for the two beeves. Though he had basted them with care and his two assistants had cranked away with a will, the beeves remained raw. The pork, however, was excellent and when the crowd was overcome with food and speeches the guests went over to the Odeon Hall to dance. At midnight the music ceased for a short time while the guests ate again. During this brief rest Mr. Cross, the hotel-keeper, surprised the band members by serving them a special midnight dinner in appreciation of what he termed their marvelous music. Just how musical they may have been is not certain, but one thing is sure: those eleven bandsmen were possessed of extraordinary physical strength. They returned to play for more dancing and when they finally finished their banging and tooting at dawn they had been at it for nearly twenty hours.

The man who had dared to invite 200,000 people to a party was not discouraged by the fact that about 199,800 people stayed home. The beef had been raw, but at least the pork was excellent. The beer held out, and although he personally preferred wine, he considered beer the appropriate drink for tunnel celebrations. Even if the bread had been burned, all the meat raw, or if a blizzard had kept everyone else away, the man who had stood alone on the platform of Piper's Opera House would have stood alone at the foot of Mt. Davidson and swung that first pick. If he had thought that the best and fastest way to get the tunnel dug was to go in himself alone with a pick, shovel, and wheelbarrow he would have done it. No one knew better than Sutro that the one job only he could do was to finance the tunnel. That job required dedication to the cause, an almost religious fervor. To advance the cause tunneling had to be commenced, and it mattered not to him that the ceremony had been less than perfect. He had had the publicity of an enormous festival but the expense of feeding a handful of people. Socially the ceremony was a flop; psychologically it was a success.

He now cut Bethel's crew to nine men. They worked in threes, eight hours to a shift, around the clock, seven days a week. Using only hand tools they were still able to lay 52½ feet of track into their header by the end of ten days. Sutro could now face financiers with facts: the tunnel was started, work was progressing around the clock, tracks had been laid, and cars were removing the waste material to a dump. This was no casual wheelbarrow operation; he had a foreman and a crew and less than four miles to go! The men with money had said they wanted home endorsements and work progress reports. Sutro knew he had only tokens, but they were honest tokens and he would use them to their full worth. He would do his utmost to swamp the newspapers with tunnel reports and let the world know that the Sutro Tunnel was under construction in the soil of Nevada as well as in his own head.

Bethel superintended the clearing away of the sagebrush for the building of a boarding house for the men and for an office. He provisioned the boarding house mainly through the $1,000 credit available at Mr. Howe's store. There were also farmers from the Walker River area who brought in produce and were willing to exchange it for tunnel company stock.

Dr. J. C. Hazlett was appointed tunnel company physician, assayer, and head of the Dayton office for selling tunnel company stock. Just how much prestige and income physicians enjoyed in Nevada in the 1870's is difficult to determine, but we do know that in 1872 at the first meeting of Nevada medical men a scale of minimum fees was agreed on which sounds exorbitant. Day visits were to be $5; night visits, $10; and detention $10 per hour. The union wage for miners at this time was $4 a day. Although Sutro got in some trouble with the miners' union when he tried to deduct a certain amount of money from the miners' pay for what would now be called "health insurance," he always, one way or another, maintained medical facilities for his miners.

His men worked under no worse conditions than those in the mines, but Sutro had a paternalistic attitude towards all of his employees. This was not a sporadic thing caused by the sudden support the miners gave him which made it possible for him to start work on the tunnel. In fact, it increased with the years. Sutro never had many men of his own intellectual level as friends, but he lived and died surrounded by employees who were utterly devoted to him.

His chief construction employee at this time was Bethel, now alone because Sutro had to go down to San Francisco. A corporation must be formed under California law to succeed the Nevada association of individuals. Sutro hoped to induce men of wealth and standing to identify themselves with the new corporation. Every possible way of raising money must be pushed. It had not been by accident that a member of the newspaper profession was chosen to receive the first pick from Sutro. The tunnel enterprise needed a favorable press and in San Francisco the projector arranged that the San Francisco papers would have weekly progress reports from the tunnel.

By November 26 the tunnel had penetrated 254 feet and on November 29 the certificate of incorporation was filed for the new Sutro Tunnel Company, a California corporation. The Board of Trustees did include men of wealth and standing. The trustees were: Dr. Samuel Merritt, Michael Reese, Abraham Seligman, William H. Sharp, Joseph Aron, John B. Felton, and Henry Barroilhet. Dr. Merritt was named President and W. K. Van Alen was elected Secretary.

In the story of the Sutro Tunnel there is not only a multiplicity of names, but occasionally persons with the same names, and even a foreman by the name of "Foreman." There was also a Mr. Savage who worked for the tunnel company and was not related to the Savage Mine, located on the Comstock Lode where the tunnel was expected to connect. The Dr. Samuel Merritt who was President of the company was a physician who also became known as a bachelor Mayor of Oakland; his name adorns the pretty lake in the heart of that city. He was also the owner of the schooner-yacht *Casco*, which was leased by Robert Louis Stevenson in 1888 and carried him to Tahiti. This Dr. Merritt must not be confused with another physician, George W. Merritt, who was destined to marry Adolph Sutro's eldest daughter,

Emma. Since Emma was herself a physician, she will become our third Dr. Merritt!

Returning to Dr. Samuel Merritt and the organization of the California corporation, some of the details of that transaction are of interest. A total of 1,200,000 shares of stock were authorized, each with a nominal par value of ten dollars. The shares were all non-assessable, quite in contrast with the prevailing practice at the time for mining stocks. The low price per share and the non-assessability were intended to help make the stock attractive to potential investors both small and large.

The tunnel franchises from Nevada and from the United States government were both made out to "A. Sutro, his heirs, or assigns." It would be necessary for Sutro to turn over his ownership of these franchises to the new tunnel company or it could not exist. He sincerely believed these franchises were enormously valuable and he expected something in exchange for them. He did not demand cash, however; he was so confident of the ultimate success of the tunnel project that he was willing to exchange them for a substantial block of stock in the Sutro Tunnel Company.

But stock must first be issued to various individuals who had subscribed money to the predecessor Nevada association, or who had paid money in return for a promise of stock when a company was formed. Fulfilling these obligations required 296,084 shares. The new company allocated 400,000 shares to the company treasury, or to trust accounts held for the benefit of the treasury. The balance, 503,916 shares, was issued to Adolph Sutro as his own property. Thus in exchange for his franchises and his many past services to the tunnel enterprise, Sutro accepted approximately a five-twelfths interest in the company. He was expected to continue as the key man in pushing the project, and he received the title General Superintendent. He was awarded no salary but was permitted to draw money from the company as needed.

Sutro now had a company and a board of trustees which included men of wealth and standing. But that alone did not assure a steady influx of money. Money was becoming more and more of a problem. Bethel was ordered to do his own surveying and to discharge the blacksmith. Sutro lingered in San Francisco trying earnestly to sell enough stock to keep work going on the tunnel. Four hundred thousand shares were available and par value was $10 per share, but there was no hope of getting anything like par value unless there were favorable reports on progress from the tunnel. Unless some money could be raised, no progress could be made at all. Only hard clay mixed with boulders was coming out, but the boss kept hoping to make a big ore strike. The doctor-assayer had only negative reports to make. If the dirt would not pay, at least Congress would soon be in session and a government loan could solve all difficulties.

The national attention which would be helpful in convincing Congress was increased after Horace Greeley read the speech given at Piper's Opera House. Sutro had visited the famous editor of the New York *Tribune* earlier, in 1867 and 1868. Greeley had been deeply impressed by the arguments for the tunnel but some of his political ideas had prevented full support. After reading the appeal to the miners, however, Greeley came out for a government loan to the tunnel company in a lengthy editorial on November 19, 1869. Not all editors agreed with Greeley's conclusions, but Sutro hoped that the widespread discussion stirred up would prove helpful to his cause. He looked forward with confidence to the opening of the next session of Congress.

CHAPTER IX

CONGRESS CREATES A TUNNEL COMMISSION

A NEW DECADE dawned and Adolph Sutro was still in San Francisco. Tenaciously he hung on, hoping to have a sizable sum of money subscribed there so that he could go to Congress and show home endorsements from both California and Nevada and tunnel progress as well. He realized that the bank ring was active in Washington but he had friends there who were vigilant. Finally he received a telegram from one of them which was so urgent he had to ignore his duties in San Francisco and take a train for the East.

This was Sutro's first opportunity to use the new transcontinental railroad. Cinders were better than crocodiles, and the monotony of clicking rails far superior to the hum of mosquitoes. In twenty years transportation between East and West had certainly improved, and on many occasions Sutro would take advantage of this fast and comfortable mode of travel.

The bank ring had sent its attorney J. C. Hillyer to Washington. Acting with extreme caution, Tom Fitch, Representative from Nevada, inserted a handwritten bill among the papers on the Speaker's desk. This was Bill 1179, which would explain away the royalty clause in the Sutro Tunnel Act. By placing the bill as he did, Fitch avoided having it printed and circulated. Hillyer helped Fitch with the lobbying. The two men anticipated an easy passage since their friends had been apprised of the situation and they presumed Sutro's friends would have no way of knowing what was going on, and would be either absent or confused by its wording.

When Sutro arrived he had the bill printed and circulated. He recognized the power of his Piper's Opera House speech and had it printed in one or more Washington newspapers along with comments on House Bill 1179. Then he called on every member of Congress whom he could reach. The countless hours he had spent on such calls up to now were in his favor, for he and his tunnel project needed no introductory remarks. He could quickly get to the concern of the moment. The effort Sutro had made during the previous summer to inform the Ways and Means Committee on its visit to the West also paid dividends. The members had heard Sharon in his efforts to overcome Sutro and knew that the bank ring was willing to do almost anything to rid itself of the threat the tunnel presented. When the vote was taken in the House it was a solid Sutro victory, 124 to 42.

In April Senator Stewart found a Senate bill relative to ditch and canal owners that was in part so obtuse that there was some possibility that it could be used against Sutro and his tunnel. Sutro was alert, however, and had his friends ready with an amendment specifically excluding him from being affected by the bill. Stewart was furious that once more the name "A. Sutro" was being incorporated into a bill and denounced it as one of Sutro's advertising stunts. Stewart asserted that instead of boring a tunnel, all Sutro did was to bore Congress. Congress adjourned without granting Sutro a loan, but neither had it revoked any of his previously granted rights nor changed them one iota.

Since Congress showed so little willingness to grant money, Sutro was desperate about the many bills coming in and he made his usual efforts to raise money with little success. After the danger in Congress was over, Sutro used his time profitably by visiting Massachusetts and studying construction progress on the Hoosac Tunnel. This projected railroad tunnel of 4.7 miles would be slightly longer than the main Sutro Tunnel and it had already experienced many setbacks. Sutro also included a visit to the machine works which made the Burleigh rock drill.

He remained in the East for four months seeking money and his hopes rose high. Nearly $3,000,000 was in sight in Paris and he planned to sail for France on July 20. Just five days before he was to leave, however, word came of the Franco-Prussian war and all hope of receiving French money was gone.

England was more stable, but Sutro's primary contact with England was one of his most trying problems. George T. Coulter of San Francisco was a second cousin of Robert and Hugh McCalmont of the banking house of McCalmont Brothers and Company, Philpot Lane, London, and his potential value to Sutro was very great. This very year, with McCalmont backing, he brought out the stock of the Sierra Buttes Gold Mining Company, Ltd., on the London market. From its inception this mine twelve miles east of Downieville, California, was a financial success, paying twenty per cent a year. Its success brought a rash of mining ventures to London — most of them dubious or worthless. These failures by rivals tended to magnify the great reputation of Coulter, the man who had promoted Sierra Buttes. No man was in a stronger position to successfully float an American mining stock in London than George T. Coulter.

The Sutro Tunnel was unlike a mine, however, in that revenue would be deferred during a long construction period of several years. The public would be impatient for dividends, but the Sutro Tunnel offered a magnificent opportunity, in Coulter's opinion, for shrewd private investors. Coulter was willing, even eager, to negotiate with his McCalmont cousins but was often offended by methods Sutro considered just. At the very moment when it seemed McCalmont Brothers might come through with a huge investment, Coulter retreated in a huff because Sutro asked for a "good will" deposit of $100,000. While talking and dreaming of huge sums the tunnel promoter managed to realize a small sum for himself. He sold some property in White Pines, Nevada, for $350. By September the three shifts of miners had been reduced to one and Sutro was in San Francisco on a similar financial mission with equally discouraging results.

In December of this year (1870) he transferred his base to Washington, where Congress was again in session. But the Sutro Tunnel was getting to be a stale issue; as the tunnel promoter himself later wrote, "It had been huckstered about too long." The time had come for a dramatic approach, and Sutro blundered into one. What he planned as a sober, intellectual investigation turned into a spectacle. He asked for a special investigating body to be sent to Nevada in order to determine the worth of his tunnel. To this both houses agreed and on April 4, 1871, President Grant signed the bill creating a Sutro Tunnel Commission. This body was to consist of three engineers who were to report to the War Department through the Chief of Engineers.

Exactly one month later Sutro was in New York in his endless quest for financial support. Relations with Coulter had been patched up and Sutro greeted him the day after his arrival from Britain. The tunnel projector also made a new acquaintance of consequence in Lewis Richard Price, who had accompanied Coulter on his voyage.

Price was a wealthy Briton aged fifty-four who had retired from mining, mercantile and related businesses in Mexico six years before. McCalmont Brothers and Company had invited him to join an investment syndicate and he had agreed. As a result he was involved in the Sierra Buttes venture from the start. Because of his mining experience, Lewis Richard Price was named chairman of the board of directors of Sierra Buttes and was soon requested to visit the mine and report on it.

Although Price's main mission was to visit a successful gold mine in California, he was inundated with information on a languishing tunnel project in Nevada. Sutro's detailed explanations of the advantages of investing in the tunnel were reinforced by the favorable opinion of the Seligmans. The Seligmans were international bankers with offices in Europe and America, including New York and San Francisco. They were advancing Sutro enough money to keep him afloat until McCalmont or some one else could be obtained to back the project. After two days in New York, Price and Coulter boarded a westbound train.

Within a month the members of the new Sutro Tunnel Commission were appointed and holding their first meeting. The law specified that two members must be officers of the Army Engineers and the senior officer was H. G. Wright; his associate was John G. Foster. Both men held the rank of Lieutenant Colonel of Engineers and Brevet Major General United States Army. The civilian member of the commission was Wesley Newcomb, Ph.D. Although Dr. Newcomb was a civil and mining engineer, he had developed a hobby which had become his profession — the collecting of sea shells. When Ezra Cornell purchased the Newcomb shell collection in 1869, Dr. Newcomb went along with his shells to Cornell University as curator of the collection.

The three commissioners met in New York on June 9, and went to visit the Hoosac Tunnel in Massachusetts. From there they went to Virginia City, where they stayed from late June until late in August. Newcomb was equipped with a small satchel and hammer to aid in collecting specimens of ore.

The commission had been directed to investigate the Comstock Lode in terms of value of bullion extracted at present and the probable future production of the mines. About the proposed Sutro Tunnel they were to ascertain its importance, feasibility, cost, and time required to construct it. In addition they were to determine its geological and practical value as an exploring work, as well as its general bearing upon national interests. The commissioners prepared a list of seventeen questions about the mines and mining practices which they submitted to the superintendents of the mines, who were also invited to comment on the question of the Sutro Tunnel.

The mine superintendents answered at length and according to their respective humors. Some were sarcastic and some facetious in their remarks about the tunnel, but they were uniformly against it. Thomas G. Taylor of the Yellow Jacket said that the geological value of the tunnel lay in the fact that it would be the most distant section from the known ore body, and therefore of scientific value. Isaac H. Requa of the Chollar Potosi said, along with others, that if the Sutro Tunnel were then in existence and all its many proposed services were absolutely free to the mining companies it would still be of absolutely no use to them.

The only real problems the superintendents admitted at all were occasional low grade ore and lack of ventilation in the prospecting tunnels or "drifts," as miners called them. All other ventilation problems had been solved satisfactorily by blowers and the tunnel could not solve the problem of ventilation in blind drifts. There were no water problems. "This is a dry country," wrote one superintendent.

The commissioners visited the Comstock area, went into the mines, and visited the tunnel. The Bank of California took a few precautions. They let miners know that they stood ready to discharge any one of them who gave information favorable to the tunnel. The superintendents issued invitations to the commissioners to visit mines when conditions were at their best. They also served excellent champagne when they entertained and there were times when they were vague about further visits. In the words of Professor Newcomb, "They didn't object; no objection was made; but we couldn't make arrangements for the purpose of going down, some way."

The superintendents walked them through so many miles of dry, fairly cool, ventilated tunnels that the commissioners never once proposed seeing more than the superintendents planned. Professor Newcomb carried with him his satchel and a hammer and took specimens of ore. He later testified that when the superintendents concluded the tours it was with relief that the commissioners finished walking and were "glad enough to get out." Where there was water, it was boarded over, or visits were impossible because "the shaft is out of order." The pumps at the Savage and the Hale and Norcross ran day and night pumping out water much of the time the commission was there, and all the while the superintendents maintained that if their mines were not bone dry, the water was at least diminishing.

Sutro found the commissioners timid. He felt that they did not know what course to pursue and they were restrained in their communication with him. Sutro was impressed with the truth and character of General Wright and Professor Newcomb but he later implied by innuendo that his opinion of General Foster was not so high.

Soon after the commissioners arrived at Virginia City another party of interested visitors appeared — Coulter and Price. They had made an extensive trip across the continent and had spent several weeks in California. They were now eastbound and the very first morning of their visit (July 6) the alert Sutro took them to see the tunnel and to visit the rich ore body being worked in the Crown Point mine. Price learned that the tunnel commissioners were making their investigation and he spoke to one of them, Professor Newcomb, who was "wonderfully impressed" with the tunnel's advantages.

The success of Sutro's propaganda efforts with one important convert is proved by Price's journal. Price noted the intense heat at the Crown Point ore body, which was down 1100 feet. He and Coulter remained down only ten minutes, and the perspiration poured off them "as though in a vapour bath." Price continued: "And in this atmosphere the poor miners have to work!!! They die in great numbers from miners consumption, but all this will be changed & ventilation be perfect if the Sutro Tunnel be carried out." The next day

Sutro took the two visitors to see the hoisting works at the Savage mine and claimed that the mine spent $65,000 a year for fuel. After recording this item in his journal Price wrote: "This will be saved by the Sutro Tunnel." That day the two men left by buggy for Reno where they resumed their rail journey.

On or about the time of this visit Coulter agreed to purchase some tunnel stock with his own money. In about a month he cabled from England and although he did not invite Sutro to come and made no firm promises, Adolph decided he must go to England. He left Nevada promptly on August 15 even though the work of the commission was not finished.

In London he found Robert McCalmont a receptive listener and before long McCalmont demonstrated that he was a sincere believer in the merits of the project. He was willing to use company or personal funds in stock purchases to the extent of $650,000 in gold coin. Whether or not Coulter was completely frank with his cousins is not known. He had left Nevada carrying an agreement that he would receive one share of tunnel stock for every four he sold. Sixteen years later in court he flatly refused to produce letters still extant between him and the McCalmonts on the ground that they had little or nothing to do with the case being tried.

Whether Coulter was ethical or not, the languishing tunnel project took on new life. Now Sutro was able to buy machinery and by December the tunnel project was in full progress with from 300 to 400 men employed. Sutro traveled to Washington in January, 1872, confident that he was "on the high road to success." The Sutro Tunnel Commission would surely issue a favorable report and then nothing could stop the long-expected loan from Congress. Such a loan would redeem Sutro's promise to the McCalmonts that government aid was imminent.

The report of the Sutro Tunnel Commission was a shock. The commissioners agreed with Sutro as to the feasibility of the tunnel and as to its value as a geological and exploring work. But when they dealt with the ventilation and drainage of the Comstock Lode, they were of the opinion that the Sutro Tunnel was "not a necessity." As to Sutro's strong claims concerning more economical working of the mines through the tunnel and reduction works near its mouth, the commission concluded that present methods would be better. They would agree to the superiority of Sutro's plan, however, if thorough surveys proved the existence of an abundant year-round supply of water from the Carson River for power and reduction purposes and if the allegedly far more efficient methods of English and German ore concentration proved successful on the Comstock.

As Sutro read the report he feared that his project had been given the kiss of death. Worse still, the mineowners on the Comstock now had official approval for their opposition. Even the miners were represented in the report as being content with working conditions. Who would see falsity behind such statements as "the miners with whom we conversed did not complain"?

A way must be found to change the report or to negate it. Sutro recognized that it was a flimsy thing which tried not to offend the mineowners and he was shocked that the army officers were "not quite up to the rascalities of that bank ring. . . . They (the commissioners) were not sharp enough for them at all." How could he keep this ridiculous report from becoming a grave marker for his tunnel? There was one possibility — get these three engineers cited before the mining committee and make them defend the report. When the chairman agreed to do just that through a series of committee hearings he set the stage for Sutro's most astonishing performance.

Sutro was advised that the hearings would proceed by the rules of the committee, not court procedure. Both sides could be represented by lawyers and the Bank of California sent Thomas Sunderland to defend its position. And who was to defend the position of the Sutro Tunnel? A battery of lawyers? Of course not. Adolph Heinrich Joseph Sutro might lack formal degrees in engineering and in law, he might speak with a thick German accent, he might be more familiar with the tobacco trade than the intricacies of a congressional committee, but when it came to the Sutro Tunnel he had no peer. He would not be relegated to the role of star witness; he would act as his own lawyer. Legal advisors he would have, but only in the background. He would examine, cross-examine, confound and confuse every witness tending to support the mineowners. In the end he would sum up his own case. Others might speak in better accents, but no one could talk with more authority.

Sunderland was no match for Sutro. He would not admit having been sent by the Bank of California, saying only that he represented the whole Comstock. What might have happened had the bank's lawyer been more flamboyant and dedicated, must be left to conjecture.

On the evening of Monday, February 12, 1872, the first hearing opened. Sutro, without any introductory remarks of any kind, started questioning General Foster. From the first sentence Foster must have thought he had stumbled into his own court martial. Sutro nailed him with a question challenging his methods of arriving at conclusions. Foster hedged and Sutro proceeded to throw the book at him. When the older man countered with evasive answers, Sutro made long statements, rattled off figures, multiplied by 2.36, talked of the cubic contents of shafts, multiplied it by tons, divided by 1,628 days, and came up with a figure of $3.80! Foster said he had not followed the calculations.

At this point the mining committee could have rebuked Sutro, and Sunderland could have asked for a copy of the figures so they might be checked and Foster could have done the same. But such was not the case. In addition to such pyrotechnics, Sutro made many solid points. One was the fact that the commissioners accepted all statements made by the mine superintendents at face value; they did not examine company books or correspondence. With this and other challenges Sutro tortured the General and then the hearing was recessed until four days later.

Sutro continued his examination of Foster and Sunderland complained peevishly that Sutro was making speeches which should not be taken down as testimony. Mr. Shober of the mining committee asked the general the distance from the tunnel to the river. A more alert witness would have deferred to the great familiarity of the tunnel projector with this subject, but Foster estimated the distance at a quarter of a mile, then raised it to half a mile when Sutro challenged him gently. Sutro concluded the exchange with the definitive announcement that it was nearly a mile.

For the three hours of that meeting and for most of the meeting on the following Tuesday Sutro did most of the questioning, but eventually Sunderland had his turn. Sutro had already shown that although he could reduce Foster to the level of a know-nothing when it came to finding and evaluating facts, yet he and the General could talk with authority about the rule books governing the miner's inch of water, friction, pumping, and hoisting. Sunderland avoided technicalities as best he could and at last, after four nights of hearings, General Foster's ordeal was ended. He had proved, without any doubt, that he had been the wrong man to send on a fact-finding mission. Otherwise, he had proved very little.

Now it was time for Professor Newcomb. Once more he had to leave his shells far above Cayuga's waters. He had written Sutro that he was to read a paper on Santo Domingo before the Geographical Society in New York City and if the chairman of the committee requested it he would then proceed to Washington. Newcomb seemed to have no great objection to coming, so long as it was understood that the Secretary of War had authority to order the other two men to appear before the committee, whereas he was appearing voluntarily.

Sutro questioned Newcomb with care, but not with cunning. Sunderland was rude to the conchologist but, as usual, the lawyer came off second best and no one could ever force the professor into making an unqualified statement he could not prove. In order to effect a total change of pace, Mr. Rice, counsel for the tunnel company conducted part of the cross-examination of Dr. Newcomb.

On February 28 Sutro started to examine General Wright, of whom he was later to say, "and a more honorable gentleman never lived." Once more he bogged down Sunderland in miner's inches. Wright had been far more careful than Foster in keeping notes, and less prone to use the "Well, possibly yes, and possibly no" of Newcomb.

Sunderland had sent home for help and so when Wright was finally finished, Sunderland produced I. L. Requa, Superintendent of the Chollar Potosi mine, and General C. C. Batterman, superintendent of two other mines. Both men admitted that they had been notified by Sharon as to the proceedings.

Next the committee asked for R. W. Raymond, U. S. Commissioner of Mines, and Sutro used him to refute the testimony of Requa and Batterman. Sutro then quoted from letters complimentary to his tunnel which he had received from world-renowned authorities such as von Cotta and von Beust, and asked Raymond to testify as to their eminence as mining engineers. Without these specific letters which Sutro had collected so earnestly and for which he had no idea of such use, he would have had a more difficult time damaging the testimony of the mine superintendents.

By Friday, March 29, the committee had met twenty times, each time for a period of 3 to 3½ hours. As if to drag it on forever Sutro brought in Charles A. Henry, General Manager of the Rocky Mountain Coal and Iron Company. The meeting ended in an argument about some sworn copies

of press copies* of letters forwarded to Sutro by Philip Deidesheimer, and every time the committee members considered admitting them, Sunderland fumed over some testimony
Foster had not been allowed to give, but the sworn copies
of press copies were finally admitted as evidence. Perhaps
Sunderland realized that the bank was clearly losing this
fight. Even before the final arguments were given, Sunderland approached Sutro and asked him to postpone any work
on a bill until the next session of Congress so that they might
both go home. Of course Sutro made no such bargain.

Sutro should have given his closing argument first, then
Sunderland would reply, and Sutro would have a small
amount of time to reply to Sunderland's statements. Instead,
Sutro managed to have Mr. Rice make a brief statement as
to the Sutro position. That meant Sunderland would have
little to reply to and Sutro would be left with considerable
time (three hours) in which to reply to Sunderland's statements. Thus Sutro would be able to present a formal, lengthy
"reply" which was really his closing argument and Sunderland would not be allowed to refute it. The bank's lawyer
apparently realized that he was unlikely to win over the
committee; he voluntarily limited his statement to one hour.

Sunderland in his closing argument continued to air his
grievances about Foster and the "copies of copies." The pamphlet published by Sutro in New York in 1866 came in for
ridicule, especially the portion where Sutro had predicted
the removal of miners, mills, and businesses from Gold Hill
and Virginia City to the mouth of the tunnel. The Piper's
Opera House speech was labeled inflammatory, and Sunderland pointed to some gross inaccuracies in a "finely bound
volume" published by Sutro. Sunderland also asserted, "In

----

*At this time copies of hand-written pen-and-ink manuscripts were
made by placing the freshly written sheet in the flat bed of a special
press with a sheet of tissue-thin paper over it. Pressure would be
applied through a screw or lever mechanism and the tissue would
usually pick up enough ink to make a legible copy.

two-thirds of the entire Comstock worked today the mines are as dry as this floor." All in all, Sunderland's argument was a collection of fragments in which he accused Sutro of bad intentions, incompetence, and having a desire for public funds for private gain. Sutro withheld all intimation of just what line of argument he would take in his "reply," so Sunderland was at the disadvantage of having to refute he knew not what.

The final three hours were at the disposal of Adolph Sutro, and he gave his real closing argument. He began with the history of the tunnel and proceeded with considerable logic from his first trip to Washoe through Mr. Sunderland's summation. Sutro took special care to refute the testimony of the mining superintendents Requa and Batterman by putting it in juxtaposition with that of Luckhardt and Raymond, who were acknowledged engineers.

By the time Sutro finished he had produced another masterpiece. The methods he used were entirely different from those of his Piper's Opera House speech. They were appropriate to his audience and he impressed the committeemen just as he had impressed the miners. Unlike Sunderland, he knew exactly what he wanted his speech to accomplish. He wanted to inform the committee of the total history of the Sutro Tunnel project, present the part of the Bank of California in what he believed to be its villainous role, to wipe away all negative reports about his tunnel and to ask for a $3,000,000 loan.

After three weeks of deliberation the Committee on Mines and Mining adopted a report full of enthusiasm for the Sutro Tunnel project. Not only did the committee overrule the conclusions of the special commission but they went so far as to distort the commission's recommendations. The committee report stated flatly: "The commissioners made a report, recommending the work to favorable consideration." The committee then drew up a bill calling for a loan of $2,000,000 to the Sutro Tunnel Company and urged that it be passed.

CHAPTER X

HE WAS THE COMPANY

IF THE SUTRO TUNNEL COMPANY had been organized along the lines of a modern business firm with Sutro as President and then a typical arrangement of line and staff positions we could readily visualize the activity resulting from the successful completion of the activities of their lobbyist. The Vice-President in charge of Publicity would launch a campaign involving publication of materials relative to the Federal commission and a series of illustrated lectures on the tunnel. The fringe benefits section of the Personnel Division would take care of a man named Riley, J. H., and a memo from them might drift upward to flutter eventually like an autumn leaf onto the President's desk. Then a personal letter to Riley's friend, Samuel Clemens, might or might not get dictated, typed, and mailed and copies filed.

Simultaneously the Vice-President in charge of Expansion (real property division) would be involved in the purchase of contiguous land along the Carson River while his peer in Building and Maintenance excluding the Tunnel would concern himself with the planning and erection of a suitable dwelling for the big boss. These projects would probably move very slowly because both men would have to spend long hours in staff meetings during which the Executive Vice-President would seek to allocate responsibility for the town of Sutro which the President had proposed. Real Property would probably need to notify Personnel about job specifications for an increased staff, but perhaps Maintenance excluding the Tunnel should be in charge of streets and parks. What they really needed was a Wild Life Man in

[103]

charge of snakes, jack rabbits and mosquitoes, but then perhaps they could shove that problem onto the Division of Animal Husbandry already in charge of horses and mules. The Vice-President for Animal Husbandry was taking up a lot of time trying to convince the members he needed a full-time veterinarian since Sutro was advocating that his miners keep cows. At this point the Vice-President in charge of Construction and Maintenance — Tunnel would break up the meeting with his question: "What are we doing, digging a tunnel or establishing a dynasty? I've got to have more mules and more men who know how to swing a pick."

The Sutro Tunnel Company suffered from no such organizational complexity. Adolph Sutro was simply *General Superintendent in Charge of Everything*. As a company secretary with many years' service testified later: "He *was* the company." So in order to see what actually went on we must look at the many activities of this man one by one and realize that he did many of them simultaneously.

We are certain to marvel at Sutro's great physical energy and might examine briefly its source. His health habits were excellent. His ideas of fresh air, recreation, and frequent bathing were in advance of his time. He enjoyed good food, wine and tobacco, but always in moderation. His stocky physique was vigorous and his immunity to disease high. He dressed with care, generally in excellent style as well as with due regard to the weather. He had great enthusiasm for his work, seldom if ever doubted his eventual success once the tunnel was started, and although his hobbies were primarily intellectual, in them he found release from tension.

Whereas the larger aspects of financing and planning were stimulating and enjoyable to Sutro, there were detailed chores which required time, patience, and a devotion to routine which he found easy to delegate. A personal secretary, a ghost writer, an errand boy, and eventually someone to read and mark newspapers were all within the scope of his ability to save time and effort without losing control of any situation.

It took a certain type of personality to enjoy the role of friend and humble employee of Sutro. J. H. Riley was such a man. Perhaps the fact that he was also Washington correspondent for the San Francisco *Alta California* gave him enough ego satisfaction to find his less stimulating jobs bearable. He served as clerk of the House Committee on Mines and Mining during two or more sessions of Congress. When Sutro was out of the capital Riley forwarded mail and sent reports on Congressional activities. He was a man of modest wants but still more modest purse. Sutro gave him no regular salary but made an occasional payment to him. While the tunnel commissioners were being examined Riley acted as clerk of the committee but received no pay and hoped, rather unobtrusively, that Sutro would compensate him. Sutro was so busy thinking in terms of millions of dollars that he forgot to pay Riley anything.

After the examination of the commissioners Riley went home to Philadelphia. Few men had a better idea of all the problems Adolph Sutro faced, and yet when Riley went to his doctor and learned that the spot on his face was cancerous he sat down and wrote to Sutro sharing his burden and asking for money. Whereas Sutro the commission interrogator had been too busy to pay Riley, Sutro the warmhearted employer responded immediately with a check for $100 and a series of friendly, cheerful letters. He took the time and trouble to visit Riley at home and wrote their mutual friend, Samuel Clemens, suggesting that he follow suit. Clemens was unable to leave home because of his wife's poor health following the recent death of their eldest child, but he too sent the dying man a check for $100. Clemens also wrote Sutro reporting on his actions. In his reply Sutro warmly thanked the author for helping Riley and also for the favorable publicity given the tunnel in *Roughing It*.

Meanwhile Sutro was sending messages to a photographer ordering stereoptican views of the tunnel, the new boarding house and the town of Dayton. These were for an illustrated lecture ostensibly on "Mines and Mining," but with a somewhat elongated introduction which took in the full sweep of the Sutro Tunnel project. Always ready to try anything new which would advance his cause, Sutro experimented with these lantern slides and found them a good drawing card. He maintained a library of them the rest of his life. President Grant enjoyed the lecture and the illustrations, and Sutro took several opportunities to call this to the attention of potential stock purchasers.

Along with stereoptican views he was also experimenting with a suitable picture of himself to be engraved and used in place of a coat of arms. Since no pictures were taken at the ceremony of "the first pick" he posed for such a picture later in London. Sleeves rolled up, collar off, and in boots that had seen more of hotel bootblacks than alkali dust he held a pick gently over his head and gazed at the ground. Unfortunately the photographer's backdrop did not quite reach the top of the synthetic hill and the whole thing looked like the fake it was.

The next attempt accomplished the nearly impossible by being even less convincing. Sleeves rolled down and cuffs buttoned, a flowing tie under a soft collar, and wearing a bowler hat, with well-deployed mustaches the honest miner contemplated a wall while holding a pick delicately over his left shoulder. Should he have swung the pick with any force while standing in either of these positions the results would have been disastrous if not suicidal.

But it was a decoration Adolph needed now, for there was the publication project to consider. The tunnel projector was a good judge of his own speaking ability and he knew that his speeches made good reading too. He had respect for the printed word, and all his life he had revered books. His weakness was in overestimating the number of books on the Sutro Tunnel which the world could absorb. Now he did a compiling job and sent two books to the printer.

The larger of the two was bound in heavy boards and the pages had handsome gilt edges. Stamped in gold on the spine was the fairly ambiguous title: *Sutro Tunnel — 1872.* The bowler-hatted miner and the words *Sutro Tunnel* were stamped in gold on the front cover. The contents included 66 pages relative to the formation of the Sutro Tunnel Commission, its report, and somewhat hidden in the debris of communications to them, the Piper's Opera House speech. Following this section were the 965 pages required to reproduce all the testimony taken at the committee hearings.

Did Sutro think anyone would read the entire book or did he plan it more for a handsome center-table piece such as his book *Mineral Resources of the United States?* The answer lies in Professor Newcomb's oft-repeated, "Well, possibly yes, and possibly no." If the compiler had expected the general public to read it he would have probably buried the Piper's Opera House speech less deep. On the other hand, if he had meant for it only to catch the eye he probably would not have made presentation copies to such a large number of libraries. The number of people who have read it in its entirety are probably few, but to a person who is interested in the Congressional investigation per se, or the behavior of some remarkable men, the reading is rewarding. The bank ring's befuddled lawyer, the indomitable professor, the weary legislators and buoyant Sutro emerge from the silt of oblivion which has long since covered them. Dr. Newcomb predicted the worth of the book in a letter to Sutro in which he said: "I want a full set of the examinations for they furnish a large amount of amusement, and not a little instruction."

The second book was merely a reprint of Sutro's Closing Argument. While the order for the large book came to less than 5,000 there were 10,000 copies of the small one destined for the state of Nevada alone, and they were bound in a variety of ways. After eighty years both books are fairly easy to obtain.

During the proceedings and subsequent activity to get the results published Sutro was, of course, in constant communication with Bethel. Sutro was trying to find a suitable telegraph system to run from Dayton to the tunnel, thence overland directly to Virginia City. Eventually the poles were set and at seven stations along this line instruments were installed which printed the message. A surface survey had been run and marked with cast iron posts. Each post was firmly placed in the ground and each top was winged. A circular hole was machined into each and a brass plug 1½ inches in diameter inserted. The posts marked the course of the tunnel and were referred to as "the line." Reports mentioned being "up on the line," and bringing visitors "down the line."

A wagon road was built from the tunnel mouth to Shaft No. 2 and from there to Virginia City an old road was placed in repair. The drop in elevation from Virginia City to Dayton was about 1,600 feet, but it was not a steady decline; the line went up and down six hills, which made the trip not only longer, but decidedly rough.

At four places along the line shafts were started in December, 1871. If they had all been completed they would have provided eight additional surfaces for tunneling as well as vital openings for air. Boardinghouses were built at each shaft, eliminating travel time for the miners. Unfortunately, though the shaft scheme cost a tremendous amount of money it was only partly successful.

All four shafts were timbered. On February 15, three days after the congressional hearings started, water was struck in Shaft No. 1 and it poured in at the rate of 3,000 gallons per day. During the next thirty days only five feet of the shaft could be dug, most of the time being used for the erection of hoisting machinery and in hoisting out the water. By March 17 Shaft No. 1 was down 110 feet, Shaft No. 2 had better luck and was down 260 feet, No. 3 struck very hard rock and was down 139 feet, while No. 4 Shaft presented the combined problems of Nos. 1 and 3 — hard rock and excessive water. Sinking was temporarily suspended at 100 feet.

The tunnel header was in 2,792 feet, and so far the problems were chiefly hard rock and water. Heat was just starting to bother the men and mules. Track was laid in the tunnel but though Sutro never failed to experiment with engines, he was always obliged to return to mules. Early in the history of the tunnel horses were tried for pulling the cars loaded with waste rock, but when anything touched a horse's ears the horse would throw up his head, hit the overhanging rock, and hurt his skull. Mules, on the other hand, would drop their heads and avoid injury. Although steam, compressed air, and finally electrically driven (storage battery) locomotives were tried, it was always "Old Peggy" and her companions who were called back and did the work. The mules were always given the best of care and had fine meadows for their use.

Sutro found the mules to be intelligent and once said in a lecture that he could write a chapter on mules. The men liked the way the mules responded to the signals for blasting. No one had to pull a mule to safety; the little beasts understood the signals perfectly and sought safety as diligently as the men.

Perhaps one reason Sutro liked mules was that they provided a bit of comic relief for the miners, and Sutro enjoyed watching his men have fun. The men shared their lunches with their pet mules. As the animals walked past the men eating their lunches, the mules would get from one man a piece of pie and from another a cup of coffee.

Sutro took good physical care of his men, but emotionally he had a bad effect on the assistant superintendents. He was unable to delegate authority and thus he frustrated a large number of men who should have had real authority to make decisions. Sutro made some men so dependent on him that they came to him for help when they should have handled the situation themselves. Other men became hostile. Sutro often ignored the advice of his superintendents, forgetting that they were doing the actual work. He was away for such long periods that he could not possibly know what was best. Even Bethel, who had served well in many capacities, was released in November of 1872.

Bethel and Sutro had had many harsh words. Ever since January one of their subjects of dispute had been a conveyance for Bethel, who pointed out that bringing the payroll in gold coins from Virginia City by horseback made his shoulders ache. Bethel asked for a buggy; but when a fancy family carriage was delivered, Bethel was furious. He wrote Sutro: "This is a damned pretty looking thing for a business man to ride around in. I wish to God the railroad company had burned it up. . . . I have no use for this thing." Sutro finally took the "fancy carriage" for himself and promised Bethel another one, but that did not solve the major problems which existed. Fortunately, Bethel came back into the Sutro picture later. He was a colorful man, and a rare one in his versatility.

Telegraphic connection between Dayton and Virginia City via the tunnel was all very well, but Sutro needed a combination home and office built near the tunnel. He could write Bethel demanding letters about getting the diamond drills to work, but he was less sure of himself when it came to ordering a home by mail. What he wanted was a large, gracious home, devoid of frills, but well lighted, heated, and with lots of plumbing. He wanted it fairly close to the mouth of the tunnel and to cost between $15,000 and $20,000. It was to be a gracious place to entertain important visitors to the tunnel, large enough for him, Mrs. Sutro and their six children, and at the same time, on the plain side. Pitch the roof high so as to take care of the heavy snows, but use plain shingles, not the fancy ones the artist suggested. And try, Mr. Bethel, to get it ready by July.

As soon as his two most recent publications were well under way, Congress adjourned and word came from Coulter that money was available in England. Sutro went to Pottsville, Pennsylvania, a coal-mining town, and did some shopping. He bought, among other things, 12 diamond drills at $1,000 each, 150 tons of "T" rails, and 13 ten-inch steam pumps.

It was July, and at last he could go "home." The house was not finished and he would have to live in Virginia City, but he had some projects to attend to which would be a lot easier to do in Nevada than elsewhere. There was a town to be established, some land to buy, and electioneering to be done for C. W. Kendall. It was an election year — perhaps Sutro himself would decide to enter politics. Yes, by all means, it was important to get back to Nevada.

The population of Nevada had been 6,857 in 1860 and rose rapidly to 42,491 in 1870. Just as many people thought the Comstock mines were inexhaustible, many thought the population of Nevada would continue to increase steadily, even dramatically. Adolph Sutro would take advantage of such a development with his model town between the Carson River and the mouth of the tunnel. He had a gridiron pattern sketched on the Hoffman map of 1866 but it was not until 1872 that the town was surveyed. After the first lots were sold a handsome black and white map was completed by Ross E. Browne, a son of the J. Ross Browne who wrote and illustrated early articles on Washoe which appeared in *Harper's Magazine*.

The gridiron pattern remained and the whole town was to be as orderly as the drawers of Sutro's filing cabinet. Eventually there would be fifty streets running east and west, each one eighty feet wide except for Twenty-seventh Street, which was to be 200 feet wide. Since it lined up directly with the tunnel opening, it would be called Tunnel Avenue. Avenues from north to south would be named for women from Adele through Zeline and would be 100 feet wide except for Florence, granted 150 feet. There were plans for broad sidewalks and four parks in the original map, which only included Adele through Jeanne avenues and Twenty-third through Thirtieth streets.

At this point Sutro started developing an interest in trees which would stay with him all the rest of his life. He had owned a few trees before, but now he saw in them a way to benefit mankind. He would have trees planted along Florence and Tunnel avenues at company expense and the sale of lots would be contingent upon the purchaser's planting and caring for a tree in front of his house. Trees were good for people. They improved the appearance of a town, they furnished shade and brought other benefits, so trees the people must have.

On September 9, 1872, the first two lots were sold at $500 apiece, one for a livery stable and one for a butcher shop. This marked the first income for the tunnel company. Some double lots sold for as much as $1,500 and Adolph wrote his brother Hugo that the town promised to become one of the largest in the state. In order to provide building materials he became involved in the construction of a brick kiln.

All during the summer workmen were urged to finish "the mansion." On its little hill it commanded a view of an artificial lake and a magnificent sweep of the valley of the Carson River and the mountains beyond. The structure was built and owned by the tunnel company and eventually cost $40,000 to build and furnish. At first it was lighted by candles. The house was planned, however, with gas lighting in mind, and a "gas machine" was ordered and eventually installed. Radiators were put on all three floors and painting the house inside and out was estimated at $1,900. Although there is no specific record of expensive furnishings, one reporter described the "large and elegantly furnished parlors" with white walls. It is known that one pair of blankets cost $30. Its occupant had not lost, nor would he ever lose his penchant for spending far more money than originally planned.

But the town and mansion were only two of Adolph's many activities. His financial backers must be kept happy and everything possible done to persuade them to invest more heavily. The unrelenting correspondence with Coulter was voluminous and not always in a friendly vein. Coulter had been working to get important English engineers to endorse the tunnel, and managed to get a model of the tunnel placed in the School of Mines on Jermyn Street, London. Sutro kept pushing Coulter to provide more money more quickly and once the reply to such a request was a brief cable: "It cannot be had from me — Coulter."

Coulter came to Nevada in September, 1872 and the two men made many bargains. Sutro tried to keep his friend Aron informed, but it seems possible that by the time Coulter returned to England, no one knew just what the other person proposed to do. Apparently Coulter's friend and associate, Colonel C. W. Brush, was also present. Brush was a retired Baltimore attorney who had been a close friend of Coulter's in the East. Brush liked California and Coulter prevailed on him to come out "just to look into things." Money was coming in from McCalmont Brothers, but the bargains by which Sutro and Coulter decided when and how the money would be delivered were, to say the least, devious.

A few months previous Joseph Aron wrote Sutro about a scheme he had for buying mining shares which would put the tunnel company in control of a large number of the mines on the Comstock. In reply he was told to have patience and in five years they would control or own every mine on the Comstock. This would indicate that the Bank of California had not misjudged the aspirations of Adolph Sutro. Apparently he did not expect to be content with just a tunnel, but might form a monopoly greater than that of the bank. By October 7 he was taking tentative steps looking toward control of the Crown Point and the Savage mines

[113]

but he was unsuccessful. So far as is known, neither the tunnel company nor Sutro himself ever had control of any major mine. Sutro owned part or all of the Sutro and the Rappahannock mines, but they were very small properties. While Adolph was maneuvering to control the mines at or near the point where the proposed tunnel would reach the Comstock Lode, he was gaining positive control of the land and water on the eastern side. By purchasing the Moore and Gee ranches he received three miles of frontage on the Carson River, with a fall of twenty-two feet useful for stamp mills. On the Gee ranch the annual production of hay amounted to 200 tons. At that time the tunnel company was maintaining stables in both Virginia City and at the mouth of the tunnel. Hay cost $30 per ton and the Gee Ranch, which cost about $11,000 brought both river frontage and some feed — in this case, 200 tons of hay already cut and stacked. There were also plans for buying five more miles of river frontage to get a fall of 100 feet.

Sutro also took an interest in political matters. He felt that he was a strong candidate for the United States Senate. He could not decide with which political party to affiliate and said it would suit him better to come out as an independent. He was wise enough to know that he was too individualistic to fit well into any existing party. If he were to run, the party would have to be made to suit him. Even so, he might not win.

It was very important to Sutro that C. W. Kendall be re-elected to Congress as the Representative from Nevada, for he had been a good friend. Sutro was on Kendall's reception committee in Reno on September 10. He wrote Pelham W. Ames, the company's new secretary at San Francisco, that he expected to go to Reno for Kendall. He did not think, however, that he could make it to return on the eleventh to greet Coulter and Brush.

Sutro continued to help Kendall throughout the campaign and his bid for re-election was successful. One can seldom attribute political success to any one backer, but at least Sutro did contribute toward Kendall's victory. Sutro was sought out by Kendall's political organization and on at least one occasion he was invited to speak at Virginia City. On the eve of election he made a speech in favor of Kendall at the Mechanics Hall which had just been completed in the infant town of Sutro.

Sutro stayed in Nevada until December, 1872. He then left for Washington, expecting things to run smoothly during the several months he would be away. Sutro was still trying to get the often-sought government loan. There were only 18 men working on the tunnel, but there were 35 on Shaft No. 1, 36 on Shaft 2, 34 on Shaft 3, and 35 on Shaft 4. The machine department had 21 men, Sutro also had 14 other "outside" workers and the Virginia City office had three men.

The ranches had only one man, "a very faithful laborer" who among other things, cut and stored over twelve tons of ice. Some idea of the immensity of the ranch project can be gained from a letter which reported that sixteen horses and two wagons were kept on the Moore Ranch solely for the purpose of hauling wood from the river to the different points on the line.

While Adolph in person (or by letter) was superintending the many activities related to tunnel construction, Mrs. Sutro stayed at "the mansion." Much of her time was occupied in entertaining any celebrity who might be snared into visiting the tunnel. Although she lived in a beautiful house, it was much like her husband — tunnel company property.

SUPERINTENDENT IN ABSENTIA

IN THE EARLY MONTHS of 1873 Adolph Sutro had two great desires, neither of which would be fulfilled. As usual he wanted a speedy hearing on his loan and a grant from Congress. Secondly, he wanted his stay in Washington to be short, permitting an early return to Nevada.

Sutro was frustrated by delay after delay. It is true that there was an adverse minority report from the Committee on Mines and Mining, but the real stumbling block was the investigation of the Credit Mobilier. This concerned the Union Pacific Railway Company, which had been commissioned by Congress to build the eastern portion of the first transcontinental railroad. Congress granted thousands of square miles of Federal lands and also loaned millions of dollars on a long-term basis to assist construction.

"Insiders" who owned only a few shares of railroad stock controlled the Union Pacific. They owned a construction company, the Credit Mobilier, which was allowed to build much of the railroad at prices amounting to several times the actual cost. A number of shares of the highly lucrative stock in the Credit Mobilier were offered to key Congressmen on easy terms, in an attempt to prevent Congress from becoming too critical of this scheme for bilking the railroad stockholders and the government.

The secret of the Credit Mobilier was exposed, however, and a Congressional investigation damaged a number of political careers. As one result, politicians were afraid to become involved in anything which concerned government loans to private enterprise. In his second inaugural address in March, President Grant made no mention, not even a veiled one, of the Sutro Tunnel.

Sutro also met frustration regarding an early return to Nevada. Although things were not going well at the tunnel Sutro could not possibly return. Lack of sufficient money was causing the majority of tunnel problems, so Sutro would have to go to Europe and try to raise more money.

Expenses at the tunnel were alarmingly high. On February 13 daily salaries and wages alone amounted to $1012.46 and as usual the assays read: "No silver — no gold." The Civil Engineer was drawing $26.66 per day, the Chief Mechanical Engineer $10.00, the Chief Miner $14.00, and five foremen were getting $6.00 each per day. Wages and salaries were not the only expenses incurred, of course, as attested by items in the storehouse such as two horizontal pumps costing $5088.51 and cordwood valued at $2990.38. Two melancholy memorials to Sutro's wastefulness were two steam locomotives for 36-inch track. They did not fit the track in the tunnel, which was 21 inches, and were never used. Even if they had been the right width, one wonders how Adolph ever expected to use steam power in a long tunnel.

Money was running low and Sutro ordered that the expenses must not exceed $1,000 a day. Even with such a rule in force all of the available money would be spent by May and the tunnel project would be faced with a grave crisis. George T. Coulter in London wrote Adolph that unless Congress granted aid to the tunnel it would be useless to try to sell a proposed new issue of $3,000,000 worth of bonds in England. Sutro replied by cable to Coulter that the work must not stop and that among other things the two locomotives cost $10,400 and must be paid for.

Sutro continued to retrench drastically, however. Shaft No. 1 was closed and no new orders were placed for pumps or boilers. The Virginia City office was closed and Shafts 2 and 4 were then closed. Sutro even had to plead with one of his backers, the banking house of Seligman, for enough money to pay the men who were discharged.

In Virginia City there was much talk about the tunnel being shut down and the presence of many ex-tunnel hands on the streets gave rise to the rumor that the project had failed. One Virginia merchant reported a loss of $1,000 a month in trade after the serious curtailment of work in the tunnel.

In April word came that Sutro had been successful in raising money in Europe. When a news item said that the machine shop would open and jobs reopen "on the line," fifty men came from Virginia City looking for employment. Hundreds of people were out of work in Virginia City and the very little work going on in Sutro required few hands but stout hearts. When Shaft No. 1 had been shut down it was within four feet of the tunnel level.

All during the many years of tunnel construction the working men were devoted to the tunnel and took its problems to their hearts. It was during this time of renewed hope that a few minor events occurred of historic interest to the fledgling town of Sutro. Twenty gum trees from Australia were set out and in May the first child was born in the town of Sutro, a girl born to a Mrs. Kelly. A tragedy occurred at Shaft No. 2 shortly after the happy news of the reopening of the shaft. On June 6 fire broke out in the boarding house at that shaft and destroyed the house in a few minutes. James Dockery, the manager of the boarding house, had seven children and one of them, a girl, was burned fatally. In addition, Dockery was left penniless.

While Adolph Sutro was keenly interested in the details of life in Sutro, Nevada, at the moment his eyes were focused on far horizons. He remained in Europe visiting mines and tunnels, including the St. Gotthard tunnel then under construction. The money problem continued urgent and he did get some, but the Seligman branch in Paris was not as cordial as the Seligman brother in Frankfurt had hoped they would be. Three weeks later even the friendly Seligmans of New York were asking Sutro to please pay them $18,000 immediately. They alluded to the "severe crisis through which New York is at present passing," and feared that Sutro would not succeed in obtaining further aid from the McCalmonts at present. In other words, the financial outlook for speculative investments such as the Sutro Tunnel was dark indeed. This general state of financial distress was hardly news to Adolph Sutro. Panic had struck the Vienna Bourse as early as May, 1873, and the decisive blow at American confidence had been the failure of the Philadelphia banking house of Jay Cooke and Company on September 18.

A few days before receiving the Seligman demand for $18,000 Sutro sat down and wrote a long letter to President Grant. Sutro was careful to say that he was not asking the President to recommend to Congress any direct aid to the tunnel but went on respectfully to request a favorable mention of the tunnel project in Grant's forthcoming annual message to Congress. In this latest attempt to influence the President, Sutro was eminently unsuccessful.

Meanwhile in London the great faith of Robert McCalmont in the Sutro Tunnel was unimpaired. In spite of the general financial distress plans were made for a public offering of bonds. The London *Times* for January 6, 1874, carried both a news item and an advertisement about the Comstock Lode and the Sutro Tunnel. First mortgage bonds backed by the "Sutro Tunnel and Railway" were being offered to the public by McCalmont Brothers and Company. The banking house of Seligman was taking some part in the offering too, for they also had prospectuses available for persons interested and the two trustees of the first mortgage would be Messrs. Robert McCalmont of Philpot Lane, and Isaac Seligman of Angel Court, Throgmorton Street, London. The tunnel company, whose current board of trustees was listed, had authorized a first mortgage of £1,600,000 or $8,000,000 but the first offering would comprise only $3,000,000 worth, to be sold at 82 per cent of face value and to bear interest at the rate of 8 per cent.

The advertisement included a great many of the usual assertions about income from town lots and water rights on the Carson, and also a statement that the railroad through the tunnel might be extended and form a junction with future railroads east and west. Much stress was laid on the actions of the Congress of the United States and the fact that the Committee on Mines and Mining had recommended a $2,000,000 loan. In fact, the prospectus quoted in the advertisement contained nearly all of the hopes and aspirations of Adolph Sutro, and none of the fears he might well have entertained. Controlling the Comstock mines was not mentioned and any difficulties with Congress, past, present, or future, were ignored.

The bonds went on sale on January 6, and subscriptions on the first day totaled £150,000 ($750,000). Robert McCalmont, however, did not make any allotments and the bonds were withdrawn. Aron reported a conversation with Robert McCalmont in which the latter said he was dissatisfied with the way Seligman Brothers and Sutro wanted the McCalmonts to pay "extravagant" commissions. Also he objected because the Seligmans, although one of them was co-trustee of the mortgage, did not subscribe one penny to this bond issue. A third reason why McCalmont withdrew the bond issue was that "the public did not deem it fit to subscribe at once on a bond offered by my house."

Although the withdrawal of the bond offering was no doubt a disappointment to Sutro, the immediate needs of the tunnel company were met by large stock purchases by Robert McCalmont personally. Apparently he was still well satisfied with the tunnel as an investment. Aron recalled his saying: "I believe in the value of the Sutro Tunnel, but my brother Hugh does not, as he believes about Sutro what Brush writes us."

The news that fresh money for the tunnel had been obtained was joyously received at Sutro, Nevada, and construction went ahead steadily. F. A. Benjamin had taken over on November 30 with the title of Assistant General Superintendent and his salary of $1,000 a month was two or three times that of previous assistant superintendents. Perhaps it was the salary, or perhaps it was because he had once been in the employ of the Seligmans, but Benjamin felt free to address the Board of Trustees of the tunnel company directly. Also he did not hesitate to criticize previous methods.

By February 28 Benjamin was ready with a report to the board in which he stated that the expenditures of the previous year were "incredible" and he blamed them on the lack of "a managing head on the spot." He had abolished six offices (Chief and Assistant Civil Engineers, Chief Mechanical Engineer, Chief Miner, Chief Carpenter, and Storekeeper) and he dismissed many of the men who had been with the tunnel company for some time. By July 7 Bluett was made foreman for Shaft No. 2 and Benjamin wrote Sutro: "He will be the last of the old crowd (and a hell of a set they were)." Good progress was made on the tunnel during Benjamin's stay but, of course, he and Sutro exchanged snappy letters; these included an offer to resign after a tenure of only five months. Sutro was then in Washington, however, and Benjamin stayed on for two or three months.

Although Burleigh compressed-air drills were introduced in the Comstock area in 1872, they were first used in the Sutro Tunnel on April 25, 1874. Operators from the Hoosac Tunnel were used to run them. Some of these men were hired in the East by Sutro but some just came west when work on the Hoosac Tunnel was finished. Benjamin was glad to get these men because they were familiar with the techniques necessary for using these new drills. It was fortunate for the tunnel that just at the time the Burleigh drills were introduced a dynamic leader like Benjamin was in charge of affairs.

During Benjamin's first three months of service Sutro was in London immersed in money matters. In spite of the importance of financial support, the projector could not ignore developments in America, especially in Washington. He received a letter from Representative C. W. Kendall with a January date saying that no movement to check the rights of the company was as yet apparent in Congress; "You ought to be here, however, as soon as possible."

Kendall's warning may have been based on rumor, but there can be no doubt that by January 12 the bank ring had under way a specific plan of action against Sutro and his tunnel. On that day in San Francisco there was a meeting of the Board of Trustees of the Ophir Gold and Silver Mining Company. The board approved a plan whereby the various mining and milling companies on the Comstock Lode would be assessed to provide for "such legal proceedings as may be necessary to secure a final judgment denying the validity" of the claim of the Sutro Tunnel Company to a royalty of two dollars a ton on ore raised from the mines. The companies agreed to be assessed amounts which could in no case exceed a total of $201,580.

Joseph Aron was a stockholder in the Ophir mine, so he examined the record book of the company and made a copy of the agreement approved by the board. He made a sworn statement that it was a true copy and sent it to Washington. Sutro was notified by telegraph at London and on February 1, 1874 he addressed letters to all Senators and Representatives warning them of this "corruption fund."

Many of the mining companies on the Comstock Lode were refusing to take out patents on their land in accordance with the general mining law because the patents would specifically mention that ownership was subject to paying royalty to the owner of the Sutro Tunnel, when completed.

[122]

Many companies that had filed for patents refused to complete the process. Sutro exposed this situation in an eleven-page pamphlet.

Sutro examined the bills in Congress and he discovered Senate Bill 16 after it had already passed the Senate and the House Committee on Mines and Mining. This bill would make all proceedings for mineral land patents then in process null and void. The mining companies preferred to take a chance and hold their lands without any patent at all rather than specifically accept Sutro's royalty claim.

In the House a friend of Sutro's offered an amendment saying that nothing in the bill should affect the rights of the owners of the Sutro Tunnel. Although adopted, Sutro felt that this was not enough, and he had Representative James S. Negley of Pennsylvania offer another amendment. This provided that mineowners on the Comstock Lode who had not yet taken out their patents must do so within six months or forfeit their rights. This stirred up the bank ring mightily, yet it passed the House with only nine opposing votes. One of these dissenters, ironically enough, was Charles W. Kendall of Nevada, longtime firm friend of Sutro whose letter had warned Sutro a few months previous.

With both amendments attached, Senate Bill 16 now returned to the Senate, where it would be studied by the Committee on Mines and Mining under its new chairman, Senator Jones of Nevada. Sutro claimed that it was the bank ring who maneuvered the former chairman, Senator Chandler, into resigning his place in favor of Jones. Sutro bided his time and said nothing.

On the day that hearings began on the bill Sutro went before the committee accompanied by his lawyer. He asked the chairman for permission to put a few questions to the members of the committee. He then asked Senator Jones if he owned any interest in the Crown Point mine. Jones admitted that he did and further questioning brought out that he was bitterly opposed to the Sutro Tunnel. Sutro then questioned Senator Sargent, bringing out the fact that he was strongly opposed to the Sutro Tunnel. Turning to the chairman of the committee, Sutro respectfully requested that the bill be submitted to another committee, where none of the members were interested parties. The committee had a stormy argument over this question, according to rumors, but finally agreed with the tunnel builder and it was sent to the Judiciary Committee. This committee examined the bill for a month and concluded that Congress had no power to interfere with Sutro's vested rights. Any controversy over his rights should be left to the courts. The committee recommended that Senate Bill 16 and its amendments be indefinitely postponed, which amounted to a victory for Sutro.

He continued to give his illustrated public lectures and to watch Congress but he could not neglect his financial backers. He assured the McCalmonts that without the pressure of the bank ring in Washington he could get a subsidy of possibly five million dollars when Congress next convened. He felt it probable that soon more than half of those now composing Congress would have been defeated. Sutro also wrote that he felt compelled to become a candidate for United States Senator from Nevada in order that William Sharon might lose the race for that office.

The McCalmonts were opposed to Sutro's running for Senator but apparently Sutro kept reiterating the "I am compelled" idea. Sutro wrote the McCalmonts that he would need $75,000 to $100,000 for the campaign expenses but would try to have his friends in California and Nevada contribute most of it. Thus Sutro opened the door for the McCalmonts to contribute pounds sterling in order to help "pack" the United States Senate to their advantage. It is altogether unlikely that they did so. They also turned a deaf ear to a second proposal suggested in the same letter — the idea that the tunnel company gain control of a mine on the Comstock Lode in order to dig the tunnel from the west as well as from the east.

But James J. Robbins, then in San Francisco, was an eager confederate in all of Sutro's schemes. He had ideas about breaking the bank ring through stock manipulation, about gaining control of mines, and about speeches for the election campaign. He told Sutro news on the legal dispute between the Crown Point and Belcher mines and the two lesser mines (the Dardanelles and the Leviathan) which claimed the rich ore bodies they were working. Robbins suggested speculation in the stock of the two lesser mines. Most of all, Robbins was enthusiastic about starting a newspaper. He reported that Sharon had bought the *Enterprise* and also had the Virginia *Chronicle* and the Gold Hill *News*. The bank ring, he said, expected to carry the state with Requa for Governor and Sharon for United States Senator.

A new paper appeared in Virginia City on or about the first of June. It was called *The Daily Independent* and was dedicated to the independent cause, but not necessarily to the Independent Party. John I. Ginn was editor of the paper with Bethel as business manager and Myron Angel and Thomas Boyce were appointed as San Francisco agents.

As the time for election grew near the Gold Hill *News* became violent in its attitude toward what it called the *Dependent*. Sutro had pledged Ginn up to $1,000 to help get the paper started and the paper was most favorable to everything in regard to Sutro, although the editor seemed to try to avoid his name. One obvious reason why Sutro sponsored a Nevada newspaper was his hope of defeating Sharon's bid for a Senate seat. Apparently Sutro also hoped to win the election for himself. He wrote to Ginn that he was determined to be elected to the United States Senate and fully believed success would crown his efforts. Fourteen years later he tried to minimize his part in this election. He asserted to one of Bancroft's writers that people said that he was running in opposition to Sharon but that this was not the case. Sutro simply opposed him.

The political season had opened in Nevada but Sutro felt obliged to remain in Washington until Congress adjourned. That event finally came on June 23, 1874, and Sutro left for the Pacific Coast a few days later. He not only had a tunnel to dig, but the bank ring had begun some law suits against the tunnel company in San Francisco. Sutro attached no great importance to them but felt that they should be defended with the best lawyer available.

As Sutro already knew, the introduction of Senate Bill 16 had been inspired by a double motive. In addition to the mineowners' reluctance to give specific recognition to Sutro's royalty right, some of the mines then in bonanza were working ore bodies east of their original locations. If compelled to take out patents based on their recorded locations they might lose everything and be liable for the large sums already extracted. In addition, the Sutro Tunnel Company had a stipulated right to anything that they might discover lying to the east of the original Comstock Lode locations. The tunnel company's right extended two thousand feet on each side of the main tunnel. One can readily see how this situation aggravated the already bad feeling existing between the mineowners and Sutro.

Thus legal moves and political attacks were closely intertwined. Sutro attacked Sharon continuously and Sharon replied in kind. One report asserted that Sutro could have had the Democratic nomination for Governor, if he had been willing to bow out of the race for Senator. He refused, however, and an Independent Party favoring Sutro was organized in several counties and Sutro was confident that Sharon would be defeated. Sutro was now less positive, however, that he would himself be the successful contender.

Sutro carried on a vigorous political campaign. Running for Senator was an especially difficult undertaking since the power to elect still lay in the state legislature. Thus Sutro would have to elect a majority of the legislators or a small but loyal minority who might find themselves in a balance-of-power position where they might dictate to the major parties. He took his lantern slides to every city, town, or camp that would hear him and his lecture called "Mines and Mining."

Piper's Opera House was once more the scene of a triumphant Sutro speech. Once more the bank ring was painted in darkest hues and the virtues of the Sutro Tunnel were extolled. This time, however, instead of exhorting his listeners to buy stock, Sutro urged them to vote the Independent ticket. If the Republicans were sent to the Nevada legislature they were sure to elect Sharon to the United States Senate. Chances were the Democrats would do the same. Vote Independent. The entire speech and thirty-six of the pictures used to illustrate it were published at Virginia City in a supplement to the *Daily Independent.*

Three days later the voters of Nevada trooped to the polls and not a single Independent was elected to the state legislature. Sutro had one source for satisfaction in that the bank's choice for Governor, Requa, was defeated by the Democratic incumbent, L. R. Bradley. But the Republicans captured the legislature and Sharon easily won the coveted position of United States Senator. One of the bitterest disappointments to Sutro in the whole campaign was the fact that Storey County went solidly Republican. That was the county in which Virginia City was located and Sutro had made strenuous efforts there.

Ironically enough, Sharon did not take his seat in the Senate the first year and was absent the last four years of his six-year term as well. His lateness in going to Washington was no doubt due to the great distress experienced by the Bank of California in 1875. But even without taking his Senate post, Sharon and his bank associates could take satisfaction in knowing that neither Sutro nor one of his allies represented Nevada in the Senate. The other Senate seat was held by John Percival Jones, the wealthy owner of the Crown Point mine, who was independent of the bank ring but who usually agreed with them where Sutro and his tunnel were concerned.

While the political campaign was still raging, Sutro had detected one disturbing development among his financial backers. The banking house of Seligman was showing signs of deserting the Sutro cause and Colonel Brush held a grudge because he had failed to become President of the tunnel company. That office had recently been vacated when the incumbent, Joseph Aron, moved to New York and Sutro had vetoed Brush as President.

But digging the tunnel went on regularly despite any storms brewing in political or financial skies. During the month of September the tunnel was advanced 310 feet, some of it being 8 by 10 and some 10 by 14. Tunnel expenses were $25,000 a month, however, and the McCalmonts were pledged to only $15,000 per month after December first. This would mean cutting the work back to a single machine drill or possibly hand labor. Then no more than 150 feet a month could be accomplished, Sutro believed, and the width and height of the tunnel would have to be reduced to that of a mere header.

Sutro wrote to Aron, who was then in Paris, laying before him the urgency of the situation and imploring him to go to London and make a more advantageous arrangement with the McCalmonts. Sutro hoped Aron could do it so as to save him a trip to London. Sutro added that as soon as they had drilled a little farther immediately west of Shaft No. 2 they would strike greenstone, where he felt sure that they would hit a mineral vein. Then there would be no difficulty in placing the stock upon the San Francisco market and the question of funds would be settled forever. But nothing turned out the way Sutro had hoped. No ore was found and Aron could not make the arrangements desired in London. Sutro left his assistant superintendent in charge at the tunnel and went to London.

The year was not quite over and progress on the tunnel was encouraging, with a spurt of 110 feet made in seven days during December. But the year ended in the town of Sutro with extreme sorrow. Two men were blown to bits early in the morning of December 30 in the header of the tunnel. John Delaney, foreman of the shift, and Samuel Richards, "boss blaster" of the shift and formerly of the Hoosac Tunnel, were killed, while four others were injured. Some loose giant powder had been allowed to collect near the blasting battery and a spark flew from the main wire and caused the loose powder to explode.

For a project of great magnitude the death rate for the Sutro Tunnel was extremely low. Sutro claimed that in the entire operation only twelve persons were killed. For a comparison Sutro used the five-mile railway tunnel in Massachusetts, the Hoosac Tunnel, which took the lives of 185 workers.

While the town of Sutro mourned its dead, Adolph Sutro sat in his room in a London hotel on the last day of 1874. He turned over a printed invitation to the creditors' meeting of Jay Cooke and Company held at Philadelphia and he listed the number of nightshirts, day shirts, socks, handkerchiefs and drawers he was sending to the laundry.

CHAPTER XII

THE GENERAL SUPERINTENDENT KEEPS
INFORMED

SUTRO'S STAY in London was short but successful. True, McCalmont Brothers had declined to make further large purchases of tunnel stock, but they agreed to continue to advance substantial sums of money in return for a first mortgage on all property of the tunnel company.

The McCalmonts insisted on an arrangement which would give them unquestioned control of the tunnel through a trust agreement embracing a large majority of tunnel company stock, but Sutro was agreeable to that. Robert McCalmont was friendly to him and his position as General Superintendent seemed assured. In fact, Sutro reflected that a first mortgage could not be in better hands. McCalmont Brothers already owned nearly half of the tunnel stock and there would be no conflict between the biggest shareholder and the holder of the mortgage.

There is one interesting implication, however, of this mortgage loan. Apparently even the ever-hopeful Sutro had given up hope of receiving a loan from Congress. He talked about giving a second mortgage for a government loan, but he undoubtedly realized that such an arrangement would be far more difficult to put through Congress than a first mortgage.

In mid-January of 1875 Sutro was on a ship entering New York and was intent on getting to Washington. He soon learned the disappointing news that his Virginia City newspaper, the *Independent,* had gone out of business on January 11. He was vexed at this action, feeling that if the editor had persevered a few weeks longer money could have been found to save the tottering journal. Sutro swallowed his disappointment but vowed that he would found another Comstock newspaper before long, which he did.

While in Washington the tunnel projector did not press the Negley amendment in the Senate, partly because he wanted to let it "hang over" his opponents. The new Congress would soon be seated and go into executive session, when Sutro would be free to leave for Nevada.

Sutro knew that the tunnel diggers were facing a problem. Water had been struck and the miners were in fear of their lives. Before leaving Washington Sutro visited the White House and engaged in conversation with President Grant's secretary, General Orville Babcock, formerly of the Army Corp of Engineers. They discussed the water problem and Babcock suggested a bulkhead. He said it should have a gate which would close automatically if there were a great influx of water. The water might be expected to gush at the time of a blast and if the miners could be on the other side of a bulkhead they would have time to escape. Sutro thought that the expense of the bulkhead would be easily offset by the fact that it would free the miners from fear.

Upon his return to Nevada Sutro found the Comstock reasonably prosperous. The bank ring was still in evidence but was being challenged by the compact group of mine-owners composed of John W. Mackay, James G. Fair, James C. Flood, and William S. O'Brien. This quartet of Irishmen had gained control of the Consolidated Virginia and the adjoining California Mine. By 1875 it was clear that they had made a real strike, the one that was forever afterward known as the "big bonanza." These four were entirely independent of the Bank of California.

In Sutro's domain construction was proceeding extremely well, except for the water problem. Ever since the Burleigh drills had been introduced the progress had averaged 300 feet per month. Because the tunnel was open past Shaft

No. 2, it was possible to effect a worthwhile saving on the cost of cordwood. In June the wood was floated down the Carson River to a point opposite the tunnel mouth. There it was corded and hauled to the tunnel mouth by teams. It was then loaded onto cars which the mules pulled through the tunnel to Shaft No. 2, where the wood was hoisted out and re-corded. This method of transportation saved the company $6 per cord, and since there were often twenty-four hundred cords to be moved the saving was substantial. It was, in fact, the type of saving Sutro had predicted. Here, at last, his gargantuan dream reached partial fulfillment.

While Sutro was demonstrating the use of the tunnel for transportation, all was not well in the world of Comstock mining shares. After the high prices of January the market became quite erratic and even the mighty Bank of California was experiencing serious difficulties. Finally, stocks fell as much as two-thirds of their former market prices, and stock in the Consolidated Virginia, although still in bonanza, dropped $200 a share in one week.

Panic swept San Francisco and on August 26 thousands of depositors besieged the Bank of California. Withdrawals were so great that Ralston closed the heavy iron doors twenty-five minutes before the usual closing time. To a group of excited newspaper reporters Ralston could only say that the bank had no definite plans for reopening. The following day Ralston resigned as an officer of the bank. Shortly after 3 o'clock he went for his customary swim in the cold waters of the Bay and he drowned. Any intent of suicide was never proved, but the mighty Ralston was dead. The bank Ralston had founded was reorganized and it reopened in six weeks, but the Bank of California never regained its former position of dominance.

On the Comstock Lode the fall of the Bank of California made way for the rule of the "silver kings" of the Consolidated Virginia and California Mines. As always, however, Adolph Sutro waited in the wings, a possible future monarch.

If his tunnel proved to be the key to the mountain that he believed it would, there was little doubt that Sutro would finally displace any previous rulers of the silver-and-gold mountain.

This year of financial revolution also witnessed a financial change inside the Sutro Tunnel Company. For five years the General Superintendent had served the company without salary, but he was permitted to draw money from the treasury as needed for his personal and business expenses. By March of 1875 the two classes of expenses totaled $27,298.65 and a different plan was adopted. Sutro would now depend on a salary of $1,000 a month and the past sums received by him would be written off. Also the trustees granted 100,000 shares of stock to the projector as his own property in recognition of the fact that the increase in capital stock from 1,200,000 to 2,000,000 shares had diluted his equity considerably. In return Sutro signed a receipt saying that these acts of the company satisfied all of his claims for past services.

As if the stock market collapse and the closing of the Bank of California were not enough, fire broke out in Virginia City on October 26, 1875, with a property loss of ten million dollars. Two thousand buildings were in ashes, including the surface buildings of the Consolidated Virginia mine. The fire started at 6:00 a.m. in a little lodging house on A Street and a fierce gale was blowing. One observer wrote that the main body of the fire streamed before the gale "as fierce as the flame of a blow-pipe."

The next morning work started on rebuilding Virginia in a hundred places at once. A week later a tornado blew down most of the work of rebuilding. Although the Consolidated Virginia Mining Company suffered a loss by fire of $800,000 the directors of the company paid the usual dividend in November and December of $1,080,000 a month.

With this sign of confidence in the big bonanza before him, Sutro could only push tunnel digging more than ever. On the last measuring day of the year there was cause for

[133]

celebration in the town of Sutro. The tunnel had advanced 3,726 feet in that year and no sign of trouble ahead.

But Adolph Sutro was frequently absent from "Sutro City," and he kept in close touch with affairs in Nevada through a voluminous correspondence. He received daily reports from many of the tunnel employees, as well as monthly reports, summaries, and expense reports. He encouraged everyone to write to him and maintained a correspondence with anyone he considered capable of keeping him informed on some item of interest to him. Since his interests were catholic his informants were numerous.

Frank S. Young was often sent by Sutro to cover either Washington, D.C., or the tunnel, whichever one Sutro was not covering himself at the moment. Young worked at many jobs at the tunnel and he probably enjoyed making general reports or clipping newspapers for Sutro, but obviously he loathed what he called "spying." In one letter he reported on the fights, gambling, and drunkenness the night following pay day and added:

I should consider myself guilty of a most contemptibly mean action in thus spying, as it were, on the actions of others, did I not, in informing you of these facts, but simply carry out your instructions.

R. S. Raw, Assistant Superintendent, was primarily responsible for keeping Sutro informed about everything connected with the progress of the tunnel. Raw had been with the tunnel company for a long time, for he had served in the Virginia office when Benjamin was Assistant Superintendent. Although Raw did not get along with Bluett very well, at least the two of them had outlasted many changes of personnel. No doubt Raw knew that practically everyone who was capable of writing a letter was, at least occasionally, sending reports to the boss. Details of fights, personality conflicts, and petty squabbles which he would not send to a man of lesser curiosity he regularly reported to Sutro knowing

[134]

that the participants' versions and those of many others might reach the General Superintendent.

Raw particularly objected to the behavior of H. B. Hanmore, the mining editor of the Virginia City *Chronicle*, because Hanmore was supposedly a secret agent for Sutro yet he would often come down to see Raw to request salary advances. Raw felt that Hanmore should not be seen in the town of Sutro and was sure the money was being thrown away at the faro tables. Although Hanmore did some reporting on tunnel people his job, as he saw it, was to interview the most important people in Virginia City in order to find out how they were feeling about Sutro and his tunnel. In order to do this and remain in the good graces of Fair (whom he called "Slippery Jim") Hanmore wrote that he "did not scruple to damn the tunnel and yourself (Sutro) after the most approved methods in Virginia."

Hanmore reported that the Burleigh agent told him the Ingersoll people had spent $1,000 to get their drills into the tunnel, and that half of the money had gone to Bluett. An investigation was held and since Bluett remained with the company it is probable that Sutro was convinced that the charge was groundless. Sutro himself refused "gifts" and would certainly not tolerate an employee accepting one. Hanmore had a weak character and may have manufactured the whole story or repeated an idle rumor.

Hanmore needed money to support his vices. The Reverend T. H. McGrath in Virginia City probably used his earnings for different purposes, but he was both a reporter-at-large and real estate agent for Sutro. For several years McGrath wrote to him about stocks, public sentiment, and even about Mr. Raw.

One of the most frequent correspondents from Sutro, Nevada, was Thomas H. Cox, M.D., who was the combination health officer and assayer for the tunnel. His reports were a mixture of broken ribs, small pox vaccinations, scalp wounds and descriptions of the type of rock at the header.

Even George Rammelkamp wrote to Sutro. George was a German immigrant who took care of the mules, the trees of the town, and who accepted numerous other duties which were placed upon him. George wrote mainly in German, with a few English words thrown in, often spelled in German syllables. One of his letters began, "I want to write you according to your regulations," and he reported on mules, wood, and the possible need for an extra water pipe in the tunnel. George took a very personal interest in everything which affected Adolph Sutro, whether it was the planking in the tunnel, or the hogs which ruined the trees in the town of Sutro. On the latter subject he grew vehement and threatened to slay the next hog he caught near one of the young trees, "even if I have to pay for it."

Of all this correspondence, none is more charming, vivid, and devoid of malice than that of Henry L. Foreman. To him life was so wonderful that he seems to have been unaware of the peccadilloes of his fellow employees.

Foreman was an engineer in his late twenties who had come to the tunnel to take a position as head of the supply department. He had resigned his position of Chief of the Signal Service Bureau in Washington, D. C., because of ill health. Foreman had a frail body, but a will to live that matched in determination that of Sutro's will to succeed. Foreman lacked Bethel's vigorous and often profane style of writing, but Foreman's reports were detailed and clearly written. Mr. Foreman went to the face of the header to watch the drills in action, check on the exploders, and talk to the men. He kept the batteries for the exploders in condition and when anything proved recalcitrant he would bring it out and conduct experiments, all of which he reported in detail. We see him as a quiet gentlemanly fellow enjoying the writing of his daily report to Sutro, whom he must have pleased with his fine descriptions.

With the aid of all these people in Nevada Sutro knew a great deal of what was going on there even when he felt obliged to be in Washington to watch Congress. By March 13, 1876, Senators Jones and Sharon were both in Washington and so was James Fair. Sutro found Fair's presence favorable because of the jealousy which existed among Fair and Jones and Sharon. Sutro felt sure that each side feared the other side would form a coalition with the tunnel company. Sutro also imagined that all of his efforts to publicize the practices of the bank ring and the mineowners had been effective and that Sharon and Jones were snubbed on all sides.

The principal measure at this session of Congress which Sutro traced to his enemies was an attempt to remove the Federal Court in Nevada from Carson City to Virginia. Sutro felt that his enemies were behind this, certain that they could control members of juries drawn from Virginia far more readily than those from Carson City. The measure failed, however, and Sutro could chalk up a minor victory.

By September Sutro had returned to the Pacific Coast and from there he went to England. Even before he left he knew the yearly progress in feet would be less than that of the year before because of the hard rock through which the men had to drill. He also knew that in spite of Young's cleverness with blowers, both men and mules faced serious heat and air problems in the days ahead.

The McCalmonts agreed to send at least $24,000 a month to the tunnel company. By mid-January of 1877 Sutro was back in Washington and registered at Wormley's Hotel, from which he carried on vigorous lobbying activities. Although the trip to England was one of his most successful, unexpected bad news from home had ruined what might have been a very happy trip.

On December 1 Mr. Foreman wrote: "Everything in the tunnel is working very well, going on from day to day with but little change to write about." On December 2 he wrote: "Everything working smoothly." On December 3 it was Mr. Raw who did the writing; Mr. Foreman had been injured seriously that morning. Although he was still alive Raw called it "a very serious if not fatal accident."

Mr. Foreman had been hanging up exploders. They came in bunches of 100 and two bunches had gone off at the same time, injuring Foreman and sending fragments of the exploder house flying in the air. Raw and Savage were nearby and rushed to the rescue. Foreman remained conscious until the doctor mercifully administered chloroform to help him to withstand the pain.

On December 16 the blind and paralyzed Mr. Foreman was sent to a hospital in San Francisco. A doctor accompanied him and he was given the best of care. A letter received from San Francisco on December 28 stated that Foreman had no doubt lost the sight of his left eye; there was hope that he might someday be able to use his right eye. There was also hope that he might again get some use of his arm. Foreman remained badly scarred and nearly blind but he was far from forgotten by Adolph Sutro. Through good years and those not so good the monthly allowance list never omitted the name of H. L. Foreman.

Bluett wrote and tried to cheer the boss. "Everything is going along all right and we are doing the best we know how to get up to the Comstock for you." Tunnel progress was excellent in February when 361 feet were accomplished, but then March had roared in with twenty inches of water and hard rock as well. Bluett described the heat as being sufficient to cook a chicken in half an hour.

Lobbying activities were so simple for Sutro compared with the more hectic days of Congressional investigations that he had time to catch up on his personal correspondence and to read his new newspaper. The town of Sutro now had a weekly newspaper, subsidized by the tunnel promoter and named *The Sutro Independent.*

Shortly after the tragic explosion which injured Foreman, the Sutro *Independent* noted the death of ex-Senator Nye, a one-time great figure in Nevada politics. In the same issue with the news of the passing of Nye it recorded a local marriage. George Rammelkamp married Anna Doherty "last Thursday," and the couple would "settle down in the cottage on Twenty-sixth Street." Miss Doherty was the "Annie" who had come from Ireland to be nursemaid to the younger Sutro children and apparently she performed her office well. She and George long remained in the hearts and minds of the Sutros, and the Rammelkamp children and grandchildren still speak of the Sutros with affection.

Adolph maintained contact with his family by mail in much the same way that he corresponded with his employees. He turned his personal letters over to a secretary who folded them into the form prescribed for all correspondence, then noted the date and writer at the top. The various Sutros reacted differently to this busy man's way of keeping in touch; each was no doubt hurt in some degree by Adolph's preoccupation with tunnel affairs. The promoter's philosophy of "first things first" was clearly expressed in a letter to Coulter in which he asserted that his main object was the honorable and successful completion of the tunnel. Where necessary he had put aside private interests and he would continue to do so until the project was completed.

Perhaps Adolph wrote his brother Hugo a similar renunciation of everything but the tunnel enterprise. Hugo was essentially a family man and took his responsibilities as a brother and uncle seriously. Hugo relayed news of the various members of the family, including Sali, on whom he registered an unfavorable judgment. Hugo felt that Sali was selfish and avaricious and blamed it on his being a bachelor. It had been Hugo's sad duty to write of the first death in the family, that of their sister Laura in August, 1869. Laura had been very dear to all her family. Judging by Hugo's description, she had the same type of amiable character as Adolph's daughter Rosa. Hugo ended his long letter with the statement, "I am in tears and can write no more." Apparently

[139]

he was not exaggerating, for the last page of his letter still looks as if tears had fallen on it.

Hugo urged Adolph not to live near the tunnel for fear the bank ring might get its "serfs" to put a quick end to his life. Hugo urged him to establish a family residence in San Francisco and concluded with these words: "You are a brave man I know, but it is folly for a man to place his life in jeopardy. You have obligations to your wife and children of more importance than even the tunnel can claim."

In replying to his family Adolph dictated his letters to a secretary who took them in shorthand, then wrote out the letters, and sometimes even signed them. Hugo thought family letters should be personally written, so as to include "any warm expression of sympathy, brotherly love, ties of friendship." Once Hugo ended a letter with: "You need not answer this unless you can find time to write a few lines yourself." Another time he suggested that if Adolph did not have time to visit he could "send your substitute; he can bring us a shorthand conversation." Hugo threatened not to write again for five years because his brother had persisted in sending "a confounded scribble with *Adolph Sutro* stuck under it."

Letters from the children and school reports (and acknowledgments for bills paid months after they were due) show that the older children were not only kept in boarding schools but also that there could have been little communication among them except by letters. During the year 1872 Emma (then sixteen years old) was apparently in school in New York — possibly at Vassar College. Rosa (fourteen years old) was making excellent grades and her usual perfect score in deportment at Miss Reinhardt's English and German School in Baltimore. Kate (ten years old) was in the Convent of Our Lady of the Sacred Heart in Oakland, and Charles (nine years) was at Saint Mary's College, in San Francisco. That would leave Edgar (seven years) and five-year-old Clara at home with Mrs. Sutro.

Five years later Edgar was failing to cope with either the curriculum or the discipline of Saint Matthews Hall in San Mateo, while Rosa, who had mercifully been transferred to a school nearer her parents' home, was making near perfect marks at Mills Seminary (later Mills College) in Oakland. Clara lived in the town of Sutro with her mother, and attended the local public school.

During the late spring and summer of '77 progress on the tunnel was going so smoothly that Adolph and his wife Leah spent some time together at the Baldwin Hotel in San Francisco. Emma was studying medicine either at the Toland Medical School in San Francisco, where she obtained her M.D. degree, or carrying on further medical studies in Paris. The other five children joined their parents for a few days at a time, but never all at once. It is easy to sympathize with parents who do not choose to spend ten days in a luxury hotel encumbered with five children between the ages of ten and nineteen. On the other hand, these children had been allowed to see little of their father and the older ones saw not much more of their mother or of each other; it seems a pity that they were entertained in shifts. The hotel bill for $191 shows Master Charley had been there four days, Master Edgar five, Miss Kate also five days and Miss Rosa eight. "Dear Papa" was always willing to spend money for good schools, but of himself, he gave only what was left over from the "great work." He certainly did not pattern himself after his own father who had made his sons welcome in the factory at Aachen.

Now when Adolph returned to the tunnel he found the work going smoothly, supplies were coming in, and there was progress in every department unless they were battling clay, which was the greatest deterrent to speed. When the tunnel had to go through clay there was no end to the work. First the clay would be removed and immediately thereafter the section would be timbered. Next the track would be laid so that the next portion of rock or clay could be removed and

[141]

placed in the ore cars for the mules to pull away. But with swelling clay the job was only started. On one occasion 48 feet of clay floor swelled as much as 7½ inches in one night and the track in that portion had to be relaid three times.

From the roof and sides the clay would ooze and swell, pushing on the timbers. If this did not cause the timbers to break, the heat and dampness would cause them to rot. At last it was found that green wood could stand the pressure and heat better than seasoned wood, but there was no permanent cure for clay — it demanded constant watchfulness. Once set, the timbers had to be eased up constantly. When the ground in front of the working face was swelling it made trouble for the carriage which held the power drills. At such times the only safe thing to do was to dispense with the machinery and set the miners to work with hand tools.

Once into solid rock, it was a relief to leave a clean, permanent passage that would not require facing, but if the rock was crumbly it had to be timbered to keep rocks from falling on the heads of the men and mules. No part of the tunneling was easy, but at least there was variety.

While the Sutros were at the Baldwin Hotel and later visiting Yosemite Valley, Jack Bluett was acting as tunnel foreman. He was running three shifts of eight hours each and keeping careful watch over his men and mules. He was devoted to Sutro and wrote, "I will go through it (the tunnel) if it is quicksand. If I can not make two feet I'll make one." He did not need to say "and do it safely," for his chief knew that old blustering Bluett was the soul of caution. When necessary he would stop work on the header and set the men to timbering a place he considered dangerous. It was he who was always ready to sacrifice the speed of the power drills for the safety of hand tools.

While giving his men optimum care, Bluett did even more with the mules — he gave them his love. Once he saw George Rammelkamp using a mule for hauling which had already done its stint for the day in the tunnel. Ignoring the great strength of the mighty little German and disregarding the fact that George was supposedly in charge of animals, Jack not only cursed George (whose use of two languages probably did not compare to Jack's superb command of profanity in one) but would have exchanged blows if Raw had not come between them. Jack went for his time card, but Raw convinced him he should stay, and George was not quite so bullheaded as to be blind to the justice of Jack's complaint.

Sutro sent Bluett one directive (probably from San Francisco) about re-deployment of his men. Bluett split his timbermen into two groups as directed, but sent a message to Sutro full of anguish. There was no pity for the men — they could work in two groups as easily as one — but the poor little mules! It was his mules which would suffer and for his mules Bluett would fight with others or even argue with his beloved master. By having an extra station to supply, the mules would have an extra trip and with fewer men at each station would have to stand longer for the unloading. Bluett felt that with all the tools, lumber and men the mules had to pull in, and all the rock they had to take out, they had enough to do. Bluett added: "Of course I calculated to do just as you direct, but . . ." Jack Bluett's heart would bleed for his little mules on many a future occasion. The air became foul, the heat intense, and Jack would plead for more mules so as not to overwork the ones he had.

While the work in the hot, slippery tunnel progressed, work on the outside went on apace. The boarding house at Shaft No. 1 was no longer needed so it was torn down and all items of value were salvaged, especially nails. Twenty-seven tons of "grass hay" and twenty-eight tons of alfalfa were baled on the ranches. Enormous quantities of castor oil were laid in because the dampness of the tunnel made castor oil and lard the best lubricants for the car axles. In November the temperature of the air at the header was 94° and the clay was 100°. It was obvious that a large supply of ice would be absolutely necessary. Both men and mules would require ice if the work were to progress. Artificial ponds were created and an ice house was built.

The ice project provides an example of the type of administrative problems created by a General Superintendent in absentia, especially one who loathed delegating authority as much as Sutro did. The accountant Sheldon felt obliged to write thus to Sutro, then in San Francisco: "George says it will take two or three more carloads of sawdust to fill spaces of ice house. Shall I order them?" A similar ridiculous situation arose when the taxes were within eight days of being delinquent and no one at the tunnel office had been authorized to pay them. Sutro had left late in August without authorizing anyone to sign checks or drafts, pay day was near, and Sheldon was concerned.

These things were but trifles compared to the problems which had already been solved. The year 1877 had been without major financial crises or human tragedy. There would be no easy way to complete the tunnel and fulfill its founder's dreams, but if some easing of the tension between the mineowners and the tunnel project could be accomplished everyone would benefit.

CHAPTER XIII

THE GREAT WORK IS FINISHED

IN APRIL, 1878, Adolph Sutro would be forty-eight years old, and connection of the tunnel with the Savage mine was imminent. With all the difficulties encountered underground, however, there was more progress there than above ground. In Virginia City public opinion was still largely anti-tunnel, and anti-Sutro. Sutro had bored through the earth for a distance of nearly four miles but he had made no headway at all with the mineowners. It was true that Sutro's rights under the Sutro Tunnel Act were unimpaired, but that law specified that the amount of royalty would be based on agreements between the owners of the tunnel and the mineowners. The agreements repudiated by the mines would probably be impossible to enforce since Sutro had failed to carry out his part of those bargains, especially the time limits with respect to raising capital and beginning construction.

The mineowners were solving their problems of heat and water to their own satisfaction and standing firm on the idea that the tunnel was unnecessary and they would not use it if it were completed. Mackay, Flood, and Fair were no more cordial to the tunnel idea than the once-mighty Ralston had been. The joy Sutro felt for the progress of his tunnel was thus qualified. The big problem he must solve was how to bring the mineowners to use the tunnel at least for drainage, and to pay a royalty. He had fought them successfully at home and in Washington; now he must have some sort of royalty agreement.

Previously he had outlined a plan in a letter to Elliott J. Moore, who succeeded Aron as President of the Sutro Tunnel Company. Sutro would, if necessary, buy stock in the various mining companies, be present at all stockholders' meetings and, if necessary, bring the subject of mismanagement of the mines before the courts. More important than that, if the mines tried to use the tunnel drain without paying royalties he would build a bulkhead in the tunnel and thus remove any chance of free drainage.

Sutro did order the erection of a bulkhead and when Isaac Requa, his long-time adversary, visited the tunnel in early May, 1878, he was surprised to find it almost ready. At a point in the tunnel where the rock was very hard, stone work had been put up to seal the tunnel, space having been left for doors through which the mule cars could pass.

The doors were not yet hung. They were made of solid blocks of a sugar pine thirty inches thick; the tree from which they were cut had 495 rings. The masonry was fifty-two inches thick, and the bulkhead was expected to withstand a column of water 5,000 feet in height and the greater the pressure the tighter the bulkhead would become. Sutro said: "It's a good thing to have a door to your house, in case of emergency."

While the bulkhead was being built work still went on at the header. The men knew that a connection would soon be made because for some time they had been able to hear noises from the nearby mines. At first they heard the explosions and finally they were close enough to hear voices. Although in the early spring of 1878 they did hit some of the softest clay they had ever had to control, and the water draining through the tunnel registered 108°, still the most monstrous of all their problems was the lack of fresh air in the tunnel and especially at the header.

The extreme conditions of bad air and heat at the header are illustrated by the experience of Biddle, one of the engineers operating the blowers at Shaft No. 2. Biddle had never been in the header and was finally taken in for an inspection tour. Overcome by the heat and foul air he sat down on a rock, only to jump up. He swore that he would never sit down in there again; he said it was so hot he had been burned. He promised to send in the other three engineers so they too could experience the heat and understand the absolute necessity for keeping those blowers going.

The men working in the tunnel started complaining. The hours were too long; the tunnel too hot, humid, and foul. They would not work more than half of the time they spent in the tunnel — spending the other part of their time resting at the blowers. Many of them quit. Bluett and another man from the office went in but both were overcome by the heat and had to be taken to the blowers to be revived. The workmen were tumbling over too, and became alarmed for fear they would all lose consciousness at once and suffocate for lack of help. The face of the header became dry, but the gas increased and finally six-hour shifts were put on. One mule driver saw his mule drop dead from heat and nearly fell himself. When his friends carried him up to the blower the man cried from fright and cramps. When a man got so sick he had to be taken out of the tunnel, the doctor was called and he applied a mustard plaster. If a mule was brought out alive the horse doctor was called, a bed of straw made for the animal and the doctor would sit with the mule and try to save him.

The spring of 1878 was an exceptionally hard one for the mules and Bluett's reports were full of details. A big mule was overcome and in falling down knocked out one of its teeth. Mr. Bishop, a shift boss, tried to get his switch mule away from the blower and the mule bit Bishop's arm. If a mule saw a man with a piece of ice in his hand, the mule would make a grab for the ice and hold it in its mouth. The mules were given ice water to drink five or six times each shift and had their heads and lips rubbed with ice as well. Still they fell and were loaded on cars and brought out.

One mule, "Paddy," died of spasms, and poor Bluett suffered greatly to see so many mules overcome and dying.

The workmen feared for their own lives because the mules did not sink down gradually, but fell over as if shot. Any man in the way of a mule could be crushed to death. At this time one or two mules died each day and the men had a real cause for concern. During this trying period Colonel Brush and George T. Coulter visited the tunnel, but there is no record that either of them was at the header.

Three months later, in July, it became apparent that the Sutro Tunnel would soon connect with the Savage Mine, and the real engineering problem would be solved. To drain the whole Comstock Lode, however, lateral tunnels would be necessary to the other mines. Transportation would be immediately available in the main tunnel, for track had been laid and in constant use since the start of the tunnel eight years before.

A small drain was in use, but the huge one, three feet square and the full length of the tunnel would still need to be cut. Sutro calculated that it would take five or six months to cut the drain, line it with three-inch redwood planks and cover it over tightly. He suggested that cold water from the outside could flow over the top to carry off the radiating heat from the water flowing from the mines.

Sutro also talked about cooling the tunnel. He said that he could lower the temperature of the air passing through the tunnel by installing, at various points, pipes with perforations every quarter-inch. These would be supplied with cold water from the surface and create a veil of cold water through which the hot air would blow.

One question would be answered by the break-through. Sutro had maintained that the current of air would ascend in the mines, having passed through the tunnel. On this point he had been alone, everyone else being certain that the air from the mines would pass out through the tunnel. There had been interminable arguments over the direction the current of air could take. Sutro had defied the experts, all of whom maintained the mine-to-tunnel direction.

As the moment for breaking through approached, Sutro was joined by the man who had stood behind him financially through the darkest of the years of trouble. Joseph Aron had moved to New York, but he came to Nevada for the ceremonies Sutro would be sure to conduct. One of the finest tributes a friend could give had been given before a committee of Congress six years before by Adolph Sutro. He spoke of Aron in these words:

> I want to pay tribute right here to a noble-hearted, far-seeing, generous, and true man, who has stood by me in the darkest hours of my trials, who has counseled and assisted me at all times . . . That man's name is Joseph Aron.

The break-through was expected momentarily. When, where, or how it would occur was uncertain. The header was pushed, men lost consciousness, mules dropped, and the compressors at Shaft No. 2 continued to pump fresh air.

Overhead on the 1640 foot level of the Savage Mine and 270 feet east of the Savage incline, the Savage miners were working a drift. It was 9:00 p.m. on July 8 when one of them removed his drill and a rush of hot air came through the drill hole. The connection had been made, and the air came from the tunnel into the mine and settled the question of which way the air would flow. The miners and tunnelmen exchanged greetings and comments such as:

Savage — Has Sutro ordered the champagne?

Tunnel — No, not yet. 'Ave ye got henny beer?

Savage — Five casks up in the works.

Tunnel — Then we must bust 'er through tonight.

Somewhat belatedly a telegram from Adolph Sutro to M. B. Gillette, Superintendent of the Savage, was read by Gillette to his men. Sutro stated that the Savage drills were heard directly over the last set of timber in the tunnel. Exact measurements showed that the header had progressed an additional sixteen feet.

A man stumbled along the Savage drift and handed Gillette another telegram. In this missive Sutro warned against enlarging any drill hole until he was notified. He explained that he feared such action would release a column of hot and foul air which might prove fatal to some of the men.

Soon another dispatch was received by Gillette. Sutro now knew about the drill-hole and he authorized blasting if the Savage miners would retire to the incline. Sutro planned to appear at 11:00 p.m.

Gillette ordered the men to wait until 10:45 before blasting. Word came that Adolph Sutro was on his way in and the foreman of the Savage directed the blasting procedure. The men withdrew and soon a dull roar shook the ground. Everyone in the Savage drift rushed for the connection, but they were met by "a blinding rush of smoke and a blast of hot air" which blew out their lanterns. Even so they made their way to the hole.

The Savage miners worked with picks and bars to enlarge the five-foot square hole made by the blast. Through the smoke and dust they could see the lights of the tunnel and each time they managed to knock down a rock the tunnel men cheered. The air blowing through the hole became hotter and more fetid. It was 110° and compounded of smells from gas, rotting timbers, perspiring mules and sweltering men. In other words, it was the climate in which the tunnel men had worked for a long time and it often drove the Savage miners to their own compressed air pipe.

When the hole was made safe, Adolph Sutro prepared to go through. He was flabbergasted to discover that two of his daughters had come to the header and wanted to go through with him. So it was that Rosa and Kate, with their brothers Charles and Edgar, followed their father through the new opening between the Sutro Tunnel and the Savage Mine.

Sutro and his party walked through the Savage drift to the incline and cooled off at the blower. Sam Davis, reporter for the Virginia *Chronicle*, noticed that when they returned to the tunnel "the crowd was very much exhausted with the exception of Misses Rosa and Kate Sutro. These ladies endured the heat and foul air much better than even the miners." The passenger car was ready for them and before they left for the mouth of the tunnel and home, Sutro dismissed the shift, but the 7:00 a.m. shift went in as usual.

At nine o'clock in the morning all of the tunnel employees and many of the townspeople got into line and marched to the mansion. Adolph Sutro came out and made a speech about the tunnel. He apologized for not having refreshments ready but said that if they would stop at the saloons in town they would be his guests. There is no indication that Leah Sutro shared her husband's hour of glory.

In the evening there were bonfires on the nearby hills and it is sometimes said that cannon were fired, but the probability is that only small arms were discharged. Like some of the other stories of the break-through, the years seem to have increased the dimensions of the bore.

On Wednesday, July 10, Sutro wrote a restrained letter to Secretary Ames in San Francisco in which he said that the draft was very powerful and at first one was in danger of suffocating. He thought that he and his companions were unwise in entering so soon after the connection was made, but fortunately they got out safely.

There were too many problems ahead to warrant great rejoicing at this point, but Sutro did get up a small party of friends, relatives, and senior employees to go to Virginia City via the tunnel. Each person packed some clothes suitable for a dinner party and the clothes were sent through the tunnel to the changing rooms of the Savage Mine. At 4:30 the air in the tunnel had cleared and two passenger cars were ready.

[151]

The following persons climbed aboard, clad in old clothes and raincoats: Adolph Sutro, Misses Kate and Clara Sutro, Masters Charles and Edgar Sutro, Joseph Aron of the New York branch of Lazard Frères, Paris; John Bluett, Peter Savage, Dr. Brierly, F. S. Young, H. H. Sargent, and F. B. Mercer, publisher of the Sutro *Independent*.

Sutro had notified Superintendent Gillette of their coming. Gillette telegraphed his San Francisco office and when the Sutro party arrived at the Savage Mine they were told that they could not proceed. But proceed they did, and later when toasting their friends they included "three groans for the directors of the Savage Mine."

The party arrived in Virginia City at 5:45 all dressed in their good clothes and ready for a gay evening. Then Sutro invited the party to dine with him at the French Rotisserie, Virginia. A bounteous meal was served, and a most enjoyable hour spent. Sutro and Aron talked over old times and many of the trying and laughable circumstances passed through during the first years of tunnel construction were related. Numerous toasts were drunk and responded to, and many who were not present were remembered and spoken of. "The party returned overland, so to speak, at about 10:00 o'clock that night."

Through the late summer and fall of '78 the tunnel company attempted three major projects. Tunneling must continue to make connection with the various mines on the Comstock. An enormous drainage ditch must be dug. Most important of all, some terms must be agreed upon between the mining companies and the tunnel company.

In January, 1879, the principal mines were having difficulty with water, and the Hale and Norcross and the Savage especially were in trouble. These mines had their apparatus ready to connect with the tunnel, but the tunnel was not ready for the water. Sutro was trying to negotiate an agreement, and both sides had made threats. Sutro asserted he would close his bulkhead. The mines threatened to release their water into the tunnel, and without the ditch being completed they would flood the tunnel and ruin it with hot water and steam. They knew the timbering and clay would be unlikely to stand protracted exposure to such a deluge.

Negotiations dragged on. Finally the Savage Mining Company secured a temporary injunction against the Sutro Tunnel. The tunnel company was to refrain from constructing, building, or maintaining a bulkhead. On Saturday afternoon, February 1, Sheriff Williamson of Storey County got dressed in miner's garb and proceeded to serve the injunction on the gang then working in the tunnel. Harry Bishop, the shift boss, sent the injunction by messenger to Assistant Superintendent Sheldon.

Sheldon was not told by the messenger that the writ had been served already and thought it was a bluff. Nevertheless he took the precaution to go to Virginia City to find out. When he was sure it was a writ he tried to telegraph home to have the workmen withdrawn from the tunnel, but the telegraph office was closed. He therefore returned to the mouth of the tunnel and sent in a messenger. It was then 9:00 p.m.

Sheriff Williamson had meanwhile sent a deputy to check on the tunnel men. When the deputy tried to pass through the opening between the Savage Mine and the tunnel, a guard in the tunnel mistook him for a Savage miner and shot at him with a revolver. The deputy quickly made his business known. The sheriff appeared and arrested all of the miners. Just then Sheldon's messenger arrived and tried to explain that he was there to bring the men back to Sutro City. But Williamson arrested the messenger and took the prisoners away.

The tunnel workers were clothed as usual in caps, pants, and boots because despite the extreme cold weather above ground they were working in a humid 100°. They protested about going to the surface without their clothes, which were in the changing room at the mouth of the tunnel. Williamson assured them they would be outfitted at the Savage changing house but when they arrived there were no clothes available. The sheriff put the prisoners in charge of his deputy except for Bishop whom he took with him. They left to go and get the men's clothes. The trip took three hours and the prisoners, of course, got extremely cold. They asked Mr. Gillette for a drink but he refused, saying he didn't want any drunks. The men believed that a drink of liquor would prevent colds and that Gillette was condemning them to pneumonia. Twelve of the eighteen prisoners subsequently had severe colds.

Finally Williamson and Bishop returned, they all had a good breakfast, and then the tunnel men were all locked in jail in lieu of $1,000 bail apiece. It must then have been between 2:00 and 3:00 a.m.

At 5:30 p.m. that day (Sunday) they were all released on their own recognizances and were to appear in court at 10:00 a.m. Monday. Various pro-tunnel factions had kept them well supplied with cigars "and other sources of enjoyment not generally enjoyed by prisoners." Now as the men climbed into carriages to return to the town of Sutro they and the large crowd which saw them off gave three cheers for Adolph Sutro.

On Monday morning Judge Rising dismissed the charge of willful contempt as far as the ordinary miners were concerned. The charge against Mr. Sheldon was dismissed the next day, but Mr. Bishop was fined $100 and costs for violating the injunction. The fine and costs were paid immediately. From the manner in which the whole episode was reported in the Sutro *Independent* the following Saturday, one can say that it was treated as a lark and special thanks were sent to the numerous friends in Virginia City for their hospitality.

For nearly two weeks all seemed quiet and no doubt the tunnel employees felt that they had made the heads of the mining companies look pretty silly. The next move, however,

[154]

was a dreadful one. Up to now there had been more than ten years of animosity between the power represented in Virginia City and the will of Adolph Sutro. Both sides had engaged in legal battles, political maneuvers and defamation of character.

Although the endless battles were far from clean, they were bloodless. Only Hugo had seemed concerned about the personal safety of his brother Adolph, and the Sutros had lived fairly contented lives while in the mansion. The youngest child, Clara, was enrolled in the local school and all the blood that was shed was confined to the local saloons.

Now however, the men in control of the mines decided on a course of action which could have resulted in the death of many innocent miners. Also it could have ruined the tunnel itself. By some odd chance of fortune no such tragic results ensued. At about 5:00 p.m. on Sunday, February 16, the pumps in two of the mines were started and the hot water which had collected in the Hale and Norcross drift was sent, absolutely without warning, into the Sutro Tunnel. An alarm was sounded and the tunnelmen and mules rushed for the daylight.

Part of the way the men were able to walk on the compressed air pipes "while the poor mules, as the miners termed it, had to 'dance a jig'." Men and mules just barely made it to the mouth of the tunnel ahead of the water. The pumping continued until Tuesday, all 120 men employed in the tunnel were out of work, and there was real concern that cave-ins would result and possibly ruin the tunnel. A week later the men were still out of work and the damage caused by the hot water (at least 130°) was still unknown.

Fortunately these wounds did not prove mortal and Sutro continued to negotiate with the mineowners. At last on April 2 an agreement was signed by twenty-four mining companies. The contracting mines were the Utah in the north through the Overman on the south. The tunnel company agreed to get the drain ditch finished in ninety days and to

[155]

accept a royalty of only one dollar on every ton of ore taken out of the mines which would mill $40 a ton or under. A two dollar rate would still apply, however, on richer ores. In other words, Sutro cut his original rate of royalty in half, except for bonanza ores.

The mines agreed to advance $70 per running foot of laterals advanced north and south to their mines, without interest, to be liquidated out of half the royalties earned on ore extracted. There was a clause which made it impossible for the mine, even if it extracted no ore, to have any claim against the tunnel company for money advanced on laterals.

Immediately a huge force was put to work in the tunnel. Even fourteen-year-old boys were working, for they were employed in the torch room. This was a small building near the mouth of the tunnel entrance which housed oil, candles, hand torches, and collar torches. The boys kept the torches filled with oil and when the mule teams came out of the tunnel the boys snatched the torches out of the mules' collars. When the mules re-entered the tunnel the boys placed lighted torches in the collars. In 1878 there were 102 mules and about 1,000 men working underground and their candles and hand torches were all in the care of these boys. It was said that while at work the boys were kept constantly on the run.

Fortunately the drainage ditch could be worked on by many men at the same time. Stations were established every thousand feet. Three blacksmiths' forges were set up inside the tunnel where picks and drills were kept sharpened. The first forge was about 1,000 feet in from the mouth and the correspondent of the Sutro *Independent* described it, saying that the glow from the forge and the half-naked blacksmiths created a picture very like what he presumed perdition to be.

This tremendous influx of men brought the town of Sutro to its zenith. A surveyor was kept busy and lots sold quickly. More stores and many rooming houses were opened. There were five saloons, of which Paul's required the services of four bartenders every evening. North and South Squares were beginning to be useful and each eleven-acre park was planted with trees as well as alfalfa. There were 2,000 Lombardy poplars in North Square and cottonwoods in South Square. On the Moore ranch a tree nursery had been established and 1,000 honey locust, 500 spruce, 1,000 elms, 500 sugar maples and 4,000 Lombardy poplars were being cared for under the direction of George Rammelkamp.

Whereas most boom towns grew up like Topsy, Adolph Sutro had made sure his town would be as rigidly determined as the line of his tunnel. Once the gridiron pattern was laid out he developed a strict building code. Messy occupations such as wagon repair could only be carried on away from the center of town and every householder must agree to plant and care for a tree on his property.

Pelham W. Ames, the tunnel company secretary in San Francisco, was harassed with procuring items for the enrichment of the town of Sutro as well as drawing up the deeds and carrying on other company business. It was he who had to deal with various seed supply houses, and explain to Sutro that the order for seeds of the arborvitae had been too large but the one for red oak too small, and tulip trees were sure to fail.

While reporting on such matters as bills for telephone rental, boiler heads, and draft books Ames was obliged to deal with an order for frogs. Apparently Sutro had an idea he could put some frogs in the pond near his home and have a supply of fresh frog flesh for his table. Ames wrote: "I can purchase frogs at $2.25 per dozen. There is no difficulty at all in finding them — but no one can tell the male from the female — so that we would have to chance it as to sex." He could not order large frogs but there were a few good-sized ones in the lots available. After finishing the letter Ames went back to the paragraph about frogs and added, "Let me know how many I shall box up and send you by express."

Poor Ames, he was forever packing things to express to Sutro, but this man of fastidious handwriting must have found boxing the cherry and plum seeds sent in charcoal from France more to his taste than popping the lid on a box of frogs.

In the pond for which the frogs were destined Sutro had already established ducks, turtles, and trout. His beautiful mansion sat above the pond — regal as Victoria on her throne. Regardless of the eddying currents around her the mansion remained slightly aloof and dearly beloved by all who knew her.

Eleven-year-old Clara was at Sutro with her parents but the other children were scattered, attending their various private schools. At vacation time, however, the mansion was full of children, laughter, and guests. Mr. and Mrs. Sutro maintained a facade as Victorian as their home, and although children always feel unpleasant undercurrents and react to any tension which exists between their parents, they can still forget themselves in parlor games and parties.

Dear Papa took time to encourage his children to read the books in his library and to use the very fine microscope he kept there. When there were visitors in the evening each person would be expected to do a trick or tell a story. Sutro would start things off by shuffling across the carpet and then raising his hand to the gas jet, lighting it with the static electricity in his body. Mrs. Sutro was preoccupied with rumors she had heard about her husband, but life went on in the mansion, and in the town, much as it did in every other wealthy home and thriving town in the United States in the spring of 1879.

May, 1879, was probably the finest month the tunnel and the town had ever experienced, or ever would experience. The ninety-day time limit was running out, but the work on the drain boxes was progressing satisfactorily. There were 1,310 men on the payroll and "pay day" extended over five days. Paying the men was a ceremony carried out in the office of the company's assistant superintendent. Mr. Sheldon sat behind a tray of $20 gold pieces and alongside him was the "croupier" for the poll tax imposed by the town of Dayton. Mr. J. P. Garnett was nearby, taking subscriptions to the hospital fund, and Mr. Herbert of the Silver City Miners' Union made sure every miner had a union card or had applied for one. Seated around the room in an impressive circle were the boardinghouse keepers, each armed with a book and pencil and a navy revolver. Also present were hotel and saloonkeepers and restaurateurs. They all had lists of the men who owed them money. So many gave false names to creditors that this procedure for collecting debts had been established. The miners were paid in sections and passed through the line at the rate of thirty per hour. Pay day started on Tuesday and ended Saturday night.

Probably it was during this boom period that the Sutro graveyard was started. Sutro later told how every death was the excuse for his men to get up a big funeral and go off to Virginia City or some other place, to bury the man. All work had to be stopped for one or two shifts, and drunkenness kept some men away longer. Sutro wanted to check this evil by establishing a graveyard at Sutro. But when the next death occurred the men objected to burying the man at Sutro, saying that he would be lonely. This went on for some time until two miners were killed at once. These two were in bad standing with the miners' union, so there were no friends to protest and no one could justly raise the issue of loneliness.

By the end of May the cemetery was not the only quiet place in Sutro. Work on the drain boxes was nearing completion so fast that fewer workmen were needed. Men were laid off in groups of two hundred and the town, so recently a promising community, went into a sharp decline.

By June 30 of 1879 the first line of boxes to receive the water was ready and a second drainage ditch was half finished. There was some concern that the enormous volume of water which had collected in the mines could not all be discharged through the drain boxes, but the fear proved groundless. Not only did the boxes hold the water, but they were sufficiently tight to contain the steam as well.

As the first water came through the open ditch at the mouth of the tunnel a great cloud of steam enveloped the men standing there. It poured over the faithful, if somewhat bumbling Assistant Superintendent Sheldon, the steady worker and lover of mules Bluett, and over Adolph Sutro, who stood thermometer in hand ready to measure the temperature of the water. As the reading rose from 101° to 104½° he calculated that the boxes were excellent. The water was losing very little heat in transit, and the tunnel was a success.

Of all the days Sutro had labored for his tunnel this was the one that should have been most free of worry. With the steam enveloping his brawny figure as he plunged the thermometer into the hot water, as he straightened up and scrutinized its slender column, it should have been the moment for someone to say, "Well done, thou good and faithful servant." But the Sutro *Independent* unintentionally used a more prophetic quotation as its headline: "It Is Finished."

CHAPTER XIV

EXIT THE GENERAL SUPERINTENDENT

NOTICE of the successful operation of the drain boxes at the Sutro Tunnel was important news around the world. In Virginia City, however, the importance of the news of the success of Sutro's "coyote hole" was only one of three important happenings. Adolph had to share his hour of glory with an old soldier and a young woman.

Former President Ulysses S. Grant was completing his world tour. He had expressed a desire to visit the Comstock Lode and plans were being made for the entertainment of him and his party. Since he had alluded to the Sutro Tunnel in his first inaugural address and had approved the act creating a Sutro Tunnel Commission, he would probably be interested in seeing the tunnel. This would be one visitor the enemies of the tunnel could hardly prevent from visiting it and Grant would be the most distinguished person who had yet visited the Comstock.

The third topic of conversation was a new resident at the International Hotel. She said her name was Mrs. George Allen. Although she dressed all in black, she was certainly not in deep mourning. In case she had once worn crepe and a widow's toque she had put them aside for feather boas and willow plumes. Nor did she confine herself to a few appropriate pearls, but sparkled with diamonds. Tongues wagged and as the trim little figure strolled down C Street, jewels blazing in the hot July sun, she was nicknamed "the $90,000 diamond widow."

Adolph Sutro was introduced to her and they dined together while gossips noted that the ever handsome Sutro was providing the widow with the acme of Comstock culinary extravagance, cold bottles of champagne and quail on toast. One evening the normal quiet of the hotel was broken by a woman's voice screaming for help. Proprietor and guests rushed to the room from which the screams came and found Leah Sutro hitting Mrs. Allen over the head with a champagne bottle.

Major E. J. Stonehill was among those who forcefully separated the two women. Major Stonehill was conversant with the fact that Leah had heard about her husband's attentions to the little lady in Virginia City. Leah had heard rumors to the effect that their meeting in Nevada was far from the first time they had met. Leah had engaged Major Stonehill as her attorney and asked him to gather evidence about possible indiscretions in Washington, D.C. The idea that her husband was sharing a bird and a bottle with that woman so close to home overcame her and for one brief moment she became judge, jury, and all but executioner.

Sentiment was on Leah's side. Adolph admitted that he had met Mrs. Allen and that he had been in her room. Mrs. Allen promptly suggested she had been using a false name and said that she was really Miss Hattie Trundle and just out of finishing school, thereby implying she had been heavily chaperoned and could not possibly have been associating with any man in Washington. While many people spoke of her disparagingly, Adolph maintained to his death that she had been falsely accused. His friends said he never saw her again, but his own marriage was ruined. Major Stonehill tried to get Mr. and Mrs. Sutro to forgive and forget, but he was unsuccessful. Apparently the rift between them had reached such proportions that there was no chance of a reconciliation, but there was no divorce. Adolph and Leah maintained separate residences thereafter and he provided handsomely for his wife and children.

In the dramatic incident at the International Hotel, morality was on the side of Leah. For Adolph the intimation of scandal was probably as painful as it must have been to his adolescent children. Imagine having to face Ulysses S. Grant with the fear that only the night before the old enemies in Virginia City might have been whispering to him about a cold bottle and a hot bird! Well, Leah had only a bottle and righteous indignation to live down. Someone had to face the general; let Leah do it.

Sutro probably did not mind missing Grant. The two men had little in common and Sutro had never been one of Grant's admirers. He had ordered, however, a handsome little car especially constructed for the Grant party. It was well padded and upholstered in red velvet and was always called the "President's Car."

At 9:00 a.m. on Wednesday, October 29, 1879, General Grant and a party including James G. Fair and Governor Kinkead left Virginia City, while Mrs. Grant stayed behind. They traveled by way of Gold Hill, Silver City and Dayton to the mansion at Sutro. There they were met by Mrs. Sutro and another party which included Mr. and Mrs. Philipp Deidesheimer; they had come directly "over the line." Grant and Kinkead stood on the porch of the mansion while Mr. A. Summerfield, a resident of Sutro City, made a welcoming address in behalf of his fellow townspeople. If the next issue of the Sutro *Independent* quoted the talk accurately it was a gem of a speech, and short enough to still reward the reader.

Mr. Summerfield said:

General Grant: In behalf of the people of Sutro, allow me to extend to you a cordial welcome. We are poor, and cannot afford to give you a reception of pomp and grandeur such as you have had all over the world; but if love, respect, honor and esteem will make up for the absence of pomp and grandeur, we give you the grandest reception you ever had. In saying so I echo the sentiment of every child, woman and man in the town of Sutro; for, General, we all love you. In a short time you will behold one of the great enterprises of the world, constructed by these brave, hard-working men before you.

While children stood below waving flags, the adult population of Sutro and most of Dayton stood waiting to hear the voice of Grant. He and the governor advanced to the steps but it was Kinkead who spoke. He said the general was pleased with the reception and would "be pleased to take all by the hand and greet them, but his time was limited."

Such a weak reply annoyed the crowd and they started shouting, "Grant, Grant, Grant!" Finally the taciturn man found his voice and thanked the people for the hearty reception. The crowd gave three cheers for General Grant, Governor Kinkead, Mrs. Sutro, Colonel Fair and lastly, three for Adolph Sutro.

Grant and Kinkead turned and went into the mansion. The general was hungry. So was little Clara Rammelkamp, the daughter of George and the former Annie Doherty. When Clara called from the top of the stairs her mother tried to remind her that all of the children had been told to keep out of sight, but the general overruled the mother. He picked up the tiny girl, carried her to the head of the table, seated her on his lap, and fed her from his own dish. The other guests at the table included Jack Bluett, H. H. Sheldon, Frank Mercer, Frank Young, and Charles Sutro.

After breakfast, General Grant and his party changed into tunnel clothes and boarded the "President's Car." So many townspeople were determined to stay with the general as long as possible that six additional cars were used by nearly two hundred men, women, and children. The tunnel was "finely lighted up," according to a newspaper account, and as the long procession moved toward Virginia City, the unexpected guests awakened "wild and cavernous echoes" with such songs as "The Star-Spangled Banner," "John Brown," and "The Sweet By and By."

Leah Sutro was not a member of this unique procession, for she was busy preparing to move out of the mansion. That very evening Leah left for San Francisco to take up residence in the spacious home which Adolph had purchased for her use one month previous. At last Leah was to have a home that belonged to her husband rather than to his company.

That duty discharged, Adolph had gone to New York. His first order of business was to see Joseph Aron on October 13, for Aron had started to challenge Sutro's business methods. That day Sutro telegraphed Pelham W. Ames, secretary of the tunnel company in San Francisco, "J. Aron admits his error."

Sutro's principal mission was to sell tunnel stock in New York to pay off certain tunnel company debts, especially one owed to Aron's firm, Lazard Frères. He tried to get Ames to sell some in San Francisco, but apparently Aron would not give his consent. The telegram Ames received from Sutro on November 11 was also brusque: "I have no further relations with Mr. Aron. Lazard Frères will deliver shares if necessary."

Trouble of another sort was brewing for Adolph Sutro and from another direction. George Coulter still believed in the tunnel project, but his relations with Sutro were bitter and became even worse as a result of the shock of the Sutro-Allen scandal. To an intimate Coulter referred to Sutro as "that arch fiend." Relations between Adolph and McCalmont Brothers and Company had been strained for over a year. Robert McCalmont had had a paralytic stroke which left him no longer able to dominate his brother Hugh, who had always been hostile to Sutro and ever doubtful as to the merits of the tunnel project.

The letters from McCalmont Brothers took on a new tone and frequently expressed displeasure with Sutro. He had not put his "shoulder to the wheel" as he had promised when last in London. They demanded that he avoid financial troubles and maintain more harmonious relationships with company executives. This was hardly the type of complaint which Sutro could long endure.

While Adolph was battling with Aron he was also getting ready to give a speech before a New York group known as the "Bullion Club." Despite the pressure of impending rifts he delivered one of his finest speeches. He told the story of the tunnel, its hardships, its victories. Whereas his Piper's Opera House speeches had been heavily weighted with invective, this speech was a simple narrative of success. He told the graveyard story and gave some observations on mules, but he also told the serious stories of Richthofen, the bank ring, Congressional committees, and success. The tunnel had succeeded in lowering the water in the mines 100 feet in 8 hours and the first royalty payment had been made on August 12. In many ways it seemed that success was at hand.

Some writers have indicated that after the breakthrough to the Savage Mine Sutro spent several years running a successful tunnel. Then, feeling the real job was finished, he sold his stock for as much as $5,000,000, and retired in a blaze of glory. There is a rumor told by less friendly people, that Sutro appropriated 300,000 shares of tunnel stock he held in trust and unloaded these and 50,000 shares of his own on some of his Jewish friends.

Letters still extant indicate that Sutro neither unloaded his stock on friends nor cleared anything like $5,000,000. The charge that Sutro appropriated stock held in his name but actually held in trust is disproved by court testimony based on company records. A similar charge that some of those who paid money into the Nevada association were defrauded by the California corporation was equally baseless. In fact, it would appear that in financial matters Adolph Sutro had a high sense of honor.

But with the tunnel completed and his own dismissal as superintendent likely, would it be honorable to sever all relationships with the company he had inspired and created? Adolph had promised to construct a tunnel and he had done it. Tunnel stock was listed on stock exchanges and there was a good demand for it. If new bonanzas were discovered regularly the tunnel company would flourish. True, the Comstock was at a low ebb right now and might never revive, in which case the tunnel would be a resounding financial failure. But Sutro had built the tunnel at the cost of endless effort and worry. He had such great faith in the project that he had accepted as his main compensation a large but then unsalable block of stock in the tunnel company. Who could blame him if he chose at this time to turn his tunnel stock into cash and let eager new shareholders reap whatever profits (or losses) operation of the tunnel might bring?

Adolph secretly sent to the company secretary in San Francisco for stock certificates representing his stock in smaller, more salable units than those he already held. He also needed a new confederate in New York and he found such a person in Edward D. Adams. Adams was a partner in the firm of Winslow, Lanier and Company, bankers of New York City. Proceeding with the utmost secrecy, Adams sold 50,000 shares of Sutro's tunnel stock during the month of January, 1880. The first two thousand shares brought $4.00 a share, but the block of fifty thousand averaged less — $3.69 a share. Adams reported that nearly all of it had been sold to speculators "on the street" who were hoping to unload it on someone else.

Sutro kept sending stock and by March 27 Adams had sold 200,000 shares at an average price of $3.189 per share, or a total of $637,825 from which a commission of $25,000 was deducted. Winslow, Lanier and Co. still held 150,000 additional shares of Sutro Tunnel Company stock belonging to A. Sutro.

Adams telegraphed in code to Sutro daily and between March 27 and May 11, he had only partial success in making sales because Sutro had instructed him to sell at not less than $2 per share. Fifty thousand of these remaining shares finally brought $96,187.50, or a total from stock sales of

$709,012.50. If Sutro ever managed to sell the other 100,000 shares of stock at $2 per share, which seems unlikely, he realized a little over $900,000 from his tunnel stock.

The last letter from Adams to Sutro is dated December 27, 1880. Mr. Adams advised Sutro against forming stock pools in New York and suggested that Mexican railroads might be a better outlet for Sutro's time, energy, and money. Adams thanked Sutro for the latter's appreciative remarks and said that if he had known the responsibilities involved, "I think I should hardly have undertaken this."

Sutro had a final task connected with the tunnel. He had to write his last report. This one was not signed "General Superintendent," but "Adolph Sutro, San Francisco." Sutro urged his successors to push the tunnel through Mt. Davidson to the north, to buy more water rights on the Carson River, to produce more ice, and he was even holding out hope for discovering bodies of ore. Although he was still on the board of trustees, there is no indication that as a trustee he tried to influence tunnel affairs.

If after he left, the tunnel had become the thing Sutro had predicted, if a thousand men had used it daily for getting to work, if the wood and ore, dynamite and machinery had been hauled through it, if the town of Sutro had become the largest city in Nevada, Adolph would have found great satisfaction in contemplating his handiwork. Just exactly how he felt about the pathetic later history of the tunnel he never said. He mentioned the tunnel as a great engineering and financial accomplishment, but he never pretended that it was a moneymaker after it was built.

The tunnel was used for over fifty years. Although as a tunnel it was a success, especially for drainage, it came too late to be of maximum aid to the Comstock Lode. The bodies of ore did extend deep into the earth but were of such low grade that mining them soon became profitless. No sizable bonanzas were found after the Sutro Tunnel began operation, so the royalties were extremely modest.

Some accounts say that the tunnel was profitable. In fact, a respected reference work, *The Dictionary of American Biography,* says that the tunnel "proved immediately and immensely profitable." The sad fact is that the Sutro Tunnel Company stock which was purchased by McCalmont Brothers and countless lesser investors became worthless. The McCalmont firm foreclosed the mortgage in 1889 and accepted a compromise settlement of $800,000 for a mortgage loan which amounted to $997,852.52 in principal and $577,-372.82 in interest.

When Adolph Sutro sold his stock he got out just in time; his stock was sold for more money than could have been realized at any later period. Sutro had devoted fifteen years to the tunnel project, lost his best friend, Joseph Aron, and sacrificed his marriage. Could he just drop the whole thing? Could he return to California and begin a whole new life? Some writers have implied as much. Crowned with success, Sutro turned his face to the West.

How could a man spend so much time, so much of his life on one thing, suffer humiliation, experience so much success, be so intimately involved with anything and just walk off and forget it forever? The Allen scandal was not enough to embarrass a man of Sutro's temperament sufficiently to explain his complete disenchantment with Nevada. Although the town of Sutro did not grow and the tunnel did not prosper, they were both accomplishments of a fair size which many a man would have found sufficient for his ego.

There must have been some final blow of sufficient proportions to make Sutro as finished with the tunnel and the whole state of Nevada as he had been with the little mill on the Carson River after it burned. He had always declared his interest in politics was not that he cared for it per se, but just to advance the tunnel cause. The fact that he truly desired public office would be shown by his actions in both 1880 and a later year.

A MAN IN SEARCH OF A CAUSE

THE HOUSE in San Francisco to which Leah Sutro moved was a large one with spacious gardens. The property extended over half a city block. San Francisco had a well-knit Jewish community and there was plenty of scope for the quiet religious and charitable activities which Leah enjoyed. No longer would there be any need for her to play hostess to people important to her husband's business. She and the children would live quietly and well. Adolph would provide.

In order to make sure his wife and children had an adequate income Adolph purchased the Reese Building on Battery Street. There were two lots in this purchase, each lot having a three-story brick building. Some idea of the value of this property may be gained from the fact that Sutro had it placed in trust and after the taxes and upkeep were paid, the income was to be used for the support of Mrs. Sutro and the children. Mrs. Sutro was to receive $500 per month for life, Emma, Rosa and Kate $200, Charles and Edgar $150, and little Clara was to have $100 a month until age 15. This latter allowance was to be raised to $150 from age 15 to 18 and then be $200 a month until Clara was 30 years old. The boys' allowances were to be paid to their father and he would pass the money on to the boys.

Adolph was not at all sure he wanted to locate in San Francisco, but since Leah and the children were there he moved into the Baldwin Hotel and started looking at real estate from the standpoint of investment possibilities.

San Francisco had seldom seemed more dispirited. Land values were low, and the real estate market so sluggish it was almost impossible to evaluate just how much or how little any one piece of land was worth. "Inside business property" held its own in the eyes of investors, but only property lying between Kearny, Front, California and Market Streets was well rented and recognized as "inside property." Transactions in Outside Lands were very dull and speculation was dead in 1879. The *Real Estate Circular* reported that the section between Jones, Van Ness, Bay Street and the bay would probably be in demand later, but not until the streets had been graded and macadamized. Now, however, they were all, or nearly all, in drifting sand. Less than half of the area of the city was occupied.

With the whole wide world to choose from, Adolph Sutro decided to invest his money in San Francisco real estate. In later years he would seem to boast when he said that he had had "faith in San Francisco." To anyone who could remember the black despair of 1879-80, however, this must have been less boasting than mere statement of fact. Other men have made fortunes in San Francisco real estate, but no one else in 1880 launched into a buying program which soon resulted in ownership of one-twelfth of the area of the city.

It is a fairly well known fact that Sutro invested heavily in the Outside Lands. What is not so well known is the fact that he also bought some exceedingly valuable real estate in the heart of San Francisco. First he purchased a place facing Market Street for fifty feet and extending 110 feet on Sixth almost to Stevenson. Eventually he purchased the corner across Market Street.

He also bought nearly one-half block on Battery Street between Jackson and Oregon and a piece of land on California between Spring and Montgomery Streets. It can hardly be said that Sutro put all of his faith in Outside Lands. It is more accurate to say that, having invested heavily in extremely well situated property in the central business section, he also acquired extraordinarily large tracts of inexpensive vacant land. As time went on Sutro bought real estate in San Mateo and Alameda counties as well as a large parcel in Napa and Lake counties, but his pride was always in the fact that he had expressed faith in the potential of San Francisco.

While he was getting things settled with his wife and trying to make shrewd investments, he received a letter from Frank S. Young who complained that Sutro had obviously forgotten him in the days of his prosperity. Far from being offended, Sutro wrote Frank a letter unusual in its length and tenderness. Sutro said that he felt the most friendly feelings toward Young and that he had hardly written a letter for months to anyone, not even to his brothers, sisters, or children, and he attributed this laxness to family troubles. He referred briefly to tunnel affairs and he took a dim view of the present management. He thought the tunnel might be forced to suspend operations before long unless a bonanza should be discovered in the Comstock, but he regarded such an event as very unlikely. Sutro did say that he might gain control of the tunnel company again some day, but doubted if he would accept its management under any circumstances. He asserted that what he wanted was rest.

Sutro continued to live at the Baldwin. He was not ready to buy a home in San Francisco or even to declare himself a resident of California. He was hoping that friends would soon be addressing him in Washington, D.C., as a member of the United States Senate.

Nevada had been conducting a gold-sprinkled campaign to elect the legislature which was to meet in January, 1881. Presumably the legislature would choose either James Fair or William Sharon as United States Senator from Nevada. Fair was reputed to have paid $40 a vote in Washoe County and as much as $80 each in Churchill County for votes for candidates who would be sure to vote for him. Sharon bought no votes, and a comfortable majority of men pledged to Fair were elected.

Into this supposedly cut-and-dried situation stepped Sutro. He rented rooms 36 and 37 at the Ormsby House in

Carson City. These were historic rooms, in which many a deal had been made and many a man broken. Sutro captured thirty-five members of the legislature, allegedly with the aid of a "big sack." He hatched an elaborate scheme in which a legislator would be charged with using money in Washoe County to purchase votes for candidates pledged to Fair. This exposure of corruption would be the excuse for Fair men in league with Sutro to break away from Fair.

One member who was in on the plot, Bob Howlands, left Sutro's rooms at 3 o'clock in the morning and went to Fair, allegedly receiving $5,000 for his services. Within half an hour a fast team left for Reno, the seat of Washoe County, and when Sutro's lawyers went to Reno to swear out warrants all of the witnesses had skipped. This burst the Sutro bubble and Fair was elected.

Sutro returned to California. There is no evidence that he ever again visited Nevada as a candidate, a tunnel visitor, or even as a friend. He had plotted a tremendous coup and had failed. For over twenty years his every success in Nevada had been crowned with failure. Sutro excised the future of Nevada from his life with the thoroughness of a surgeon removing a well defined tumor.

Shortly after his return to California Adolph took a fateful buggy ride. On the second of March, 1881, he and his daughter Emma rode out past the western edge of the city, through the area where John McLaren would later do wonders with a large tract of sandy land known as Golden Gate Park. They went on toward a bluff overlooking the ocean and on its crest they found a small white cottage they had never seen before. Emma and her father got out of the carriage and both of them were "almost overcome" with the magnificence of the view.

The house and its plot of about one and one-half acres belonged to Samuel Tetlow, proprietor of the Bella Union, whose business had declined in recent years. The two Sutros found Mr. Tetlow at home and Adolph immediately entered into an agreement to purchase the house and land for fifteen thousand dollars. Sutro now had a home of his own. Compared with the mansion in Nevada the cottage was a very humble dwelling and to a person who had become accustomed to the immensity of Nevada, a piece of ground only one and one-half acres in extent was very cramped.

The surrounding land was for sale and bit by bit Adolph acquired not only 21.21 acres for an estate, but the shore lands north and east for 1½ miles with 80 acres bordering Fort Miley and part of the future Lincoln Park. Cliff House was directly west of his little cottage and had an unsavory reputation. He solved that problem with ease. He purchased Cliff House and turned it into a family resort of utmost respectability. He continued to invest in other parts of the city and in August he extended his already large holding in San Miguel Rancho by a second major purchase. In time he came to own virtually all of this 1,150-acre rancho which embraced Twin Peaks and large areas encircling them and to the south.

If Sutro had elected to tear down the Tetlow cottage and erect a massive monument in its place he would have been behaving in a manner typical of many of his contemporary millionaires. As real estate prices rose he could have had his share of ghastly turrets, solid gold bathrooms, or vaulted ceilings. Nob Hill was studded with enormous homes, many of which owed their existence to Comstock fortunes. San Francisco had grown accustomed to the wealthy spending their money and their lives in erratic ways and took little note of Sutro's behavior. What another man might have spent on a dwelling, he spent on the gardens around his home. While Flood, Fair, Crocker, and even Mark Hopkins built costly homes, Sutro made do with the old Tetlow cottage.

Sutro added on rooms, he glassed in the rambling porch, and he kept it all in excellent repair, but he never changed its character. He had spent his childhood and youth in a fine

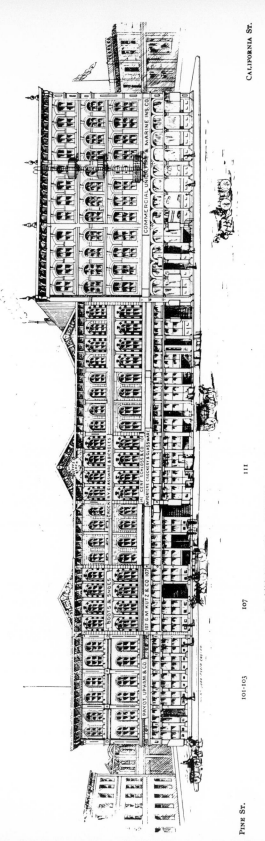

101-103   107   111   CALIFORNIA ST.

BATTERY ST.—WEST SIDE—FROM PINE TO CALIFORNIA ST.

101-103. PAVOT, UPHAM & CO. Importing
Booksellers and Stationers
Commercial Printers and Blank Book Mfrs.

107.   G. M. KUTZ & CO. Boots and Shoes
Manufacturer and Wholesale Dealers
Factory, Mission and Spear Sts.

111.   CERF, SCHLOSS & CO. Mfrs' Agent
Crockery, Glassware, Lamps, Chinaware,
Gas Goods, Silverware, etc.

COMMERCIAL UNION ASSURANCE CO.
Limited, of London
Chs. F. Mullins, Mgr.

Sutro's property on Battery Street included nos. 107-115 of the Reese (or "Reeves") Block. This business building supported Sutro's wife and children and later housed part of the Sutro Library. (*California Historical Society*)

Even twelve years after Sutro's death many of the "outside lands" were largely sand dunes. This view is from S.W. corner of A Street and 45th Avenue looking north and east up 46th Avenue, showing A Street and Block 240. *(University of San Francisco)*

Another view in the Richmond district, 1910. The photographer stood at A Street and 33rd Avenue looking south and west at Block 316. *(University of San Francisco)*

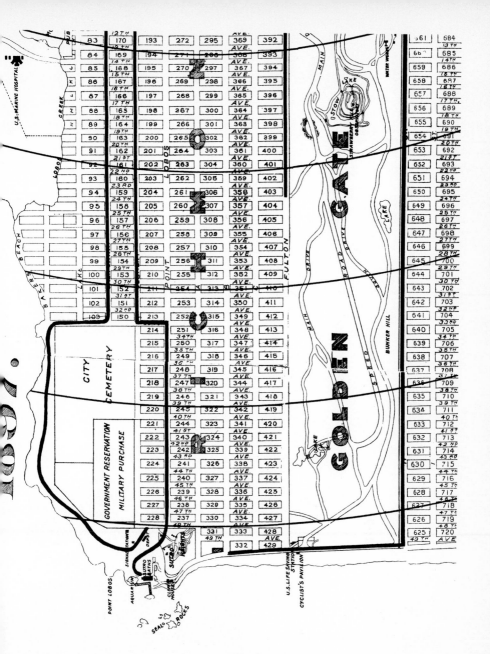

Sutro Heights and vicinity. This map shows the Heights and Sutro Baths in relation to the three street railways serving them in 1897. At the left is the scenic route, the Ferries and Cliff House Railroad, which ran along the shore and in California Street. One block right is Clement Street and the Sutro Railroad. To the right of Golden Gate Park in Lincoln Way is the Park and Ocean Railroad. A portion of the present United States Presidio is in the upper left corner. Government reservation at lower left is now Fort Miley. City Cemetery and tract adjoining it are now Lincoln Park. The rugged shore lands (but not Sutro Baths) were purchased by the city from the Sutro heirs in 1920 and Dr. Emma Merritt deeded Sutro Heights to the city. The arcs are at half-mile intervals from the city hall; the arc at bottom marks 5 miles. The two sandy blocks pictured on page opposite can be identified here by number. *(California State Library)*

The Telegraph Hill Cable Railroad was financed in part by Adolph Sutro and was extremely steep (1 foot rise for each 3½ feet). It was a single track line in Greenwich Street using two cars which passed at the turnout shown. Service began in 1884 but the line lost money steadily and it was abandoned in about two years. *(Roy D. Graves Collection)*

The first Cliff House from the hill which eventually became Sutro Heights, with Seal Rocks in the distance. The barn to the right was for the horses and carriages of patrons, for there was no other mode of transportation in 1865. *(Society of California Pioneers)*

The "second Cliff House" was actually the first Cliff House with wings added. By the time this picture was taken Sutro had developed his Heights and provided "Bath chairs" so that visitors could enjoy the view and be shielded from the wind. On days of little or no wind they could sit on the little concrete mushrooms. Note the wind breaks below the driveway. This Cliff House belonged to Sutro for about twelve years before it burned on Christmas Day, 1894. *(Society of California Pioneers)*

People have gone to the various Cliff Houses for a variety of reasons for nearly a hundred years but few, if any, have not looked at the rocks to see if the seals were in residence. The state law protecting them was inadequate and Sutro was influential in having the Seal Rocks transferred in 1887 from the United States to the City and County of San Francisco to be held in trust for public purposes. *(Society of California Pioneers)*

This ornate gateway was the entrance to Sutro Heights. It provided a preview of the statuary and trees to be seen within, which Sutro dearly loved to collect in variety and profusion. (*V. Covert Martin Collection*)

North Seal Rock

PACIFIC

Aquari

Seawall

Swim
P

Fishing Rock

Cliff

Repose Rock

Arch Rock

Cliff
House

Hermit
Rock

Cone Rock

OCEAN

Seal-Rocks

North

|—|—|—|—|—|—|—————|—————|—————|—————|
0 50 100   200   300   400   500 engl. Feet

PLAN OF SUTRO HEIGH

Terminus of
& Cliffhouse -

Ocean Terrace

Ferries-
Railroad

Windmills

Trout Pond

to Trout Pond

Lobos Road

Lover's Lane

Shady Path

Ocean Drive

Stables

Serpentine Drive

Woodland

Ivy Lane

Maze

Palm Avenue

Boarding House

1

3

8

19

20

17

15

North Esplanade

Parapet

Shady Lane

13

14

16

24

21

7

6

9

10

11

12

Site for proposed
Library or Museum

South

Esplanade

Drive to Park

Dolce far niente Balcony

23

22

Road

48th Avenue

Carl Gartef. Leipzig!

HOUSE & SEAL ROCKS

This plan was published about 1891. Among the numbered items are: 1. Main Gate; 2. Gatekeeper's Lodge; and 3. The Oval. Numbers 4 through 18 refer to special items of statuary. 19. Lower Gate; 20. Rosarium; 21. Sutro's Residence; 22. and 23. Stairs to "Dolce far niente" Balcony; 24. Observatory. *(California State Library)*

A great San Francisco photographer of this period, Taber, came to Sutro Heights in 1886 and took a series of views which Sutro later had made into a souvenir booklet. Above is shown the Main Drive, and below, the Conservatory. *(University of San Francisco)*

The gardens at Sutro Heights, showing some of the floral tapestry. This photograph seems to have been taken from a spot very close to the area where Sutro proposed to build a library and museum. He had visions of scholars relaxing from their studies by strolling through the gardens. Had he not been persuaded the climate would ruin his books, he might have built the library and thus saved it from fire and controversy. *(Society of California Pioneers)* Below, the parapet, observatory, and a portion of the residence at Sutro Heights. *(University of San Francisco)*

Sutro's home and observatory were architecturally so modest they were almost out of place in their elegant surroundings. *(University of San Francisco)*

Left: Only the exterior of the house was modest. The interior was replete with elegant clutter. *(University of San Francisco)*

Not only was the rock wall used as a base for statuary, but even the parapet
was adorned with replicas. Although Sutro defended his choice of statuary
vehemently, he had enough of a sense of humor to climb out on the rocks
himself and pose for Taber. *(University of San Francisco)*

View of Sutro's retreat in Napa County which he called "Arcadia." He began buying property in this area in 1893 and kept the buildings quite simple. *(University of San Francisco)*

The employees of Sutro Heights in 1886 pose with their employer, who wears a top hat. *(California State Library)*

home and had built one in Nevada, but he lived for the rest of his life in a little white cottage on a cliff. He never became disenchanted with the view and the soaring imagination which had envisioned a tunnel revenue of millions annually was quite comfortable with the pleasant task of dreaming about and creating a garden paradise.

He named his new home "Sutro Heights." There was much to be done about improving the grounds around his home; providing windmills to water the gardens, and similar routine undertakings. Sutro decided to leave the details to employees and go away on a trip. In order to provide for his family in case of his death he would have to make a will; otherwise, everything was in order.

If Sutro had gone to one lawyer he probably never would have written a will of such complex design. He probably did what he was said to have done about a later will — asked the opinion of several lawyers, then went off and did exactly as he meant to do all along. If a lawyer had drawn up the will he would have probably included Mrs. Sutro, but Adolph apparently considered that the trust fund already executed was sufficient and needed no further mention and therefore the name of Leah Sutro is not found in the will.

If Adolph had died on that trip, the will would have made the erstwhile Mrs. Allen $50,000 richer. The will explained that this bequest was partial reparation for the injury done her by a "false and malicious" charge brought at Virginia City in 1879. This was the largest specific bequest, with second place held by three $30,000 bequests to Adolph's sisters and a similar amount to his brother Hugo.

No one living in Nevada was named, but Henry L. Foreman was remembered with $5,000. Eight members of the United States House of Representatives of 1870 were to receive $3,000 each in recognition of their "disinterested and honorable position" taken in Sutro's behalf during his days in Washington. One clause conveyed $5,000 to Judge Solomon Heydenfeldt, to be divided after his decease equally among his children "whether they be legitimate or not." Another specific amount granted was five thousand dollars to Dr. Felix Adler of New York, "for his own private use." This bequest will be discussed later.

Sutro also made provisions looking toward the sale of Sutro Heights to the city at twenty per cent below the market price provided that it be kept perpetually as "a place of public resort." His extensive holdings in the San Miguel Rancho were left bound with enough red tape to confound the most learned estate lawyers. Briefly — and it is difficult to be brief about any of Adolph Sutro's more complex ideas — briefly, it was to be conveyed in trust, and after a period of years a board of trustees, headed by the Governor of California, would offer the land for sale as directed in the will. The board would offer prizes totaling $3,000 for essays about how the bulk of the money received from the sale of the land should be spent. It was further stipulated that no money whatsoever from the land was to go to anything even remotely sectarian. It is not stated whether the board was to follow the directions of the first prize winner or of all three.

Even after paying the many specific bequests and setting aside Sutro Heights and San Miguel Rancho, the residue of Sutro's estate would be very valuable. Sutro was quite clear as to his desires on this subject. The residue was to be divided equally among his six children. He was very clear as to what he wanted done with those countless thousands of papers he had accumulated. To his daughter Emma would go all "books, papers, scrap books, manuscripts," etc.

Having executed his will, Sutro was now free to leave on his world tour. He left Elliott J. Moore and W. R. H. Adamson in charge of his affairs. They maintained his office in the Montgomery Block, kept the downtown rental properties repaired, and made out the monthly checks. They also took care of the land deals, which often required litigation to establish clear titles. Besides the money to family members and their own salaries of $150 a month each there was the

[176]

beginning of what would become a large number of benefactions. One of the earliest was $20 a month to the Silver Street Kindergarten. And of course, as in the days of the General Superintendent, Moore and Adamson filed the bills and sent reports to their employer.

Sutro went by ship to Japan and then on to Singapore and India. After a short time in Indian ports he went on to the Red Sea and passed through the Suez Canal. This gave him a chance to inspect at first hand one of the engineering wonders of the nineteenth century, a waterway then only twelve years old. Not long after that he was in Paris. His daughter Emma was married to George W. Merritt, M.D., in London in 1883, and her father may have attended the wedding since his tour was a protracted one.

Adolph was undoubtedly sorry he could not be in New York for his mother's eightieth birthday celebration on March 14, 1883, but fifty-three of her children, grandchildren, great-grandchildren and relatives by marriage were present at the dinner party held at Pinard's Restaurant in New York City. The lovely "Rose of Düren," as she was often called, sat in a large armchair in a parlor which was decorated with immense plants, masses of flowers, and that lovely trailing vine, without which few parties were considered elegant — smilax. This tribute came just in time for she died six months later.

In April of 1884 Adolph wrote his daughter Emma from Jerusalem. His letter shows a surprising naiveté concerning the history of Judaism and it indicates clearly that he had been buying books in large quantities. In May he was in Paris with his daughter Katie and sending scathing letters to his son Charles, who was trying to get established in some kind of work in Europe. Neither Charles nor Edgar was a dynamo like his father and Adolph was vastly displeased with them. It seemed as if neither of them took to heart the motto emblazoned on their father's stationery — *"Labor omnia vincit."* In his letter to Charles the father ended by saying that he wanted his son to write frequently and tell what he was doing and not doing intimating that the latter would require more space than the former.

Sutro often told his children that if he ever became rich he would devote part of his wealth to establishing a free public library. He liked to tell them how as a boy he had read the best English and German novelists, and collected a reference library of scientific works. He exhorted them to use the books in his library in the mansion and he dreamed of the day when he could own thousands more. When he had been in London on tunnel business he had purchased some books, but when he went back with no other business than his own whims and with his pockets jingling with the gold pieces he always carried, he bought books by the thousands.

He would hail a cab for a sight-seeing trip to Windsor or Hampton Court, but since he found it difficult to pass by an antiquarian book store he seldom reached his destination. He would pile the cab so high with books that often there would be no room for him to sit down. The servants and guests at his hotel grew accustomed to see "the California Book Man," as they called him, standing up in a hack as he brought back another load of books.

Sutro spent so much time among the booksellers he came to know the short cuts through the courts and lanes of London better than he knew San Francisco. He spent long periods of time high on ladders examining books and on several occasions was taken for the owner or his clerk. He even impaired his health temporarily from inhaling too much dust. Auctions attracted him greatly, especially the one where the Sunderland Library was offered for sale by the Duke of Marlborough. Here Sutro acquired about 9,000 broadsides and pamphlets dating from the times of Charles I, Cromwell, Charles II, James II, and Queen Anne.

Only after Sutro discovered that he had purchased 35,000 books did he realize that he had done a good deal of buying and that housing the books might become a problem. It was, in fact, a problem which Sutro was never able to solve completely and for which an adequate solution would not be found until sixty-two years after his death.

The desire to purchase was not diminished by the problem of housing the collection, however, so as Sutro traveled from country to country he took advantage of auctions, visited booksellers, and then hired agents to carry on the work after he left.

Sutro's buying methods were unusual, to say the least. In Italy he visited bookshops with from 10 to 15 thousand volumes, and bargained for the lot. In monasteries he would ask the monks to sell their treasures, knowing that they would refuse. He also knew the poverty of some of the orders and this was one reason why he had his pockets full of gold coins. He did not argue or beg, he just dribbled a big handful of double eagles through his fingers onto the table. More often than not he got the books.

No one ever knew exactly how many books Sutro and his agents did buy. The most conservative estimate was made by Sutro's librarian, George Moss, who said there were 125,000 bound volumes and at least an equal number of pamphlets. The collection was heterogeneous to a fault, but there were some magnificent items. Sutro owned almost 3,000 of the 20,000 books still existing from the dates 1455-1500. (Unfortunately the 1906 fire destroyed all but 42 of these incunabula.)

The dust from thousands of books had given Sutro a sore throat, but it had also replaced the alkali of Nevada. "The California Book Man" was not a very handsome title, but it was better than "the Assyrian Carpet-bagger" and "the Great Bore," as he had sometimes been called in Virginia City. So Sutro instructed his London agent to buy no more than $2,000 worth of books per month and sailed home to tackle the job of making his books available to scholars.

At last he had found a major cause.

CHAPTER XVI

A TUNNEL TO THE SEA

UPON HIS RETURN to San Francisco Adolph found that Sutro Heights was beginning to look attractive. He refused to call in any experts to tell him how to landscape the place, but taking into consideration wind, weather, and soil, he planned gardens to surround the house and to cover the twenty acres. A stone wall was erected to give some shelter from the wind and a driveway was cut out of the rock. The flower gardens were formal and were changed according to the seasons. In 1885 the grounds were opened to the public.

Eventually Sutro bought statuary and huge urns to be placed in the garden, on the walls, and even on the face of the cliff. These were primarily plaster copies of statues which had taken Sutro's fancy in Europe. They were chosen more for their instructional qualities than for their artistic merit. The statues in the gardens had appropriate floral tapestries planted at their bases and, although several hundred rustic chairs were available for visitors, they could also rest on iron toadstools along the carriageway. In the center of the gardens was a large conservatory used for the propagation of tropical plants and for the growing of flowers for cutting.

Of course such a spectacular garden aroused the interest of San Francisco and the considerable volume of comment was not all in praise. The statues were often criticized, but an unknown writer has left an impression of a visit to Sutro Heights which by its confusion may give as accurate a picture as can now be found:

Figures were to be seen on all sides, artistically arranged, and surrounded with lovely grass lawns studded with trees. Settees were invitingly placed to tempt one to rest and behold its grandeur. A living fawn grazed the succulent grass as far as the rope he was tied with permitted. A reclining statue of a large buck, with his long antlers suggested hunter's sport in the mountains. At a short distance stood a row of busts upon pedestals, in a circle, of eminent men of the past.

With many people wanting to visit such a place, transportation was a problem. For those who could afford it, there were carriages. The problem of public transportation was partly solved when the Park and Ocean Railroad Company built a street railroad operated by steam west from the terminal of the Page Street branch of the Market Street cable railway. This Park and Ocean line ran mainly along the southern edge of the land reserved for Golden Gate Park. This was a welcome improvement, but a trip from downtown San Francisco to the Heights cost at least two fares, or ten cents. This was a period when an ordinary clerk earned twelve dollars a week, and Sutro felt that a round-trip fare of twenty cents was exorbitant.

Transfers were unusual but not unknown in San Francisco, for "Layman's Folly" used them. Frederick O. Layman had interested Charles Kohler, Jacques J. Rey, and Adolph Sutro in building a single-track cable car line with a short turnout from Powell Street to the top of Telegraph Hill. Mr. Gustav Walter built a four-story resort at the top of the hill where patrons could enjoy the view, eat, drink, and dance. After they opened in 1884 both the resort and the railroad steadily lost money and were abandoned in a few years.

There were no doubt several reasons why Sutro became involved in this venture with Layman. He was becoming more and more interested in ways to provide wholesome entertainment for the masses and he was no doubt intrigued by the engineering problems of a street railroad which had a rise of one foot for each three and one-half feet. It was not "the crookedest railroad in the world" but it was hailed as the steepest.

At the same time Sutro was active in promoting a much longer street railway. Although the franchise was issued in 1884 to Adolph's cousin, Gustav Sutro, a usually reliable witness asserts that Adolph was behind it and invested $40,000 on grading and other preliminary work at the western end on his own land. This railroad was designed to insure a single fare from the ferries to Cliff House by means of transfer to one or more lines it met at Presidio Avenue (then called "Central Avenue"). It also embraced a branch line in Seventh Avenue to provide economical access to Golden Gate Park.

In addition to saving money for the public it would be pre-eminently the scenic railroad of the city. The first few miles going west in California Street would not be unusual but at Thirty-third Avenue the route planned to curve north around the old cemeteries and run on Adolph Sutro's land along the rugged shore. Except when in an occasional tunnel the visitor would have excellent views of the Golden Gate, Fort Point, the headlands of Marin County, and many other points of interest.

Sutro did the already mentioned grading in 1886 but in the following year he sold his franchise and the work already done to the Powell Street Railroad Company. An important stipulation provided that the company must provide service from the downtown area to Cliff House or the park for a single five-cent fare. Construction was pushed vigorously and service began in 1888. The five-cent fare was a reality.

With that problem solved, Sutro could now spend more time at the Heights. His fondness for animals and quiet amusements soon led him to watching the seals out on the rocks near Point Lobos. He grew very fond of the seals and led a movement determined to protect them and their home more securely than they already were by an inadequate state law. The effort was successful in 1887 when Congress passed an act granting the Seal Rocks to the City and County of San Francisco "in trust for the people of the United States."

Sutro also spent hours north of Fisherman's Cove watching the waves hit the rocks. There was a place where the rock was hollowed out and Adolph liked to watch a wave fill it full, and then as the waves receded the water would gradually spill out of its little catch basin.

A tide pool is a watery world whose population depends on the sea. Small fish may come and go with the waves while the more sedentary animals such as the bivalves and sea anemones accommodate themselves to the various levels of water. Here was a ready-made museum of natural history that Sutro would like to share with the public. After Papa and Mama and the little ones had visited Sutro Heights and marveled at its formal beauty they could walk down to the ocean and see the natural garden of the sea.

If only the tide pool were larger! It would take at least a million years for the waves to hollow out enough rock for tide pools big enough for all the visitors at the Heights to crowd around. Sutro didn't have a million years, but by now his land had increased in value and he had considerably more than a million dollars. He decided that he would go into partnership with the sea and build a tide pool. Although he called it an aquarium, it was to have no roof, it would be stocked solely by the animals delivered voluntarily by the sea, and it would be filled by the waves. Sutro thought that a tide pool three acres in extent would serve.

The aquarium was to be situated in a cove with a break-water facing the sea, then a circular wall 15 feet thick and 14 feet high would enclose the area. Sea water in huge amounts would be allowed to come into the area at high tide, then when the marine life had settled to the bottom all but the last four feet of water would be drained off. Visitors could walk around on rock pathways uncovered when the water was let out.

This left only two problems: how to get the water in, and how to get it out. A tunnel eight feet high and 153 feet long was cut through the rock so that the sea water would spill in during four hours of high tide. There was a door to control the amount of water delivered. In one corner of the basin was a subterranean outlet which allowed the water to return to the sea. In the course of construction Sutro built a little tramway on a nearby bluff to deliver the rock taken from the tunnel to other projects of his devising.

Although this tunnel project was difficult enough, it was the sea wall that gave the real trouble. The breakwater was no sooner built than it sank into the sand. Another was placed upon it with the same result, and $70,000 worth of concrete lay buried. So a third wall was placed above the other two and it remained where it was intended to be and the aquarium was complete.

Of course a single project such as the aquarium could not engage all the attention of a man of Sutro's great energy. Normally he was busy with several projects at once and he was assisted by a sizable staff. Operation of the library was placed in the capable hands of George Moss, there was a trustee to handle the routine of Sutro's business affairs, a head gardener at the Heights with numerous assistants, and a private secretary. With the forester growing trees by the thousands Sutro also began considering ways of getting them planted and growing all over the city.

One person to whom Sutro talked about trees was Joaquin Miller, the poet. Sutro asserted that the idea of transplanting trees in February was all wrong, that it should be done in December so they would get the full benefit of the winter rains. Together they planned California's first Arbor Day, November 27, 1886, and with a large group of state officials they went by government boat to barren Yerba Buena Island and planted 30,000 trees. Simultaneously the school children of San Francisco were holding similar exercises and planting trees given by Sutro at the Presidio and at Fort Mason. Eventually Mt. Parnassus (now known as Mt. Sutro) was also planted. Sutro continued to provide trees for the children each year, and is estimated to have given away millions of seedlings of cypress and of *Pinus maritima* which he imported from the coast of the Black Sea.

Of all his trees, there were at least two not planted as Sutro had planned. An epidemic struck just as the trees were being readied for delivery and many children were absent from school. Two of the children attending one of the free kindergartens died. Their mothers went to the school, found the trees already tagged with the names of their dead children and asked if they might have the trees to plant on their children's graves. The teacher felt that would be quite all right with Mr. Sutro, but sent him a letter explaining what she had done and telling how the mothers had held the little trees in their arms as if cradling their lost children. Sutro often boasted of his trees and called them the children of his old age, but he was not the kind of man who would tell this poignant story. The letter was folded and placed in his files.

Trees were but one of Sutro's many interests. He was able to look south through the windows of his house and see the beach and the government Life Saving Station. On several occasions when ships were in distress Sutro noticed what he regarded as lack of readiness and poor management on the part of the Life Saving personnel. A most flagrant example occurred on December 17, 1886, when the whaler *Atlantic* was stranded within a few hundred yards of the beach. Captain Warren was swept off the deck of the wrecked steamer and managed to reach the Life Saving Station and arouse the men. Even then they did not go out in their surf boat but after half an hour's delay they shot a useless line to the steamer and patrolled the beach. Of the crew of thirty-eight, twenty-eight perished. Characteristically, Mr. Sutro supplied those rescued with clothing and other necessaries and gave each a small money present to tide him over until he could get another job.

Sutro made some strong statements in newspaper interviews and in letters to the regional Life Saving officer as to the inefficiency of the station near Sutro Heights. Many of these words went out on the Associated Press wire and there was correspondence with national officials of the service. The net effect was an improvement in efficiency.

A dramatic incident occurred on that same windy and dangerous shore a month later which had little bearing on the Life Saving quarrel. On January 16, 1887, the schooner *Parallel* reached Mile Rock and a heavy swell began driving it ashore. Knowing what their cargo was, the captain and crew abandoned the ship and went ashore in a small boat. They reached Pt. Bonita at 10 p.m. but warned no one about their ship.

At 9 p.m. Sutro learned a vessel was on Seal Rocks and he gathered thirty of his employees so as to render any needed assistance. He could see no one on the vessel so at 10 p.m. he returned to his cottage. At 12:30 there was a tremendous explosion which badly damaged Cliff Cottage and Cliff House and caused minor damage in every room in the Sutro residence except the one in which Mr. Sutro was sleeping. "I thought the end of the world had come," Sutro told a *Call* reporter. "If my men and myself had remained there until the explosion occurred, a vestige of us would never have been found."

The cargo included forty-five tons of giant powder, one ton of black powder, and one box of caps. Fortunately the explosion did not touch off Mr. Sutro's powder magazine; the boxes and cans of dynamite were only scattered on the floor. When Sutro learned that no lives had been lost, he did not seem to care a particle about the damage done to his property.

Ship disasters and improved rescue service were a very minor part of Sutro's life. He delighted in books and he was also interested in works of art, especially those which might adorn Sutro Heights or his adopted city. While in Europe he had been delighted with an enormous statue by Wirtz entitled "Triumph of Light." He bought the statue and had it sent in sections to San Francisco. Despite the fact that the original name was chiseled in the base, he renamed it "Liberty Enlightening the World." In 1887 he placed it on a fourteen-foot pedestal on top of Mt. Olympus, a rather high peak in the geographical center of San Francisco on Sutro-owned land. In a flood of oratory the statue was presented to the city. Judge Solomon Heydenfeldt did the actual unveiling while with a wreath in hand Miss Addie Sevey of the Sanchez School promised that she and her schoolmates would be the guardians of the "noble figure" made of "imperishable stone." No little girl should ever be asked to make ridiculous promises and it is to be hoped that Miss Addie never found out that her promises were futile.

Sutro had adorned his city's central peak and he had charmed the little fishes out of the sea, but he still had a nagging problem — how to house his library. When the books first began to pour in by the thousands they were sent to a loft on Battery Street. But as the tide of books continued this space was insufficient and Sutro rented twenty-four suites of offices in the Montgomery Block. This included a huge space which had formerly been a billiard room. It was two stories high with faded old murals and frescoes on the wall. Adolph Sutro's office adjoined the library and sometimes Mr. Sutro could be found "lying in great comfort on a sofa," resting and reading books from his collection or poring over dealers' catalogs.

But much as Sutro enjoyed himself at the Montgomery Block, he knew that it was not a permanent solution to the problem of housing his library. For a while he talked of building a huge library at the Heights, using the stone he took from the sea tunnel. Unfortunately he was persuaded that the damp air would ruin the books. He had envisioned scholars using his library, then strolling through the gardens for recreation. He talked so much about his library and how he was going to give it to the public that on at least one occasion the *Evening Post* of San Francisco poked fun at him for his rainbow-tinted promises. By the time he died the press had become very outspoken in its reactions to Sutro's lack of action regarding a library building. Whereas the newspapers seldom referred to him as a Jew, a cartoonist's pen sometimes traced a veritable Shylock.

Sutro found a temporary answer to the conflicting ideas about a library building early in 1889 when he suddenly decided to take a trip to Mexico, Yucatan, Cuba, and some of the states of the South. Within less than forty-eight hours his secretary, Archibald C. Unsworth, Sutro's son Charles, and Sutro himself were on their way.

On this trip Sutro behaved in his usual way, constantly investigating anything which interested his far-ranging mind. Near Fresno he visited vineyards and asked many questions on the raisin and wine industries. He also tried to find out why the fig culture was less successful than in the Near East. On the train he met a lawyer employed by the Interstate Commerce Commission, whom he talked with for hours. Near Torreón, Mexico, he sought out a cock fight as well as a cotton textile mill.

Although Sutro always traveled in the best accommodations available, he was his usual democratic self. He was easy to approach and was just as likely to be found in conversation in the chair car as in the Pullman car. During the whole journey he never made any effort to display or call attention to his great wealth. Inevitably he did spend large sums of money for his favorite objects — trees, shrubs, and books.

At home in San Francisco Dr. George Merritt had little time for his specialty, the diseases of the nose and throat, for he was in charge of Sutro's many business activities. It was he who had to see that the head gardener took proper care of the plants, that the grading of streets near the Statue of Liberty went forward, that certain lands were sold, etc. He was also expected to send almost daily communications to his father-in-law. This was a strange task for a medical doctor and it is remarkable that he was able to serve his employer as well as he did. Besides such routine tasks as collecting rents and repairing buildings Dr. Merritt had various difficulties over customs duties and shipping charges. One problem concerned some antiquities included in a book shipment, which could not be removed from Mexico without a permit.

Although Dr. Merritt was far from idle, at least the problem of housing the library was postponed by Sutro's absence. Sutro prolonged this happy state of indecision upon his return when he promptly left for Europe and stayed five or six months. By January of 1890 he was back in San Francisco, however, and the stubborn library problem remained.

He could not come to terms with himself about a library, but the fishes swimming in their man-made pools gave him a bigger idea. He would build an indoor swimming pool for the public. The Sutro Baths were Sutro's last great building project, his last effort to name something for his family and perpetuate the name "Sutro." In many ways the baths were a summation of all of Sutro's objectives.

First Sutro offered a prize of $500 for a design for the building. The entrance was a small classical temple which opened into an enormous glass-enclosed pavilion enclosing five salt water swimming pools and one fresh water pool. Of course the primary reason for the baths was to provide wholesome activity for the people of San Francisco. The baths could accommodate as many as 10,000 persons at one time. Besides swimming meets there were band concerts, exhibitions of swimming and diving, and occasionally free days for all school children. The opportunity to instruct as

[189]

well as entertain was not overlooked. The entrance to the baths was so designed that it accommodated glass cases for stuffed birds and animals, Egyptian mummies, and other educational objects including paintings and statues. Potted palms were placed throughout the building and eventually Sutro managed to crowd in examples of nearly all of his hobbies except books.

The baths were a unique piece of engineering. The water from the ocean came in through the tunnel cut for the aquarium and was allowed to settle in a large catch basin. Pumps were installed so that during neap tides they could be used to pump in sea water. After settling, the clear water was pumped into the pools, each one of which was heated to a different temperature. The water was drained off constantly and was piped far enough out into the ocean to avoid any re-use of the water. The laundry equipment could handle 20,000 bathing suits and 40,000 towels per day.

Hundreds of people desired work in the baths and wrote Sutro asking for jobs. Others wanted to sell him grandmother's coverlet, a live bear, or a four-legged turkey preserved in spirits. All of the letters were treated with the same care given letters from Sutro's family and business associates; each one was folded, labeled, dated and filed away.

Hard times came to San Francisco again and as "the Old Man" walked down Montgomery Street he was accosted on all sides by former acquaintances and even by strangers. He carried his gold coins, as always, and seldom failed to open his purse when asked. Finally even Sutro could not carry enough for all who wanted help, so he purchased meal and bed tickets from the Salvation Army. At first these tickets were distributed from his office, then when the corridors of the Montgomery Block became so crowded with men waiting in line for the free tickets that no one else could come to Sutro's office, the tickets were distributed outside the office. Finally during the panic of 1893 Sutro gave up all control of the

Once more Sutro visited a London photographer. No longer was it necessary to pose as a miner or worry about the tunnel. He had started to collect books and art objects and his joy in his new projects brought a bright gleam to his eyes. *(University of San Francisco)*

At left, Sutro Baths, looking west, as they neared completion. *(Society of California Pioneers) Below, left,* the interior of Sutro Baths. Note spectators' benches in upper right hand corner. *(Roy D. Graves Collection)*

It was not, however, until aerial photography was perfected that the magnitude of the baths could be appreciated. *(University of San Francisco)*

The scenic route. The Ferries and Cliff House Railroad ran along the rugged ocean shore west of Thirty-third Avenue. This land was owned by Sutro and later became part of Lincoln Park. Note the man pointing to a landmark; the Golden Gate is clearly seen in the background. *(Roy D. Graves Collection)*

The Ferries and Cliff House Railroad was a steam operation which connected with several cable street railroads at Central (now "Presidio") Avenue. The franchise was obtained by Gustav Sutro in 1884 and Adolph spent $40,000 on grading. In 1887 he sold his rights to the Powell Street cable group who completed construction and began steam service ten months later. The photograph below was taken in 1905, shortly before the line was electrified. *(Roy D. Graves Collection)*

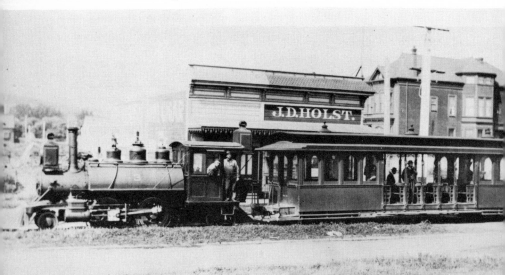

A car of the Sutro Railroad Company. Adolph built this line after electric traction had proved itself in many cities, so it was an electric operation from the start. *(Roy D. Graves Collection)*

The third Cliff House, as built by Adolph Sutro. This is the type of architecture one might have expected him to use for the Nevada mansion or at the Heights. He limited his own dwellings with admirable restraint, but provided the public with this enormous fantasy. Built near the end of his life, it burned in 1907. *(California Historical Society)*

Sutro purchased the statue "Triumph of Light" by the Belgian artist Wirtz.
He had it sent in sections to San Francisco and when reassembled he called
it "Liberty Enlightening the World."

The benign Sutro. The original of this picture was seldom, if ever used by Adolph Sutro. Apparently he preferred a sterner view, but he did have his moments of kindness and friendliness. *(Bancroft Library)*

The Honest Miner stands midway between his Pacific dreams and his Nevada accomplishments on the book plate still used by the State of California for their Sutro Library. *Below:* At home, in his own library, Adolph Heinrich Joseph Sutro planned for the future. *(California State Library)*

tickets he purchased and the distribution was turned over to the Salvation Army itself. His secretary estimated that during 1893 Sutro purchased at least 10,000 tickets.

The man who seldom before had delegated authority, much less completely relinquished control, had two excellent reasons for doing so at this time. The panic was no less severe for the wealthy than the poor, and Sutro was hard hit. On February 9 he borrowed $120,000 from the Hibernia Savings and Loan Society of San Francisco at the rate of 6½ per cent per year and in December the Society sent a terse note to the effect that payment of interest on the loan was three months past due. Sutro sent the check for $1,950. In January of 1894 he wrote to his brother Ludwig saying that he had planned to manage his property holdings in such a way that he could sell off about $100,000 worth a year for his living expenses but the remainder would go up in value and he could maintain his standard of living throughout his lifetime. Until the past year his plan had worked well, but now it was impossible to sell real estate.

It should be noted, however, that during 1893-94 Sutro was buying parcels of land in Napa County. He wanted a "hideaway" and despite the fact he had already spent over a quarter of a million dollars on the baths, he felt he could afford to spend money on real estate near Calistoga.

The other reason for releasing his control to an organization can be seen in the founder of the Salvation Army. General William Booth was a dynamic personality with many of the same interests and behavior patterns as Sutro. The General, Mrs. Booth and their children always visited Sutro Heights when they were in San Francisco. Their host would have many questions ranging from Army policies in dealing with the homeless and released prisoners to problems of labor and capital. They also discussed those whom they referred to as "the submerged tenth." General Booth had more than good stories to tell; he had the facts and figures which his host liked. What is more, they shared a philosophy of life.

Sutro avoided organized religion while at the same time he supported their charities, their leaders, and their members. Both the King's Daughters and the Home for Aged Israelites received building lots. The Fruit and Flower Mission, The Channing Auxiliary and Society for Christian Work and the Little Sisters Infant Shelter, were among those he entertained or to whom he loaned his estate for benefits. He said repeatedly that charity and kindness are the true religion of the world.

Normally he did not discuss the more intimate aspects of his religious beliefs, but he was pushed to do so by the interviewers sent by Hubert Howe Bancroft, the energetic San Francisco bookseller who assembled a unique collection of books and manuscripts on the Pacific Slope in general and California in particular. Bancroft was determined to use his materials in writing a monumental history of the Pacific Slope and in due course he completed his self-imposed task.

When Sutro returned to California after twenty years in Nevada, Bancroft was enriching his sources through oral interviews with pioneers and men who had made their mark in contemporary California life. Quite naturally Sutro was sought out and one or more interviews with assistants of Bancroft followed. Hubert Howe Bancroft was puzzled by Sutro's attitude toward religion. Time and again his interviewers quizzed Sutro so that eventually the Bancroft folder held six separate items.

Actually, Sutro's relationship to his co-religionists is not hard to understand once the full import of one of the items in his will is comprehended. The Ethical Culture movement was founded by Dr. Felix Adler seven years before the will was written. If Sutro had wanted any relationship with a group, certainly this was one that would have appealed to his intellect and to the liberal teachings he had learned from his mother. He was not willing, however, to help promote this organization per se but instead he willed a sizable sum ($5,000) to its founder "for his own private use." No doubt

Sutro was well aware that this bequest would probably aid the Ethical Culture movement indirectly.

In religion, as in business and pleasure, Adolph did not ask anyone's advice. If he liked what a society or organization was doing, he made it possible for them to use his property to raise money or he helped them entertain their charges. He avoided indiscriminate gifts, even to non-sectarian organizations, and preferred to help people individually. Obviously this tremendous desire to benefit mankind coupled with a total rejection of what H. H. Bancroft must have felt *should* be the motive of charity, had the historian puzzled. Sutro was not hoping for stars in his crown, nor for a memorial to his family, but in the age-old manner of men he was simply trying to do the kind of thing his mother had taught him to believe in. So it was that when the interviewer pressed him on religious issues he spoke not of himself so much as he did of his family, saying over and over again that they were thoroughly liberal.

One clause in his will has given rise to the idea that Sutro was opposed to everything sectarian. The clause directed that no institution in any way governed by a clergyman could benefit from the sale of certain parcels of land held in trust for a period of years. So this was not a general directive but applied to only a portion of his property. If he had been opposed to organized religion he hardly would have allowed his children to be educated in church-related schools, but his children attended both Episcopal and Catholic institutions. If he had any specific objections to any religious group he kept remarkably silent about them.

In essence, then, Sutro was not a religious man, but a charitable man. He found no pleasure in joining groups, but took great delight in entertaining individuals. Like many individuals of Jewish lineage he was a free thinker, but unlike many who were interested in the reform of Judaism or creation of a new religious movement, he remained aloof. It must have amused even the relatively humorless Sutro to note the intensity with which certain individuals tried to connect his behavior with their own ideas of religion.

Hubert Howe Bancroft wrote of hm: "If Sutro had addressed himself to statesmanship, he would have become to America what Disraeli was to Great Britain." Perhaps Sutro could have learned to be diplomatic, but diplomacy would have come hard for him. Ever since he had been a child visiting his father's woolen mill he had demonstrated his ability to be sociable with working men, but had never relinquished his role as a superior. He was cut from the cloth of kings, not prime ministers.

His methods were usually dictatorial yet many of his beliefs were radical and democratic. For years he shared the table at the Heights with his servants saying: "Why should they not eat with me? They are as good as I, and while they work for me they must eat as well as I do." He finally conformed to social custom and ate separately, but he insisted that the servants' table be supplied as generously as the family table. Sutro's radical ideas also shone forth when several thousand unemployed men were demonstrating in the city. Sutro said:

> A man has a natural right to the work needed for the support of himself and his family. It is the duty of the State to see that the men who will work can get it.

Although generous in his views on meeting human needs, Sutro was an exacting taskmaster and an implacable foe of what he regarded as wasteful. If an employee purchased twenty-five cents worth of sand paper when ten cents worth was needed, the old man would take him to task for it. If the bookkeeper was only ten cents long or short he must keep after it until the accounts balanced perfectly. If a workman was slow in asking for his wages, Sutro was indignant.

All of his life Sutro had been obstinate or persevering, depending on whether you were for him or against him. The bank ring thought him obstinate, but men who wanted the tunnel had hailed his perseverance. He showed this trait in the little things as well as the big ones. For example, while in Yucatan he saw a vine growing on a house. He roused the owner and tried to make it clear that he wanted to know the name of the vine. The owner spoke only Spanish and Sutro did not have the vocabulary necessary to express himself easily. Eventually he made it clear that he did not want the vine, only its name. On finding it was a passion flower which bore edible fruit, he obtained some seeds to take back to the Heights.

In the years Adolph Sutro had lived at Sutro Heights he had kept away from mining except to prospect for coal and bluestone on his own property. He had kept away from tunneling except to make an entrance to his aquarium. He had kept away from politics except to try to improve the Life Saving Service at Point Lobos and to have Seal Rocks made into a public reserve. He was engaged in a series of law suits relative to his land holdings and whenever he had to be in court his behavior was reminiscent of his experiences in Washington.

Sutro stayed out of the litigation in the Federal court in Carson City when Joseph Aron charged fraud in the reorganization of the tunnel company. Aron's object of attack was Theodore Sutro, Adolph's youngest brother, who practiced law in New York. Theodore Sutro had led a crusade to save the rights of the stockholders of the tunnel company, threatened by annihilation through a foreclosure suit brought by the holders of the mortgage, McCalmont Brothers and Company.

Theodore Sutro had faith in the future of the tunnel and he urged stockholders to buy off McCalmont Brothers by voluntarily subscribing fifty cents a share for the purpose. By this and other means a fund was raised, McCalmont Brothers and Company accepted $800,000 for the tunnel, and Theodore emerged from the affair with a fee for services of $100,000 (one-third paid in cash) and became President of a new tunnel company styled the Comstock Tunnel Company.

The rights of the subscribing stockholders were preserved, but Aron charged that the reorganization was very expensive and that Theodore had betrayed his trust.

Adolph Sutro could have become actively engaged in this suit, or at least emotionally involved, because Aron printed two pamphlets which accused his former friend of everything from whoring to stealing 300,000 shares of tunnel company stock. He also asserted that Adolph had given up the tunnel idea before it was even started, whereupon Aron talked him into continuing.

Aron's pamphlets were not at issue in the trial except that they included dozens of letters and other documents which were entered as evidence in the trial. The judge obviously found some amusement in the case and wrote: "What shall be said of the facts when the testimony — independent of exhibits of almost equal length — consists of about 6,000 typewritten pages, and the printed briefs of counsel over 800 pages?" Judgment was entered against Aron of whom the judge said the evidence showed "by a careful reading between the lines, that in Mr. Aron's opinion" the scheme was "only preposterous and wicked because someone by the name of 'Sutro' was connected with it."

It has been asserted that Aron's first publication, satirically titled *The History of a Great Work and an Honest Miner,* was rigidly suppressed, but if this was done at Adolph Sutro's order he made no mention of it. Quick to speak against those he considered enemies, he gave Aron the unkindest cut of all — silence.

Sutro continued to use the device he had adopted years before, a miner swinging a pick under the motto "Labor Omnia Vincit." He carried quantities of personal stationery wherever he went with this device engraved upon it. For his bookplate he had it superimposed upon a background showing Seal Rocks, Cliff House and Sutro Heights to the left, the tunnel entrance, warehouse and mansion to the right. At last the miner had a firm grasp on the handle of the pick.

At home Sutro had a routine for living which provided opportunities for meeting many people. At 6:30 a.m. he had a cup of coffee brought to his bed and while he drank it he observed a period of reflection. At eight he arose and took a bath. He was convinced that everyone should take a daily tub bath and he not only owned a collapsible tub which he used while traveling, but he also sent one to his daughter Rosa when she was in school and another to Charles in Spain.

As soon as Adolph was dressed he went to the office in his home, went through letters and arranged for answering them, answered questions which had been submitted to him, and signed checks. He also received the heads of his various departments, gave orders for supplies, and saw visitors by appointment. If a quick decision was needed he was very shrewd in getting to the heart of the matter without hesitation. If there was no need for an immediate answer he would take a great deal of time and look at the matter from all sides.

Next Sutro would call for his favorite horse, Max, and ride over his estate and along the beach. He would chat with his workmen, all of whom he treated in a friendly manner. Many of them were acquaintances from Nevada or immigrants from Europe, who when down on their luck would apply for a job. Occasionally Sutro tolerated a poor workman because of the man's need for the job, and occasionally he set up a spy system to see if the men really worked. Although he could allow for a poor gardener, he demanded excellence from his cook. She was given many special privileges and her cooking was superb.

Breakfast was at 11 a.m. and this was Sutro's time to entertain. Although sometimes he dined with only his secretary or some of his children, more often he invited guests. The conversation was interesting, sometimes brilliant. The topics were generally dictated by the interests and accomplishments of the guests.

Kate Douglas Wiggin and her sister talked about kindergartens, William Jennings Bryan about free silver, and three astronomers from Lick Observatory outlined the work they planned to do in astronomical and chemical research with the spectroscope. Andrew Carnegie talked about public libraries and Denis Kearney, with his long hair and queer clothes, asserted "the Chinese must go." Unfortunately, we have no record of what Sutro and Oscar Wilde discussed. Of all of Sutro's many guests, the one who attracted the most attention for the newspapers was Benjamin Harrison, President of the United States. Harrison visited Sutro Heights on April 27, 1891, and the newspapers covered Sutro's luncheon in exhaustive detail.

Whereas the smaller entertainments always included visits around the grounds of the Heights, there were other times when large groups were entertained primarily out-of-doors. Sixty ladies actively engaged in the free kindergarten work of San Francisco strolled through the gardens with Sutro and then had breakfast. On Froebel's birthday 220 kindergarten children and their teachers were given free transportation to the Heights, where they played on the grass and were served cakes, pies, oranges and nuts. A high point for adults was the occasion when the Channing Society presented the Stockwell Company with Rose Coghlan as leading lady in an outdoor performance of Shakespeare's *As You Like It*.

Sutro Heights was closed to the public and work stopped on the Sutro Baths for a few days in December, 1893, when Leah Sutro died. The previous April her doctors had indicated that she would not live more than two or three days. Her husband visited her immediately and continued to visit her regularly during the remainder of her life. It was assumed that some sort of reconciliation had taken place, because Sutro took every opportunity to tell his friends how good and sweet she had been. He also said: "I was constantly aided and encouraged by my wife, and but for her confidence in

[198]

me I think there were times when I would almost have despaired."

Sutro's German accent and habits of speech were well known in San Francisco and it is probable that many people who read Leah's obituary paid little attention to the qualifying words in the statements attributed to Sutro. Such readers most probably accepted the reports of a reconciliation at face value. There can be little doubt that Leah deserved praise, but she had not been an active part of Adolph's life for fourteen years.

While the Sutro Baths were under construction Sutro again became concerned about the people who came out from the city by public transportation. In 1893 the Powell Street company was absorbed by the Market Street company, which was controlled by the Southern Pacific Railroad, and the policy of a single fare promptly ended. Polite requests to the street railways failed and Sutro decided to fight again on the issue. He knew that he was taking on no minor opponent, for nearly all of the street railways were controlled by the Southern Pacific Railroad, the biggest single monopoly in the state. The man who dominated the Southern Pacific was Collis P. Huntington, and Huntington would require a good fight.

Sutro dramatized his declaration of war by erecting a high fence and charging twenty-five cents admission to the Heights and to Cliff House if the visitor came "on the cars." Those who came by foot, however, or by means other than the cars were admitted free.

Huntington stood firm and Sutro threatened again to start a street railroad of his own. He obtained a franchise to build a line to Presidio Avenue mainly in Clement Street, which lay one block south of and parallel to the rival line in California Street. He would also build a branch in Eighth Avenue to serve the park. He arranged for free transfers at Presidio Avenue to the Sutter Street line, which was independent of the railroad monopoly. Electric traction had recently proved itself, so Sutro's railroad would be an electric one from the start.

This railroad was but the latest of a long series of contributions which had been made or would be made by Sutro to his adopted city. There was hardly a person living in San Francisco whose life was not already or would be enriched in some way by Adolph Sutro. For those who were down and out there was scrip; for families with a little money there was promise of a five-cent fare to the beach, and for just a little more a promenade or swim at the nearly completed baths. There would again be free entrance through the ornate gates of Sutro Heights, and for those with more money there was entertainment at the Cliff House. For everyone there were the seals barking on their rocks. And of course, for invited guests the breakfasts at Sutro Heights continued. Even Collis P. Huntington came and the two old men had a good lunch and good conversation as if there had never been a harsh word between them. Then they parted to renew their fight.

Sutro was attacking Huntington now not only on the single-fare issue but also regarding the Funding Bill then before Congress. In the 1860's the Federal government had loaned twenty-seven million dollars for construction of the Central Pacific Railroad, the first unit in the Southern Pacific system. These millions were now due with interest, but the railroad thought that it was an inconvenient time to repay. Friends of the railroad introduced a bill refunding the amount due for ninety-nine years at one-half of one per cent interest. Sutro and many others regarded this as tantamount to cancellation and regarded it as a great fraud on the Federal taxpayers. In addition to attacking the Funding Bill directly, Sutro asserted that the railroad was constantly exploiting the public through excessively high rates and mismanagement. Sutro referred to the railroad as "the Octopus" and seemingly the full vigor of his tunnel days returned.

Now Sutro had money of his own and plenty of time to devote to fighting Huntington. He had envelopes printed carrying slogans in red, such as "Huntington wouldn't steal a red hot stove," "Down with the Octopus," and "How Huntington fixes up committees." Sutro hired a newsman named Charles Sumner to play watchdog in Washington. They devised a code and telegraphed each other at length.

There was one great difference between Sutro's early days in Washington and the fight with Huntington. This time he was not alone. William Randolph Hearst sent Ambrose Bierce to Washington and Homer Davenport's cartoons were as effective against Huntington as Bierce's pen and Sutro's slogans. There was another notable difference between this fight and the earlier ones — this time Sutro was on the winning side.

LABOR CONQUERS ALL

O NE SUNDAY in July, 1894, there was a breakfast party at the Heights. Among those with Sutro were acquaintances, relatives, and two delegates from the Executive Committee of the People's Party, the radical "third party" of the period. Adolph Sutro was now sixty-four years old and engaged in enough activities to overburden a man half his age. His enormous land-holdings required constant supervision and although Sutro directed his business managers, he never really delegated much authority. At this time he had a place in Napa County which he was using as a retreat. He called it "Arcadia" and was more interested in the trout pools he established there than in the living quarters, which were rustic.

Sutro had just "declared war" over the five-cent fare and and Funding Bill issues, preliminary work was going forward on the Sutro street railway, and the baths had absorbed over $250,000 and would not be finished for at least a year. Sutro had not yet come to any decision as to how to house his library nor how to convert it into a lasting memorial. His health was poor and a wiser man would never have invited those two politicians to breakfast.

Sutro knew what they wanted and played coy. It was common knowledge in the city that the People's Party was determined to win the coming election for Mayor and they knew they could not win unless they could present a candidate who had tremendous popular appeal. Who was known better than the former tobacco dealer and tunnel builder — owner of one-twelfth of San Francisco's land and the kindly possessor of an open purse? Where else would they find such a "man who"?

Of course if these Populists, as they were often called, had been more careful in analyzing the needs of the office they would have known Sutro was the wrong man. The first consideration should have been health, physical and mental. The office was a demanding one and required better health than Sutro's. They should have wanted a man who could get along with many different kinds of people — a suave leader, not a General Superintendent. They would have done well to look for a person whose political experience was something more than a short list of complete failures. Perhaps the key Populists were aware of Sutro's limitations, but the first rule of politics is to win elections. They wanted a well-known, benevolent citizen who could pull in the votes and Sutro was their man.

At the breakfast the two delegates sounded out their choice. Sutro invited the other guests to discuss the matter and they agreed unanimously — Sutro should be Mayor. As the guests departed did any one of them realize that once more the kiss of death had been given at the table? Sutro was no Savior and there was not a Judas among his guests, but they had urged their host to make what was to become the saddest, the most profound mistake of his life and one which may well have hastened his death.

There were five other candidates for Mayor including the incumbent, L. R. Ellert, and Coroner C. C. O'Donnel (who had hoped to be the Populist candidate). Sutro campaigned vigorously, saying that most of the planks in the Populist platform were things he had been advocating for many years. He used all the mastery of oratory he had developed in his many speeches for the tunnel.

Sutro was convinced that the Southern Pacific Railroad was crushing San Francisco. At one meeting he said, "Arise then, workingmen, and do not vote for a single man who wears the collar of the Octopus." Sutro accused the Octopus of controlling the newspapers because only one newspaper was outspoken in favoring him. Even his enemies, however, admired his pluck and his phenomenal vigor.

Election day was spent quietly at the Heights. Almost 60,000 persons voted and 31,254 cast their votes for Adolph Sutro. Long before this Sutro had written, "And then commenced the tug of war." He should have said it again, because the legislative body of the city-county, the Board of Supervisors, proved neither docile nor pro-Sutro.

The supervisors started out politely enough that January day in 1895 when they applauded Sutro's inaugural address while they sat beneath festoons of smilax thoughtfully provided by the new Mayor. Sutro read his speech in earnest tones and advocated the usual things, saying honesty in government is essential, boss rule is a great evil, and the public schools should inculcate patriotism. He also said that gymnastic exercise for boys and girls should be a part of the school program and that there should be technical training for both boys and girls including shorthand and typing for girls. He also favored kindergartens as a regular part of the school system as soon as revenue permitted. He also said that the city should develop its own water system as well as a gas and electric system. Sutro said that the streets of San Francisco were lamentable and the sewer system a disgrace. He outlined a large number of problems in need of solution and included a warning about the fire department saying, "Our climate makes us particularly susceptible to a general fire." Sutro had an excellent grasp of the needs of the city, none whatever of the supervisors.

This unfortunate situation was soon made evident by the newspapers. The twelve supervisors pulled and tugged at each other and usually found that Sutro was opposed to whatever they might decide to do. San Francisco needed civic leadership and had maneuvered herself into a situation which could result in nothing but repeated deadlocks. Problems were magnified because times were hard and depression cloaked the entire country in gloom. Previous poor administrations had done little or nothing to prepare San Francisco for bettering her fiscal situation.

The administrative policies of the city were outmoded, and a destitute woman in her final hours of pregnancy could apply to the city-county hospital and be refused. But she could appeal to the Mayor in person and, if given a letter, go back and be admitted to the hospital. At the same time the debts of the hospital, jail, and almshouse were so great that merchants refused to deliver food for the inmates, or hay for the horses that pulled the patrol wagons and ambulances. The inmates and horses did not starve, but it took a specific emergency like this to get some semblance of action out of the chaotic municipal leadership. On problems lacking the element of crisis, however, Mayor Sutro was simply not the man to work with a group to whom he could not dictate.

For one thing, Sutro was far too involved in the decisions to be made by the supervisors to be an impartial public official. There was the matter of a franchise for his own street railway. The supervisors went along with that, but when other interests wanted to construct other street railways Sutro bellowed that they were destroying the beauty of the city's streets.

Sutro referred in his inaugural address to the deplorable condition of the city's pavements, but where to put better paving and how to do it were problems of great personal concern to the Mayor. For years he had been selling lots in the Outside Lands and promising buyers that their streets would soon be improved. That the streets were flooded during the rainy season and full of sand when the wind blew was common knowledge. So was the fact that any improvements would add to the tax burdens of the men and women who owned homes on small lots, but would greatly increase taxes of the man who still owned whole blocks. To do a satisfactory job the streets would have to be graded and finished not only in front of the houses, but all along those streets where Sutro owned every foot of block after block of unimproved lots.

Sutro could not agree with the supervisors about how to select materials to pave downtown streets, or how to inspect materials which were purchased. To make matters worse, he considered himself an engineer. He was an authority on everything, including materials and methods for paving streets and alleys.

Even if Sutro had been able to lead the supervisors by democratic processes rather than functioning as a general superintendent, and even if there had been a good city charter and money in the public treasury, he was far too involved personally in the growth and development of San Francisco to be a suitable mayor for the city he loved. His faults lay not in selfishness, corruption, or laziness but in his stubbornness. He knew exactly what the city needed to force it into a mold he himself conceived. He knew where the streets should be, which should be improved, and where street cars should run.

He believed that street improvements which would push him into a land-poor near-bankruptcy (as finally happened) were not good for the city. He was positive that the householders out near the park were better off with unpaved streets if they were thereby assured of a public benefactor with millions to pour into a street railroad, public baths, and a new Cliff House to replace the drab little one burned on Christmas Day of 1894. In his own mind Sutro was certain that the only people who knew what San Francisco needed were the 31,254 who voted for him, and himself. That the supervisors might also know what was good for San Francisco does not seem to have entered the head of the old man.

It seems likely that the very inefficiency and incompetence of an administration headed by thirteen feuding men resulted in San Francisco soon getting what she sorely needed — a far better Mayor and a new city charter. In the meantime the city struggled along with a man who loved being Mayor but could not behave like one. As the San Francisco *Examiner* said later: "The Mayor's power is barely more than that given by his tact. . . . He passed his term in a state of exasperation."

Gone were the days when Sutro could leave for Mexico on forty-eight hours' notice or spend his time watching the waves on the beach. He still communed with the seals, but even that pastime was interrupted with telephone calls. He did, however, have means of escape.

Best of all, there were his books in the Montgomery Block. But even in this enjoyable sanctuary he could not forget all the books still housed on Battery Street. He finally arrived at a solution. He would give twenty-six acres of San Francisco land up on Mount Parnassus to the Regents of the University of California. One-half of the land could be used for their affiliated professional schools (including the Toland Medical School from which his daughter Emma had graduated) and the other half would be just right for a library building which he would erect. He liked that site because of the view, the fine plantings of his own trees above it, and the fact that it was out of what he believed was the fire area. Still it was far enough away from the ocean to avoid extreme dampness.

Unfortunately Sutro was growing old and his mind was beginning to deteriorate. Even five years before he might have made the gift to the university one they could accept with speed. Now, however, he bound up his gift with so much legal red tape that the Regents barely managed to accept the gift and start the work on the medical school. By the time that quarrel was over Sutro had lost the necessary drive to commence his library. There is no doubt that he meant to give the library to the public. He had discussed three methods of handling the matter of deeding the library to the university with James Taylor Rogers in December 1896. Rogers was secretary to Sutro, and one of his lawyers. After Sutro's death Rogers remembered the conversation and said Sutro had decided to make a will leaving the books to the university and naming the trustees. Rogers was sure that Sutro then made a will.

There were many reasons why the old 1882 will was out-moded. Many of the persons mentioned in it were dead, including the one who was to receive the largest specific bequest — Mrs. Allen. Emma Sutro Merritt was still her father's chief ally and would certainly inherit the papers; Rosa Victoria was happily married to Pio Morbio and living in San Francisco. Katie had married a Professor Nussbaum and lived in Germany. Of the girls only Clara remained at home unmarried. The two boys had never been much like their father, but at least Charles was devoted to him.

Sutro had spent little money on his own home at the Heights and kept Arcadia simple in the extreme, but during the last of his two years as Mayor there was an elegant home on the northeast corner of Steiner and Clay streets about which neighbors were gossiping. The neighbors wondered about Mrs. Kluge, who lived there with her two children. They thought it remarkable that Mrs. Kluge mixed with no one, yet received visits from the Mayor nearly every day. The children said they were close relatives of the Sutros. Later Mrs. Kluge had a great deal to say to newspapermen about a will she was certain Sutro had made.

Although the library was always at the top of his list of unfinished business, Sutro managed to cross off a few of the other items. The railroad monopoly granted a five-cent fare five days before the election in which Sutro became Mayor. Sutro did not trust the railroad management, however, and continued work on his own street railway. Its completion in March of 1896 made the single fare doubly sure. The cars of the first train were painted red, white and gold; flags and bunting draped not only the cars but houses along the route. The magnificent Sutro Baths had opened one week previous, so two of Sutro's major promises had become realities. But in spite of such great public contributions, a year in the office of mayor had amply demonstrated that Sutro was too ill for the job and unsuited for it by temperament. As the end of his two-year term approached no one asked him to run again.

He entertained again at the Heights on New Year's Day, 1897. He knew it was going to be a good year for him because he would continue as Mayor of San Francisco for less than a week. The exhaustion which had sent him to Arcadia leaving the business of the city in other hands was gone and in a genial frame of mind he said: "What have I accomplished as Mayor? Very little. The Mayor is little more than a figure-head." He knew exactly where he had failed. "I have always been master of a situation; I have always had a number of men under my employ, and they did as I told them. I could not manage the politicians."

Sutro happily turned over the responsibilities of office to his able successor, Mayor James Phelan. A few days later Sutro had the great satisfaction of learning of the final defeat of the Funding Bill. The Governor of California, James H. Budd, attached so much importance to it that he proclaimed a one-day public holiday for Saturday, January 16.

Sutro was now back at the Heights and well pleased with his home overlooking the sea. He wished to spend the remainder of his days here close to his beloved seals. He liked to wander in his gardens and watch the fog roll in. His children watched him carefully knowing that he had been worn out by the annoyances of public life, and that diabetes had caused a marked lessening of his physical strength. They also feared that his mind was weakening faster than his sturdy physique.

Adolph Sutro was now in his late sixties and had accomplished more than most men could have done in a hundred years. Born into a rich family, he had seen his own financial pendulum swing many times. Denied a thorough education, he had never ceased reading and learning. Although he had often been far away from his mother, brothers, and sisters, he had maintained contact with them. Although he and his wife were formally separated, he had been able to share with her the upbringing of their children. He had dreamed of a four-mile tunnel to drain the mines of the Comstock Lode. Despite the organized resistance of a most powerful and wealthy interest group the tunnel had been completed.

His attention shifted to San Francisco and he affirmed his great faith in the city's future. This was not mere rhetoric, for he risked his fortune by investing nearly all of it in San Francisco real estate. His judgment was vindicated and the rewards were sweet. He succeeded in parlaying less than a million dollars into five, ten, perhaps twenty times as much.

But he was no absentee landlord; he had invested more than money. He had invested his time, his thoughts, his very life in the welfare of the people of San Francisco. The red-headed beggar on crutches, the dilapidated-looking widow, and the promising student were as comfortable in his presence as presidents and millionaires. Behind a rather formidable exterior beat an over-generous heart. Quick to become angry over the squandering of a dime, he had poured forth his greatest wrath at a corporation which demanded an extra ten cents from the working man. He was especially angry at an economic system which failed to provide a willing man with work.

Only a year after Sutro left public office his six children had to petition for the appointment of a guardian for their father. The court appointed Emma, his favorite daughter and the one who knew the most about his affairs. She was also an able physician and business woman and was considered best suited to be his guardian and in possession of all his papers, legal and otherwise.

The mind that had conceived and built a great tunnel was legally dead. It was a sad ending, for the physical body lingered on. One month later a newspaper reporter interviewed Mrs. Kluge and published her story, but the wasted body at the Heights was unaware of it. Clara and Charles were living at the Heights and took turns sitting at their father's bedside. There had always been a good staff at the Heights and to it were added several nurses. All seemed to be going well when one day Emma strode into the sickroom and announced that she was taking her father by ambulance to her apartment immediately. Clara and Charles remonstrated to no avail.

The ambulance attendants came in, rolled the feeble old patriarch into coverings and carried him to the porch. Clara dashed for the ambulance, grabbed the whip, and lashed the horses. She hoped that they would panic, overturn the ambulance and give her time to summon help and deflect the determined Emma. The horses merely bolted and were soon caught, so Adolph Sutro and Emma proceeded to the daughter's apartment.

Later Emma gave a variety of reasons for this move. She said that the Heights would only remind her father of his many battles waged there. He would, she thought, relive the problems of the sea wall, the burning of Cliff House, the Funding Bill, the five-cent fare, and his mayoralty. Another time she said he needed to be nearer medical assistance and that when he was at the Heights he liked to wander around the garden and refused to return to the house at rest time. She felt it was too exhausting for him to put up a fight and stay outdoors and finally be obliged to give in and be returned to the house.

None of these arguments seems very convincing. The Heights was the scene of many of Sutro's labors, but also of many joys. If he was going to relive his struggle with the Octopus, he might also relive his breakfast with President Harrison, his success in having the seals protected, and his successful introduction of tropical trees, shrubs, and flowers. As for doctors, they had been coming to the Heights for a long time.

Public sentiment, the newspapers, and the other children were against both the manner in which Emma moved her father and the move itself. Had she said "I am a doctor and I know this is the correct thing to do" and refrained from further comment, there would have been less room for conjecture. By giving such varied and not entirely logical reasons, she leaves the reader of the newspaper accounts wondering if perhaps she had some reason she was unwilling to disclose. If so, the secret died with her.

Adolph Sutro was only sixty-eight years old, but his strength had been used up in a long series of struggles. His younger brothers Otto and Emil were both dead as were his cousins Gustav Sutro and Bernard Frankenheimer. Adolph's powerful body remained alive but God in His infinite mercy bestowed the blessing of senile dementia.

Sutro thought he was back at the Heights. He could not see the terrible commotion that was going on there. He did not know that the children were back in court now fighting Emma's guardianship. He was oblivious to the newspaper reporters who were denied any statements about his health, and of course he could not know anything about the long and involved litigation which would follow his death. Many persons would assert that there was a recent will. Perhaps Adolph never did write a new will, even though he had discussed the possibility with many people, especially his lawyers. Perhaps he had tried to set straight his vast quantity of papers, and in the way of elderly people whose minds are failing, he destroyed the new will thinking it was the old one. Perhaps he had pondered over it so long he deemed it written when actually he had not reduced it to words on paper. There are dozens of possibilities but no positive evidence, and only the outmoded will of 1882 could be produced. He would never know how the family fought Emma, Emma fought the lawyers, and Mrs. Kluge would fight all of them.

Sutro was blessed by never dreaming that all of the things he had so proudly named "Sutro" would seem to be pursued by a jinx. Guided by this evil influence the city would virtually abandon his Statue of Liberty to vandalism. Worse than that, instead of revering his beautiful Heights the city would tear down the house and let the gardens deteriorate. Even his precious library was destined to suffer partial destruction in the fire of 1906. How could anyone have guessed that in another sixty years the only monument existing in the way Sutro had conceived it would be the Medical Center, which was never named for his family? Adolph would have applauded his children's fidelity in giving his depleted but still remarkable library to the state of California, but would have had to live another sixty-two years to see it housed beautifully and with due respect for the care and use of the golconda of treasures it contains.

Such a look into the future is accorded no man, and in the case of Adolph Sutro it was a blessing. He looked through the window of Emma's apartment on Van Ness Avenue and thought he saw the fog roll in on the Heights; he thought he heard the barking of his beloved seals.

Early in the morning of August 8, 1898, Emma finally agreed to allow her father to return to Sutro Heights; he had died a few hours before. The children announced that they wanted a simple funeral and except for a vast number of floral pieces it was certainly simple. Rabbi Jacob Nieto joined the family at the Heights at 10 a.m. on August 10. He read a Hebrew psalm and made a short address. Then the mourners filled twelve carriages waiting behind the hearse and proceeded to the crematory at Odd Fellows' Cemetery.

A man who during his life was a national figure, millionaire, mayor, and public benefactor could expect a different kind of ending. He could hope the newspapers would comment more on his good deeds than on old scandals, promises, and mistakes. He would certainly expect his children would remember to find pall-bearers among his devoted employees even if he did not have enough close friends to carry the casket; they left the job for the undertaker's assistants. Adolph Sutro had never had the time or the interest to be concerned with anything so trivial as his own funeral, but he would have liked the setting that August day. The fog-shrouded gardens of Sutro Heights were his temple and the plaintive barking of the seals his funeral dirge.

The following paragraphs list the most important references and sources for each chapter in this book. Specific documentation for Sutro and his career to 1880 will also be found in Robert Ernest Stewart, Jr., "Adolph Sutro: A Study of His Early Career" (Unpublished Ph. D. dissertation, Dept. of History, University of California, Berkeley, 1958). The following notes include a few sources not consulted in preparing the dissertation and they also indicate the sources used for Sutro's life after 1880.

CHAPTER I. HO FOR WASHOE!

Sutro's own account of his trip to Washoe and return was published in the San Francisco *Daily Alta California* in three installments on April 11, 13, and 14. It has also been reprinted as the book by Adolph Sutro, *A Trip to Washoe* (San Francisco: White Knight Press, 1942). Facts on the discovery of Comstock silver and Virginia in 1859 and 1860 will be found in Chapters 3 and 4 of Eliot Lord, *Comstock Mining and Miners* (1883; reissued 1959 by Howell-North Books, Berkeley, Calif.).

CHAPTER II. FROM PRUSSIA TO CALIFORNIA

The principal source for the boyhood and youth of Adolph Sutro is the biographical narrative in the collection of typed sheets (originals or carbons) herein referred to as the "Lewis transcripts." They are in the possession of the authors through the kindness of their former owner, Oscar Lewis of San Francisco. This collection of a thousand or more sheets consists mainly of copies of manuscripts and other primary sources and was prepared under the direction of Sutro's daughter, Emma Sutro Merritt. Where it has been possible to compare these copies with original materials the copies have been found accurate. Emma compiled these materials as the basis for a biography of her father which was completed but never released. More than a hundred pages in this Lewis collection are continuous portions of a detailed biographical narrative, which is cited hereinafter as "biographical narrative, Lewis transcripts." It is also the principal

[215]

source for Sutro's life in Memel and the decision to leave for America. A few facts were gleaned from the shorter narrative in "Autobiographical Manuscript Folders, Adolph Sutro. Folder 4" at Bancroft Library, University of California, Berkeley. This interview is cited hereinafter as "Sutro dictation (1)," Bancroft Lib. "My son, live ever near to nature's heart" is from the "Unsworth Memoir," Part II, p. 15, at Sutro Branch, California State Library, San Francisco. For full citation see notes for Chapter XVI.

CHAPTER III.   FIRST YEAR IN THE NEW WORLD

Principal source for this chapter is biographical narrative, pp. 23-67, "Lewis transcripts." Also see "Sutro dictation (1)," pp. 11-12, Bancroft Lib. Some facts on the Isthmus crossing are from John Haskell Kemble, *The Panama Route, 1848-1869* ("University of California Publications in History," XXIX [Berkeley: University of California Press, 1943]), pp. 166-178. Appendix I has technical data on the *Cherokee* and the *California* and many other steamships. The *Gulnare* story is from the S. F. *California Courier*, Nov. 22, 1850, p. 3. The S. F. *Pacific News*, Nov. 22, 1850, p. 2, tells of picking up six survivors of the French expedition. For details on that episode see William Miles, *Journal of the Sufferings and Hardships of Capt. Parker H. French's Overland Expedition to California* (Chambersburg, Pa., 1851). Some facts on Stockton are from George H. Tinkham, *A History of Stockton* (San Francisco, 1880) and Col. F. T. Gilbert, *History of San Joaquin County, California, with Illustrations* (Oakland, Calif.: Thompson & West, 1879). The latter is notable for its wealth of illustrations. A detailed account of Charles M. Weber's life prior to the gold rush is in Harry D. Hubbard, *Building the Heart of an Empire* (Boston: Meador Publishing Co., 1938), pp. 65-99. A few facts are from the 1851 and 1852 files of the Stockton *Journal*.

CHAPTER IV.   THE TOBACCONIST-ENGINEER

Theo. Barry and B. A. Patten, *San Francisco, California, 1850* (1873; reissued 1947 by Biobooks, Oakland, Calif.) contains a copy of the official city map drawn Jan. 15, 1851, which shows Long Wharf. Again the principal source for Sutro in this period is biog. narr., "Lewis transcripts." The smoking Turk story is

[216]

from the S. F. *Bulletin,* Feb. 7, 1857, p. 4, col. 1. The knifing attack is from the S. F. *Daily Alta,* March 28, 1855, p. 2. Some facts are from "Sutro dictation (1)," Bancroft Lib., and from "Autobiographical Manuscript Folders, Adolph Sutro, Folder 5," Bancroft Lib. Folder 5 will be referred to hereinafter as "Sutro dictation (2)," Bancroft Lib. The year of Adolph's marriage is given in biog. narr., p. 77, "Lewis transcripts" as 1855 but the information card at California State Library filled out in 1911 by Emma says 1856. A popular sketch of the first Fraser River gold rush is in Bruce Hutchinson, *The Fraser* ("Rivers of America" series [New York: Rinehart & Co., 1950]), pp. 53-68. "Adolph Sutro, Receipt Book," California State Lib., Sacramento, contains receipts issued by others to the Sutros in the period April 13, 1860 to March 3, 1862. Adolph's two letters to the S. F. *Bulletin* were published May 16 and 19, 1860. The Sutro-Randohr agreement is in "Sutro Correspondence — I," Bancroft Lib. The Sutro Mill is described in [Myron Angel, ed.], *History of Nevada* (Oakland, Calif.: Thompson & West, 1882; reissued 1958 by Howell-North Books, Berkeley, Calif.), p. 502, and in J. Wells Kelly, *Second Directory of Nevada Territory* (Virginia, 1863), pp. 383-4. The statement by Sutro is in "Sutro dictation (2)," pp. 1-2, Bancroft Lib. The notebook containing assays is at the California Historical Society, San Francisco. The Mark Twain quotation is attributed to the Virginia City *Territorial Enterprise* and is from C. B. Glasscock, *The Big Bonanza: The Story of the Comstock Lode* (Indianapolis, 1931), pp. 122-23. The burning of the Sutro Mill is noted in Angel, *History of Nevada,* p. 502.

CHAPTER V.   THE HIGH ROAD TO SUCCESS

Sutro is listed as a member of the Washoe Stock and Exchange Board in Charles Collins, *Mercantile Guide and Directory for Virginia City, Gold Hill, Silver City, and American City* (Virginia, 1864-65), p. 37. Stock quotations for the Sutro Mine are in Gold Hill *News,* May 3, 1864, p. 3; location of the mine is shown on 1866 map of Sutro Tunnel and Comstock Lode drawn by Chas. F. Hoffmann, San Francisco. The best estimates of Comstock production of bullion are in Grant H. Smith, *History of the Comstock Lode, 1850-1920* (Reno: University of Nevada, State Bureau of Mines, 1943). Smith is the careful scholar who estimated that legal costs were one-fifth the product of the mines. Many of the facts on Virginia City in 1864 are from Charles Collins, *Mercantile Guide and Directory* (1864-65). For Lincoln and statehood see F. Lauriston Bullard, "Abraham Lincoln and the Statehood of Nevada," *American Bar Association Journal,* XXVI (1940), 210-13, 313-17. Most entertaining on Ralston and on Sharon is the sometimes inaccurate volume by George D. Lyman, *Ralston's Ring: California Plunders the Comstock Lode* (New York: Scribner's, 1937). For a balanced summary on these men see Grant H. Smith, *History of the Comstock Lode.* Sutro's Nevada franchise is in *Nevada Statutes* (1864-65), Chap. 26. The phrase "a few thinking men" is from pp. 866-67 in *Sutro Tunnel, 1872.* Full title is *Report of Commissioners and Evidence Taken by the House Committee on Mines and Mining in Regard to the Sutro Tunnel* (Washington, 1872). Whole volume cited hereinafter as *Sutro Tunnel, 1872.* Pages 864-951 contain an autobiographical speech made by Sutro before the committee and often published separately as Adolph Sutro, *Closing Argument.* References to this speech cited hereinafter as "Sutro, *Closing Argument.*" The notebook with directors' names is also at the California Historical Society. The 1865 pamphlet is Adolph Sutro, *The Advantages and Necessity of a Deep Drain Tunnel for the Great Comstock Ledge* (San Francisco, 1865). The legal history of the Nevada association of individuals can be found in an advertisement of the Sutro Tunnel Company in Virginia City *Territorial Enterprise,* Oct. 6, 1869, p. 1. The reference to parchment "to last a great many years" is from Sutro, *Closing Argument,* p. 868. Copies of the agreements with the mining companies can be found in Adolph Sutro, *The Mineral Resources of the United States* (Baltimore, 1868), pp. 173-88. Richthofen report is cited in bibliography under "Richthofen, Ferdinand." For the text of Ralston letter to Oriental Bank Corp. see Sutro, *Closing Argument,* p. 869. For the Sutro Tunnel Act see *U. S. Statutes at Large* (1866), chap. 244 (pp. 242-43). The New York pamphlet is Adolph Sutro, *The Sutro Tunnel* (New York, 1866). The two letters of Senator Stewart to Huntington and Bennett are among the "Cavalier Autographs" in the possession of Mr. William Cavalier, Jr., of Oakland, Calif. For the text of the letter of the Eastern financiers and all signatures see *Sutro Tunnel, 1872,* p. 53. For the two resolutions of the Nevada legislature see *Nevada Statutes* (1867), pp. 147-48. The report of the Mechanics' Institute is in A. Sutro, *Mineral Resources of the U. S.,* pp. 143-68. Quotation on "fair prospect of raising $1,000,000 in San Francisco" is from Sutro's *Closing Argument,* p. 873.

CHAPTER VI

"BUT NOW COMMENCED THE TUG OF WAR"

The title quotation and "full road to success" are from *Sutro Tunnel, 1872,* p. 54. On the same page are Sutro's touching account of his humiliation and mention of his "sacred vow." "An absconding bank clerk" is on page 55. For Aron's timely support see Joseph Aron, *The History of a Great Work and of an Honest Miner* (Paris, 1892), pp. 6, 7, 9, 16, 18, 19, 21. The original petition sheets signed by a thousand persons are in the possession of Mr. John H. Thies of Oakland, Calif. For Nye letter and Bismarck note see Senator Nye to Sutro, July 18, 1867, and Graf von Bismarck to Sutro, Oct. 28, 1867. Both are in "Sutro Correspondence — I," Bancroft Lib. Mark Twain's letter to the *Alta* was published on Jan. 21, 1868. Adolph Sutro, *Mineral Resources of the United States* (Baltimore, 1868) has already been cited. Quotation on "votes enough to pass" is from Sutro to Aron, May 15, 1868, in Aron, *Great Work,* p. 7. For Sutro's School of Mines proposal see *U. S. 40th Congress,* 3d sess., House Resolution 1657 (Jan. 11, 1869), "A Bill to Aid in Ascertaining the Value of Public Lands Containing Mineral Lodes, and for the Endowment of a National School of Mines," pp. 5-6. Also see substitute bill titled "Amendment" (Jan. 20, 1869), pp. 5-6. For Grant's inaugural address see *U. S. 41st Congress,* 1st sess., Senate Journal (1869), pp. 6-7.

CHAPTER VII. RALLY AT PIPER'S OPERA HOUSE

A convenient account of the Yellow Jacket fire is in C. B. Glasscock, *The Big Bonanza,* pp. 186-94. For the V. & T. Railroad see Lucius Beebe and Charles Clegg, *Steamcars to the Comstock* (2d rev. ed.; Berkeley, Howell-North Books, 1957) and Chap. 3 of Gilbert H. Kneiss, *Bonanza Railroads* (3d ed.; Stanford, Calif.: Stanford Univ. Press, 1946). The phrases "near fainting" and "subscribed $50,000 then" are from Sutro's *Closing Argument,* pp. 887-88. The joint union meeting of August 25 and its subscription of $50,000 are recorded in the Carson *Daily Appeal,* Aug. 29, 1869. For Julian's proposed visit see the *Territorial Enterprise,* Aug. 20 and 21, 1869. For the text of Sutro's speech at Piper's Opera House see *Sutro Tunnel, 1872,* pp. 48-66. The estimate of two hours is from the *Territorial Enterprise,* Sept. 21, 1869, p. 2

CHAPTER VIII. THE "FIRST PICK"

Bethel's telegram is in biog. narr., Chap. 6, p. 3, "Lewis transcripts." The account of the "first pick" ceremony is based on *ibid.*, pp. 1-5, and the Carson *Daily Appeal,* Oct. 21, 1869. Construction in late 1869 is based on biog. narr., Chap. 7, pp. 1-5, "Lewis transcripts." The medical meeting is from Chap. 25, "Medical History," by Henry Bergstein, M. D., in Sam P. Davis, ed., *History of Nevada* (1913), I. Original trustees of the Sutro Tunnel Co. (of Calif.) are listed in *Mining and Scientific Press* (San Francisco), XIX (Dec. 4, 1869), 361. For President Merritt see Henning Koford, *Dr. Samuel Merritt, His Life and Achievements* (Oakland, 1937). For the division of the 1,200,000 shares upon incorporation see *McCalmont v. Sutro Tunnel Co.* (Case 454), "Depositions," pp. 225-7, testimony given in 1887 and based on company records. These manuscript materials located in the U. S. District Court at Carson City are voluminous and valuable. For Sutro's lack of salary but privilege of drawing out money see *ibid.*, "Testimony," vol. 1, pp. 397-402. The Greeley change is based on biog. narr., "Lewis transcripts."

CHAPTER IX.
CONGRESS CREATES A TUNNEL COMMISSION

For Bill 1179 see Sutro's *Closing Argument,* pp. 889-90, and the Virginia City *Daily Independent,* Supplement, Oct. 31, 1874, p. 1, col. 5. For the ditch and canal bill see *ibid.*, cols. 5-6, and *The Sutro Tunnel in Congress* (n. p., n. d.), p. 30. For the expected $3,000,000 loan from France see Sutro's *Closing Argument,* p. 891. For George T. Coulter and the Sierra Buttes mine see W. Turrentine Jackson, "Lewis Richard Price, British Mining Entrepreneur and Traveler in California," *Pacific Historical Review,* XXIX (Nov., 1960), 337-48. For Coulter's position in London see Lewis R. Price to J. W. Gashwiler, Oct. 19, 1871. Coulter's enthusiasm for the Sutro Tunnel project is recorded in letters to Lewis R. Price of Oct. 17, 1871, and Aug. 29, 1872. The Price Papers are in the County Record Office, Shrewsbury, England, and many of them have been microfilmed for Professor W. Turrentine Jackson, University of California, Davis, who kindly loaned the reels to us. They are cited hereinafter as "Price Papers." For the "good will" deposit see Aron, *Great Work,* pp. 19-20, incl. Coulter letter to Sutro of Apr. 27, 1870. For "huckstered about too long" see Sutro to Aron, May 28, 1871, in *ibid.*,

p. 22. For Price, Coulter, and Sutro in New York see W. Turrentine Jackson, "Journal of Lewis Richard Price," *Pacific Historian,* IV (Aug., 1960), 97-99. For a biog. sketch of Wesley Newcomb see *Appleton's Annual Cyclopedia, 1892. Sutro Tunnel, 1872* is a storehouse of information on the tunnel investigation and the later cross-examination of the commissioners. "This is a dry country" and "They (the miners) didn't object" are from pages 27 and 182. "Glad enough to get out" and "the shaft is out of order" are from pages 183 and 182. The account of Coulter and Price at the Comstock and quotations from Price are from W. T. Jackson, "Journal of L. R. Price," *Pacific Historian,* IV (Aug., 1960), 110-11. Coulter's purchase of stock before McCalmonts came in is based on the testimony of Coulter in *McCalmont v. Sutro Tunnel Co.,* "Depositions," p. 64. Coulter's statement that he did not invite Sutro to England is in Coulter to Price, Aug. 26, 1871, "Price Papers." For Coulter's stock commission of one share for four see Sutro to Aron, July 8, 1871, in Aron, *Great Work,* p. 23. Coulter's refusal to produce his correspondence is in *McCalmont v. Sutro Tunnel Co.,* "Depositions," after p. 60. The $650,000 in gold coin is in Sutro's *Closing Argument,* p. 895. "On the high road to success" is from Sutro to Aron, Sept. 23, 1871, in Aron, *Great Work,* p. 23. For the report of the Sutro Tunnel Commission see *Sutro Tunnel, 1872,* pp. 3-23. "Did not complain" quotation is from p. 7. "Rascalities of the bank ring" is from Sutro's *Closing Argument,* p 898. For a transcript of the hearings in which the commissioners were questioned see *Sutro Tunnel, 1872,* pp. 1-951. For the report of the committee and its bill see *ibid.,* pp. 955-65.

CHAPTER X. HE WAS THE COMPANY

Title quotation is from testimony given in 1887 by Secretary Pelham W. Ames in *McCalmont v. Sutro Tunnel Co.,* "Testimony," vol. 1, p. 400. Ames had served as Secretary since Aug. 2, 1872, according to company records cited in *Symmes v. Union Trust Co.* (Case 527), "Testimony for respondents," vol. 3, p. 744. The manuscript records of this lawsuit tried in 1891 are of value and are also located at the U. S. District Court at Carson City. For a sketch of J. H. Riley written before his fatal illness see the chapter titled "Riley — Newspaper Correspondent," in Samuel L. Clemens, *Sketches New and Old* (New York, 1875). Riley's clerkship and forwarding of letters are referred to in letters from Riley to Sutro in the MSS formerly owned by Mr. Dudley Gordon of Los Angeles and now at the California Historical Society, San Francisco. Copies of letters between Sutro and Clemens are in "Lewis transcripts"; dates range from June 6 to June 30, 1872. The tunnel appears in *Roughing It* on p. 382. President Grant's attendance is noted in Sutro to McCalmont Bros., April 30, 1874, p. 7, "Lewis transcripts." For "amusement, and not a little instruction" see Wesley Newcomb to Adolph Sutro, March 8, 1872, in collection of original letters in the possession of the authors. Referred to hereinafter as "Stewart MSS." Facts on the four shafts are from Sutro Tunnel Co., *Report of the Superintendent for the Three Months Preceding March 1, 1872* (Washington, 1872), pp. 3, 24-6. The projector referred to the tunnel mules in Adolph Sutro, *The Sutro Tunnel: An Address Before the Bullion Club, November 6th, 1879* (New York, n. d.), p. 11. Bethel's words ending "I have no use for this thing" are from Bethel to Sutro, Jan. 4, 1872, "Lewis transcripts." Quotation "It cannot be had from me — Coulter" is from Coulter to Sutro, July 25, 1872, "Thies MSS.," in possession of Mr. John H. Thies of Oakland, Calif. Facts on Col. Brush and words "just to look into things" are from *McCalmont v. Sutro Tunnel Co.*, "Depositions," pp. 56-7. "A very faithful laborer" is from Ames to Aron, January, 1873, pp. 2-4, "Lewis transcripts."

CHAPTER XI. SUPERINTENDENT IN ABSENTIA

Quotation on "the severe crisis through which New York is at present passing" is from J. & W. Seligman, New York, to Sutro (at London), Nov. 13, 1873, "Thies MSS." Quotations from Robert McCalmont are from Aron, *Great Work*, p. E. For text of Benjamin's report see "F. A. Benjamin, Asst. General Supt., to President and Board of Trustees of the Sutro Tunnel Co., Feb. 28, 1874, Report," p. 3. This manuscript (probably a press copy) is among the "Stanford Univ. MSS" pertaining to Sutro in the Jackson Library of Business at that university. For letter quotation see Benjamin to Sutro, July 7, 1874, p. 1, "Lewis transcripts." "You ought to be here" is from C. W. Kendall to Sutro, Jan. 31, 1874, "Thies MSS." The agreement Aron copied is in Adolph Sutro, *The California Monopolists Against the Sutro Tunnel* (Washington, 1874). The Supplement of the Virginia City *Daily Independent* containing Sutro's speech is dated Oct. 31, 1874. Printed invitation to creditors' meeting is in "Ephemera, Adolph Sutro Papers," Huntington Library, San Marino, Calif.

CHAPTER XII.

THE GENERAL SUPERINTENDENT KEEPS INFORMED

For a collective biography of Mackay, Fair, Flood, and O'Brien see Oscar Lewis, *Silver Kings* (New York, 1947). For a convenient account of the closing of the Bank of California see Chaps. 35 and 37 of G. D. Lyman, *Ralston's Ring*. For the financial relationship of Adolph Sutro and the Sutro Tunnel Company see *McCalmont v. Sutro Tunnel Co.*, "Testimony," vol. 1, Ames, pp. 397-404, 431-33. "Flame of a blow-pipe" is from William Wright [pseud., Dan de Quille], *The Big Bonanza* (New York: Knopf, 1947), p. 451, orig. published in 1876. Quotation by Young is from Frank S. Young to Sutro, Aug. 9, 1876, "Lewis transcripts." Hanmore quote is from H. B. Hanmore to Sutro, Feb. 17, 1876, *ibid.* Rammelkamp quotations are from Rammelkamp to Sutro, July 13 and Aug. 13, 1876, "Stewart MSS." Next quotations are from H. L. Foreman to Sutro, Dec. 1, 1876, "Lewis transcripts," Foreman to Sutro, Dec. 2, 1876, "Thies MSS," and R. S. Raw to Sutro, Dec. 3, 1876, "Thies MSS." Bluett quote is from Bluett (per J. F. B.) to Sutro, Jan. 22, 1877, "Lewis transcripts." References to the Rammelkamp-Doherty marriage are from the Sutro (Nev.) *Independent*, Dec. 30, 1876, p. 3. Quotation "I am in tears" is from Hugo to Adolph Sutro, Aug. 14, 1869, "Thies MSS." "You are a brave man" is from Hugo to Adolph Sutro, June 9, 1872, "Lewis transcripts." Pleas for a "warm expression of sympathy" and "send your substitute" are from Hugo to A. Sutro, June 20, 1872, "Stewart MSS." "You need not answer this unless" and quotation condemning "a confounded scribble" are from letter of June 9, 1872, "Lewis transcripts." "I will go through" is from Bluett (per J. F. Banks) to Sutro, May 24, 1877, *ibid.* "I calculated to do just as you direct" is from Bluett (per Young) to Sutro, Oct. 15, 1877, *ibid.* Sheldon quotation is from Sheldon to Sutro, Nov. 19, 1877, "Thies MSS."

CHAPTER XIII. THE GREAT WORK IS FINISHED

"It's a good thing to have a door to your house" is from the *Lyon County Times* (Dayton, Nev.), July 13, as quoted in the Sutro *Independent*, July 20, 1878, p. 2. For the tribute to Aron see Adolph Sutro, *Closing Argument*, p. 943. Savage-Tunnel dialogue and quotes "blinding rush of smoke" and "these ladies endured the heat and foul air" are from the Virginia City *Chronicle*, as quoted in the Sutro *Independent*, July 13, 1878, p. 3. Sutro's comments on his rashness in going into the Savage connection so soon are in A. Sutro to P. W. Ames, July 10, 1878, in "Sutro Letterbooks," Bancroft Library. This collection of over 50 volumes is mainly press copies of Sutro correspondence ranging in dates from 1870 to 1890. "Three groans for the directors" and "the party returned overland" are from the Sutro *Independent*, July 13, 1878, p. 3. "Other sources of enjoyment not generally enjoyed by prisoners" is from the Sutro *Independent*, Feb. 8, 1879. Ames' references to seed orders and comments on frogs are from P. W. Ames to A. Sutro, Mar. 19 and Apr. 30, 1878, "Stewart MSS." "It Is Finished" is from the Sutro *Independent* for June 30, 1879.

CHAPTER XIV.   EXIT THE GENERAL SUPERINTENDENT

The phrase "$90,000 diamond widow" is from the San Francisco *Examiner*, Aug. 13, 1898, p. 8. Contemporary sources for the Mrs. Allen incident are the July 9, 1879, issues of the San Francisco newspapers — *Chronicle, Daily Alta California*, and *Daily Stock Report*. For ex-President Grant's visit see Sutro *Independent*, Nov. 3, 1879, p. 3, cols. 3-4. Clara Rammelkamp's presence at the Grant breakfast is from Clara Rammelkamp Masterson as related to Mrs. Clara Beatty in Nov., 1957. Leah's departure from Sutro, Nevada, is in the Sutro *Independent*, Nov. 3, 1879, p. 3, col. 2. Adolph purchased the San Francisco home for Leah on Sept. 22, 1879, according to Adolph Sutro Safe Book, "Stanford Univ. MSS." For Sutro's principal mission see board meeting of Nov. 11, 1878, in *Symmes v. Union Trust Co.* (Case 527), "Testimony for Respondents," vol. 3, pp. 933-35. For "Aron admits his error" see P. W. Ames, Secretary of Sutro Tunnel Co., to A. Sutro, Oct. 13, 1879, "Stewart MSS." "No further relations with Mr. Aron" is in *ibid.*, Nov. 11. "That arch fiend" is from Coulter to Price, Sept. 30, 1879, "Price Papers." For Robert McCalmont's paralytic stroke see *ibid.*, Nov. 20, 1878, and Aug. 5, 1879. "Shoulder to the wheel" is from original letter, McCalmont Bros. to A. Sutro, July 17, 1879, in "Sutro Letterbook no. 21," Bancroft Library. Speech is in A. Sutro, *Address before the Bullion Club, Nov. 6, 1879* (New York, n. d.). The $5,000,000 figure is from the semi-official sketch by Eugenia K. Holmes, *Adolph Sutro* (San Francisco, 1895), p. 28. The unfriendly rumor that Sutro sold his tunnel stock to friends is printed in C. C. Goodwin, *As I*

Remember Them (Salt Lake City, 1913), pp. 243-4. It is refuted by the Edward Adams letters cited below. The charge of misappropriating 300,000 shares is in J. Aron, *Great Work*, p. 18 and note. It is refuted by company records cited under Chap. VIII. Theodore Sutro was close to Aron for over a year [*Symmes v. Union Trust Co.* (Case 527), "Respondent's Proofs," vol. 4, pp. 1791-96] and Theodore thought that there might be something to Aron's charge that some subscribers to the Nevada association had been defrauded. Later, when Theodore was president of the successor tunnel company, he examined all relevant company records and failed to find any irregularities "even in the remotest degree." See *ibid.*, pp. 1229-30. For transfer of shares to New York see Ames to Sutro, Oct. 21 to Nov. 22, 1879, "Stewart MSS." For the sale of Sutro's stock see the undated account of Sutro with Winslow, Lanier & Co. and letters of Edward D. Adams to A. Sutro, "Thies MSS." Key letters are dated Feb. 2, March 27, and May 11, 1880. Sutro's last report as General Superintendent is in the Sutro *Independent*, March 22, 1880, p. 3. "Immensely profitable" quotation is from "Adolph Sutro," *Dictionary of American Biography*, XVIII, 224. For the compromise accepted by the McCalmont firm see *Symmes v. Union Trust Co.* (Case 527), "Synopsis of the Answer of the Comstock Tunnel Co.," p. 31.

CHAPTER XV. A MAN IN SEARCH OF A CAUSE

A description of the property and facts on the trust fund and allowances paid are from Statements of E. J. Moore and W. K. Van Alen, Trustees, for Oct. 31 and Dec. 31, 1880, and Jan. 31, 1883, in "Cavalier Papers." This mass of bills, receipts, etc., is in the possession of Mrs. William Cavalier of Piedmont, California. Article from the *Real Estate Circular* is quoted in San Francisco *Morning Call*, Jan. 3, 1880, p. 1. For a plat of Sutro's Market Street lots see Hicks-Judd Co., *Handy Block Book of San Francisco, 1894*. His properties in Alameda, San Mateo, Napa, and Lake counties are described in the printed record titled "Transcript on Appeal, In the Matter of the Estate of Adolph Sutro, March, 1907," pp. 67-73; hereinafter cited as "Transcript on Appeal, Sutro Estate." For reply to Young see Sutro to Frank S. Young, Oct. 13, 1880, in "Adolph Sutro, Letterbooks," v. 43, pp. 164-68, Bancroft Library. The story of Sutro's unsuccessful try for the Senate in 1880 is from Elko, Nev., *Free Press*, Jan. 16, 1897, in "Adolph Sutro Scrapbooks" at California Historical Society,

San Francisco. His discovery of Sutro Heights is based on various accounts including a newspaper interview of Emma in the San Francisco *Chronicle*, Nov. 19, 1933, p. 6. The date in the latter account has been corrected to 1881 in accordance with the agreement between A. Sutro and S. Tetlow dated March 2, 1881, in Adolph Sutro, Safe Book, Agreements, p. 51 in "Stanford Univ. MSS." August, 1881, deed for part of San Miguel Rancho is in A. Sutro, Deeds, *ibid.* For the 1882 will see "Transcript on Appeal, Sutro Estate," pp. 170-188. Moore and Adamson salaries and kindergarten allowance are from "Cavalier Papers," 1882. Facts on voyage to Orient and Europe are from E. J. Moore and A. Sutro, 1882 letters, "A. Sutro, Personal Material, Autobiographical," Bancroft Library. A brief sketch of Emma Merritt's life is in the interview she gave on her 80th birthday in San Francisco *Chronicle*, Dec. 15, 1936, p. 14. For the 80th birthday celebration of Adolph's mother see program in a Sutro scrapbook at California Historical Society, San Francisco. Letter from Jerusalem is dated Apr. 5, 1884, and is in "Adolph Sutro, Personal Material, Autobiographical," Bancroft Library. Letter from Paris to Charles is dated May 17, 1884, and is in "Lewis transcripts." A good source on Sutro's assembling of the Sutro Library is George Moss' statement of Aug. 30, 1888, in "Sutro Documents," Bancroft Library. The phrase "California Book Man" is from Moss, p. 2. A detailed and scholarly article on the library, its holdings, and its vicissitudes is Richard H. Dillon, "The Sutro Library," *News Notes of California Libraries*, v. 51 (Apr., 1956), pp. 338-52.

CHAPTER XVI. A TUNNEL TO THE SEA

A full and usually accurate source for nearly every statement in Chapters XVI and XVII is a 148-page typescript at Sutro Branch, California State Library, San Francisco. It is titled *Material on Adolph Sutro, Vol. 1.* The authorship is not given but it is the reminiscences of Archibald C. Unsworth, who became Sutro's secretary and traveling companion in 1886; this source will be cited as "Unsworth Memoir." Additional sources and references which should be cited for Chapter XVI include the accurate article by Donald C. Biggs, "Sutro Storms the Heights," *The Pony Express*, XXI (Feb., 1955), 3-6, 11. Layman's early cable railway is sketched in Edgar M. Kahn, *Cable Car Days in San Francisco* (rev. ed.; Stanford, Calif., 1944), pp. 62-63. Quotation "Figures were to be seen . . ." is from the "Lewis transcripts."

The "usually reliable witness" is Unsworth in his "Memoir," Pt. VII, p. 70. Franchise to Gustav Sutro is in San Francisco *Municipal Reports, 1883-84,* Appendix, pp. 138-9. Words from act of Congress granting Seal Rocks are from *ibid., 1886-87,* Appendix, pp. 252-3. For the dedication of the statue see the 30-page booklet *Triumph of Light* (San Francisco, 1888). For the Montgomery Block quarters of the library see Idwal Jones, *Ark of Empire: San Francisco's Montgomery Block* (Doubleday: Garden City, N. Y., 1951), pp. 212-13. The cartoon about rainbow-tinted promises was in the San Francisco *Evening Post,* Oct. 15, 1894, p. 1. For Sutro's plan to sell $100,000 worth of land annually see A. Sutro to Ludwig Sutro, Jan. 3, 1894, in "Adolph Sutro, Personal Material," Bancroft Library. The figure of a quarter of a million dollars for the baths is in the same letter. A detailed description of the Napa County hideaway was published in the magazine *Industry,* no. 86 (Sept., 1895), pp. 515-17. For Sutro's views on religion see "Sutro Dictation (1)," "Sutro Dictation (2)," and "Notes on Character of Adolph Sutro," Bancroft Library. The last-named also contains the quotation referring to Disraeli on page 3. Quotations "Why should they not eat with me?" and "A man has a natural right to work" are from an interview with W. R. H. Adamson and A. C. Unsworth in San Francisco *Examiner,* Aug. 14, 1898, p. 5. The Yucatan incident is from Unsworth and found in *ibid.* For Theodore Sutro's crusade to save the tunnel stockholders see Theodore Sutro *The Sutro Tunnel Co. and the Sutro Tunnel* (New York, 1887). Joseph Aron's two critical pamphlets are *A Great Work* and *A Few Considerations, Respectfully Submitted to the Members of the Bar Associations* [n. p., n. d. (prob. 1893)]. For the judge's opinion see *Symmes v. Union Trust Co.* (Case 527), "Opinion of the Court," esp. pp. 5, 61. For Leah Sutro's death and funeral see San Francisco *Examiner,* Dec. 10, and San Francisco *Call,* Dec. 12, 1893, p. 7. Quotation of Adolph praising Leah is from the *Examiner* cited. Many facts on the street railways of the 1890's are from Bion J. Arnold, *Report on the Improvement and Development of the Transportation Facilities of San Francisco* (1913). See especially "Historical Review," pp. 411-21, map of railways operated, 1893-95, on p. 419, and "family tree" of street railway corporations, p. 320. A wealth of additional facts on the funding bill fight can be found in the Funding Bill scrapbooks at California Historical Society, San Francisco. Envelopes bearing slogans against the funding bill are at Sutro Branch, California State Library, San Francisco.

CHAPTER XVII. LABOR CONQUERS ALL

The "Unsworth Memoir" is a basic source for nearly all of this chapter. Additional sources and references include biographical narrative, "Lewis transcripts" for the breakfast at which Sutro agreed to run for Mayor. For the bills of Drs. Mayer (Jan. 5, $360), Calderón (Jan. 12, $1170), and Herzstein (Jan. 20, $300), see account vouchers, 1894, "Cavalier Papers." The quotation referring to the "collar of the Octopus" is from "Lewis transcripts." For election results see official statement of the Registrar of Voters, San Francisco *Municipal Reports, 1894-95*, p. 56. Mayor Sutro's inaugural address is in *ibid.*, Appendix, pp. 8-13 and in San Francisco *Call*, Jan. 8, 1895, p. 12, with added details. Letters of the Mayor demanding admission of individuals to the city-county hospital are in the Sutro papers at the California Historical Society, San Francisco. "Mayor's power is barely more than . . . his tact" is from San Francisco *Examiner*, Aug. 9, 1898. Statement of J. T. Rogers is in *ibid.*, Aug. 13, 1898, p. 8. For the Sutro Railway see San Francisco *Daily Report*, Jan. 23, 1896, and "Lewis transcripts." Quotation beginning "What have I accomplished as Mayor?" is from San Francisco *Call*, Jan. 2, 1897, p. 10. As to diabetes, laboratory analyses of urine were made frequently between Nov. 1894, and Sept., 1896, and all but seven revealed sugar; see medical reports, 1894, "Cavalier Papers." For the claims of Mrs. Kluge and her two children see the San Francisco *Chronicle*, March 10, pp. 1-2, and March 11, 1898, p. 12, and other San Francisco newspapers; also see San Francisco *Call*, Jan. 11, 1900, p. 1. In 1960 the Sutro Library obtained excellent quarters offered by the University of San Francisco on a long-term, no rent basis. The space is physically separate from the University library, is open to the public, and is operated by the California State Library. For Sutro's death and funeral see newspapers of Aug. 8-11, 1898. A full page of illustrations and reminiscences of Sutro appeared in the San Francisco *Examiner*, Aug. 14, 1898, p. 5.

~~~ BIBLIOGRAPHY ~~~

MANUSCRIPTS AND PUBLIC DOCUMENTS

Bancroft Library, University of California, Berkeley, has perhaps half of Adolph Sutro's voluminous papers.

California Historical Society, San Francisco, is also rich in Sutro papers, especially scrapbooks.

California State Library, Sacramento, has some Sutro MSS.

Cavalier Autographs. A collection of autographs in the possession of Mr. William Cavalier, Jr., of Oakland, Calif.

Cavalier Papers. A collection of some of Sutro's business papers in the possession of Mrs. William Cavalier of Piedmont, Calif.

Huntington Library, San Marino, Calif., has a few Sutro MSS.

Lewis transcripts. *See* "Notes – Chapter I."

Lord, Eliot. *Comstock Mining and Miners.* (U. S. Geological Survey, Monograph IV. U.S. 47th Cong., 1st sess., H.R. Misc. Doc. 51, Vol. 16.) Washington, 1881. Reissued 1959 by Howell-North Books, Berkeley, Calif.

McCalmont v. Sutro Tunnel Co. (Case 454). Foreclosure suit circa 1887 in U.S. District Court, Carson City, Nev.

Nevada. *Statutes, 1864-65.*

————. *Statutes, 1867.*

Price Papers. County Record Office, Shrewsbury, England. *See* "Notes – Chapter IX."

San Francisco *Municipal Reports, 1883-84.*

————. *Municipal Reports, 1894-95.*

Stanford Univ. MSS. A collection of Sutro manuscripts in the Jackson Library of Business, Stanford University.

Sutro Tunnel, 1872. See U.S. Cong. H.R. Com. on Mines and Mining, *Report of Commissioners, 1872.*

Symmes v. Union Trust Co. (Case 527). Aron-inspired suit challenging the Theodore Sutro reorganization, tried in 1891 in U.S. District Court in Carson City, Nev.

Thies MSS. A collection of Sutro manuscripts in the possession of Mr. John H. Thies of Oakland, Calif.

Transcript on Appeal, In the Matter of the Estate of Adolph Sutro, March, 1907.

U.S. *Statutes at Large, 1866.*

U.S. Congress. House of Representatives. Committee on Mines and Mining. *Report of Commissioners and Evidence Taken by the House Committee on Mines and Mining in Regard to the Sutro Tunnel.* Washington, 1872. Usually cited as *Sutro Tunnel, 1872.*

U.S. 40th Cong., 3d sess., House Resolution 1657 (Jan. 11, 1869), "A Bill to Aid in Ascertaining the Value of Public Lands Containing Mineral Lodes, and for the Endowment of a National School of Mines." Also substitute bill titled "Amendment" (Jan. 20, 1860).

U.S. 41st Cong., 1st sess., *Senate Journal,* 1869.

Unsworth Memoir, in *Material on Adolph Sutro, Vol. 1,* at Sutro Branch, California State Library, San Francisco.

UNPUBLISHED THESES

Davies, David William. "History of the Sutro Tunnel to Its Completion." Unpublished Master's Thesis, Department of History, University of California, Berkeley, 1941. Pp. 85.

Henderson, Virgil M. "The Sutro Tunnel." Unpublished Bachelor's thesis, University of Nevada, 1912. Pp. 21.

Stewart, Robert Ernest, Jr. "Adolph Sutro: A Study of His Early Career." Unpublished Ph.D. dissertation, Department of History, University of California, Berkeley, 1958. Pp. 289.

BOOKS AND ARTICLES

[Angel, Myron, ed.] *History of Nevada.* Oakland, Calif.: Thompson & West, 1882; reissued 1958 by Howell-North Books, Berkeley, Calif.

Appleton's Annual Encyclopedia, 1892.

Arnold, Bion J. *Report on the Improvement and Development of the Transportation Facilities of San Francisco.* 1913.

[Aron, Joseph.] *A Few Considerations, Respectfully Submitted to the Members of the Bar Associations.* n.p., n.d. (circa 1890).

————. *The History of a Great Work and of an Honest Miner.* Paris, 1892.

Barry, Theo., and Patten, B. A. *San Francisco, California, 1850.* 1873; reissued 1947 by Biobooks, Oakland, Calif.

Beebe, Lucius, and Clegg, Charles. *Steamcars to the Comstock.* 2nd rev. ed.; Berkeley, Calif.: Howell-North Books, 1957.

Biggs, Donald C. "Sutro Storms the Heights," *The Pony Express,* XXI (Feb., 1955), 3-6, 11.

Bullard, F. Lauriston. "Abraham Lincoln and the Statehood of Nevada," *American Bar Association Journal*, XXVI (1940), 210-13, 313-17.

Clemens, Samuel L. *Roughing It.* 1872.

————. *Sketches New and Old.* New York, 1875.

Collins, Charles, *Mercantile Guide and Directory for Virginia City, Gold Hill, Silver City, and American City.* Virginia, 1864-65.

Davis, Samuel Post, ed. *History of Nevada.* 2 vols. 1913.

Dillon, Richard H., "The Sutro Library," *News Notes of California Libraries*, LI (Apr., 1956), 338-52.

Gilbert, Col. F. T. *History of San Joaquin County.* Oakland, Calif.: Thompson & West, 1879.

Glasscock, C. B. *The Big Bonanza: The Story of the Comstock Lode.* Indianapolis, 1931.

Goodwin, C. C. *As I Remember Them.* Salt Lake City, 1913.

Hicks-Judd Co. *Handy Block Book of San Francisco, 1894.*

Holmes, Eugenia K. *Adolph Sutro: A Brief Story of a Brilliant Life.* San Francisco, 1895.

Hubbard, Harry D. *Building the Heart of an Empire.* Boston: Meador Pub. Co., 1938.

Hutchinson, Bruce. *The Fraser.* ("Rivers of America" series.) New York, 1950.

Jackson, W. Turrentine, "Journal of Lewis Richard Price," *Pacific Historian*, IV (Aug., 1960), 97-99.

————, "Lewis Richard Price, British Mining Entrepreneur and Traveler in California," *Pacific Historical Review*, XXIX (Nov., 1960), 337-48.

Jones, Idwal. *Ark of Empire: San Francisco's Montgomery Block.* Garden City, N. Y., 1951.

Kahn, Edgar M. *Cable Car Days in San Francisco.* Rev. ed.; Stanford, Calif., 1944.

Kelly, J. Wells. *Second Directory of Nevada Territory.* Virginia 1863.

Kemble, John Haskell. *The Panama Route, 1848-1869.* ("University of California Publications in History," XXIX.) Berkeley, Calif., 1943.

Kneiss, Gilbert H. *Bonanza Railroads.* 3rd ed.; Stanford, Calif., 1946.

Koford, Henning. *Dr. Samuel Merritt, His Life and Achievements.* Oakland, 1937.

[231]

Lewis, Oscar. *Silver Kings*. New York. 1947.

Lyman, George D. *Ralston's Ring: California Plunders the Comstock Lode*. New York, 1937.

Mercer, Frank B. "A Few Memories of the Late Adolph Sutro — As I Recall Them at This Late Date," *News Notes of California Libraries*, XIII (July, 1918), 271-5.

Miles, William. *Journal of the Sufferings and Hardships of Capt. Parker H. French's Overland Expedition to California*. Chambersburg, Pa., 1851.

"The Retreat of the Mayor of San Francisco," *Industry*, no. 86 (Sept., 1895), 515-18. On "Arcadia."

Richthofen, Baron Ferdinand. *The Comstock Lode: Its Character, and the Probable Mode of Its Continuance in Depth*. San Francisco, 1866.

Shinn, Charles Howard. *Story of the Mine*. New York, 1896.

Smith, Grant Horace. *History of the Comstock Lode, 1850-1920*. Reno: University of Nevada, State Bureau of Mines, 1943.

Sutro, Adolph. *The Advantages and Necessity of a Deep Drain Tunnel for the Great Comstock Ledge*. San Francisco, 1865.

————. *The Bank of California vs. the Sutro Tunnel*. n.p., n.d. 14 pp. Circa 1870.

————. *California Bank Ring against the Sutro Tunnel. Opinion of Judge Black*. Washington, 1874. 2 pp.

————. *The California Monopolists Against the Sutro Tunnel*. Washington, 1874. 6 pp.

————. *Closing Argument*. Washington, 1872.

————. *The Comstock Companies Defy the Execution of a Law of Congress*. Washington, 1874. 11 pp.

————. *The Mineral Resources of the United States*. Baltimore, 1868.

————. *Style of Warfare As Carried on by the California Bank Ring. Outrageous Attacks on the Honor and Integrity of Mr. Sutro. What Money Will Do!* Washington, 1874. 5 pp.

————. *The Sutro Tunnel*. New York, 1866.

————. *The Sutro Tunnel: An Address Before the Bullion Club, November 6th, 1879*. New York, n.d.

————. *The Sutro Tunnel in Congress*. Washington, 1870. 24 pp.

————. *A Trip to Washoe*. San Francisco: White Knight Press, 1942.

"Sutro, Adolph Heinrich Joseph," *Dictionary of American Biography*, XVIII, 224.

Sutro, Theodore. *The Sutro Tunnel Company and the Sutro Tunnel. Property, Income, Prospects, and Pending Litigation. Report to the Stockholders.* New York, 1887.

Sutro Tunnel Co. *Report of the Superintendent for the Three Months Preceding March 1, 1872.* Washington, 1872.

Tinkham, George H. *A History of Stockton.* 1880.

Triumph of Light. San Francisco, 1888.

Wright, William [pseud., Dan De Quille]. *The Big Bonanza.* 1876; reissued 1947 by Alfred A. Knopf, New York.

NEWSPAPERS

Carson Daily Appeal
Lyon County Times (Dayton, Nev.)
Elko (Nev.) Free Press
Gold Hill News
Times (London)
Reno Gazette
Daily Alta California (San Francisco)
San Francisco Bulletin
California Courier (San Francisco)
Morning Call (San Francisco)
San Francisco Chronicle
San Francisco Examiner
Pacific News (San Francisco)
Evening Post (San Francisco)
Daily Report (San Francisco)
Daily Stock Report (San Francisco)
Stockton Journal
Sutro (Nev.) Independent
Virginia City Chronicle
Daily Independent (Virginia City)
Territorial Enterprise (Virginia City)

PERIODICALS

Mining Journal (London)
Mining and Scientific Press (San Francisco)
Pacific Coast Annual Mining Review and Stock Ledger (San Francisco, 1878)

[233]

Aachen, 9-14
Adams, Edward D., 167-168
Adamson, W. R. H., 156, 176-177
Adler, Dr. Felix, 176, 192-193
Aix-la-Chapelle, 9-14
Allen, Mrs. George, 161-162, 175, 208
Ames, Pelham W., 114, 151, 157-158, 165
Angel, Myron, 126
Antelope, 2-3
Aquarium, 183-184
Arbor Day, 184
Arcadia, Napa county retreat, 172, 191, 202, 208-209
Aron, Joseph, 63, 67, 86, 113, 120, 122, 128; present for breakthrough, 149-152; challenges Adolph, 165; charges fraud, 195-196
Ashley, D. R., 68
Astor, William B., 57
Atlantic, sinks off Sutro Heights, 185

Babcock, General Orville, 131
Baldwin Hotel, 141, 170
Bancroft, Hubert Howe, 125, 192-194
Bank of California, 73-74; opens, 46; backs Sutro, 59-60; rescinds backing, 60-62; notifies New York, 64; exposed by Sutro, 79; and Sutro Tunnel Commission, 94; sends Sunderland to Washington, 97; correct in judging Sutro's hopes, 113; plot against Sutro, 122; law suits, 126; closes doors, 132

Bank ring. *See* Bank of California
Barry and Patten's, 31
Belmont, August, 57
Benjamin, F. A., Assistant Superintendent, 121-122
Bennett, James Gordon, 56
Bethel, John D., 81, 86, 108, 110, 125, 136
Bierce, Ambrose, 201
Bismarck, Count von, 65
Bluett, Jack, 121, 134-135, 138, 142-143, 147, 152
Books, 11, 178-179, 187-189, 207-208, 213
Booth, William, of Salvation Army, 191
Boyce, Thomas, 125
Browne, Ross E., 111
Browne, J. Ross, 38, 111
Brush, Colonel J. W., 113, 120, 128, 148
Bryan, William Jennings, 198
Budd, Governor James H., 209
Bullion Club, New York, 166

California, 24-26
Carnegie, Andrew, 198
Carson *Appeal*, 75
Carson City, 1, 137
Central Pacific Railroad, 69, 89, 200
Chandler, Senator, 123
Channing Auxiliary, 192, 198
Cherokee, 20-21
Clemens, Samuel: in Washoe, 38; quoted, 39-40, 66; writes to Sutro and Riley, 105

Cliff House, 174, 186, 199-200, 206
Coghlan, Rose, 198
Comstock Tunnel Co., 195-196
Concord coach, 3-4
Conness, Senator John, 67
Cooper, Peter, 57
Coulter, George T.: his background, 91; meets Sutro in New York, 92; arrives on Comstock, 95; cables from London, 96, 111; visits Nevada, 113; writes about Federal aid, 117; visits tunnel, 148; turns against Sutro, 165; refuses to produce correspondence in court, 96
Cox, Dr. Thomas H., 135
Credit Mobilier, 116

Davenport, Homer, 201
Dayton, Nev., 37, 59, 81-83, 159
De Quille, Dan (William Wright), 83
Doherty, Anna, 139

Ethical Culture Society, 192-193

Fair, James G., 131, 137, 145, 172
Federal loan. See U.S. Congress
Five-cent fare. See Street railways
Flood, James C., 131, 145
Folsom, Calif., 2, 3, 8
Foreman, Henry L., 136-138
Foster, Major General John G., 93; examined, 98-99
Frankenheimer, Bernard, cousin, 27, 212
Frankenheimer cousins in Ala., 13
Fraser River, first gold rush, 2, 32-33

Frémont, John C., 21, 32, 57
French, Parker H., expedition, 25
Fruit and Flower Mission, 192
Funding Bill, 200, 202, 209

Gillette, M. B., 149-152, 154
Ginn, John I., 126
Gold Hill, Nev., 38, 61, 73
Gold Hill News, 125
Grant, Ulysses S., 68-69, 106, 117, 119, 161, 163-164
Gulnare, 25

Hanmore, H. B., 135
Harper's Magazine, 38, 111
Harrison, Benjamin, 198
Hazlett, Dr. J. C., 85
Hearst, William Randolph, 201
Helbing, August, 26
Home for Aged Israelites, 192
Hoosac Tunnel, 90, 93, 121, 129
Huntington, Collis P., 56-57, 199-202, 208

Ice, 144, 147
Independent Party, formed by Sutro, 126

Janin, Louis, 48
Johnson, President Andrew: signs Sutro Tunnel Act, 54; impeachment trial, 68
Jones, John Percival, 71, 123, 127, 137

Kaapche, O. G., 13
Kearney, Denis, 198
Kendall, C. W., 111, 114-115, 122-123
King, A. J.: knifes Sutros, 31-32
King's Daughters, 192
Kluge, Mrs. Clarissa, 208, 210, 212

Layman, Frederick O., 181
Life Saving Station, 185-186
Lincoln, Abraham, and Nevada statehood, 42, 44-45
Little Sisters Infant Shelter, 192
London *Times,* 119
Long Wharf, San Francisco, 30

McCalmont, Hugh, 165
McCalmont, Robert, 96, 130, 165
McCalmont Brothers and Co., 91-93, 96, 119-120, 124, 128, 130, 137, 165-166, 169, 195
McGrath, Rev. T. H., 135
Mackay, John W., 131, 145
Maguire's Opera House, 43
Manogue, Rev. Father, 70
Mechanics' Institute: report, 58, 66
Memel, East Prussian port, 13-15
Mendelssohn, Felix, 11
Mercer, Frank B., 152, 164
Merritt, Emma Sutro. *See* Sutro, Emma Laura
Merritt, Dr. George W.: marries Emma, 86, 177; Sutro's business manager, 188-189
Merritt, Dr. Samuel, 86
Miller, Joaquin, 184
Mills, Darius O., 73
Mills Seminary, Oakland, 141
Mines, Comstock: Belcher, 125; California, 131-132; Chollar, 43; Chollar Potosi, 100; Consolidated Virginia, 132; big bonanza, 131; rebuilt after fire, 133; Crown Point, 59-60, 113; visited by Coulter and Price, 95; Robbins reports on, 125; Dardanelles, 125; Gould & Curry, 37, 41, 43; Hale & Norcross, during visit of Sutro Tunnel

Commissioners, 95; trouble with water, 152, 155; Kentuck, fire, 70-72; Leviathan, 125; Mexican, 42; Ophir, 42, 122; Overman, 155; Rappahannock, 114; Savage, 43, 113; signs agreement with Sutro, 59; refusal to ratify agreement, 64; visited by Sutro Tunnel Commissioners, 95; connection with Sutro Tunnel, 148-151; water in, 152; injunction incident, 153-154; Sutro mine, 41, 114; Utah, 155; Yellow Jacket, fire, 70-72
Montgomery Block, 176, 187, 207
Montgomery Street, 30-31, 190
Moore, Elliott J., 146, 176-177
Morbio, Pio, married by Rosa Victoria, 208
Moss, George, 179
Mules, 109, 142, 147

Napa county property (Arcadia), 172, 191, 202, 208-209
National School of Mines, 69
Negley, James S., 123
Negley amendment, 123, 131
Nevada, admission as state, 42, 44-45
Nevada legislature: grants Sutro a tunnel franchise, 47; resolution favors Federal aid, 57-58, 61
Nevada Territory, 44
New World, 2-3
Newcomb, Wesley: examined, 99-100; quoted, 107
Newspapers. *See* cities of publication
Nye, Senator James W., 64, 66; death, 138

O'Brien, William S., 131
Ormsby House, 172

Panama, Isthmus of: crossed by Sutro, 1850, 21-25; crossed by Sutro, 1866, 53
Panama Railroad, 53
Parallel, explosion of, 186
People's Party (Populists), 202-203
Phelan, Mayor James, 209
Pioneer Stage Co., 1
Piper's Opera House, 43; Sutro's tunnel speech, 77-80; political speech by Sutro, 127
Placerville, Calif., 1, 7
Pony Express, 6
Populist Party, 202-203
Price, Lewis Richard: meets Sutro, 92; visits Comstock, 95
Pyramid Lake battle, reported by Sutro, 34-35

Ralston, William C., 46, 48, 52, 59, 60-62, 66, 72-73, 132
Rammelkamp, Clara, 164
Rammelkamp, George, 136, 142-143; married, 139
Ranches, Gee and Moore, purchased by tunnel company, 114-115
Randohr, John, 26, 36-37
Raw, R. S., 134-135, 137, 143
Raymond, R. W., 100
Reese Building, 170
Requa, Isaac H., 94, 100, 125, 127, 146
Revolutions of 1848, 12-13
Richthofen, Baron Ferdinand, 47, 49, 50-51, 66
Riley, J. H., 105

Robbins, James J., 125
Roberts, Bolivar ("Ball"), 39

Sacramento, 2-3
Sacramento Valley Railroad, 3
Salvation Army, 190-191
San Francisco: in 1850, 26-27; in 1880, 170-171
San Francisco *Alta California*, 2, 105; Sutro's articles in, 5-8; Mark Twain quoted from, 66
San Francisco *Bulletin*, 2; Sutro's account of battle of Pyramid Lake, 34-36
San Francisco *California Courier*, 26
San Francisco *Call*, 186
San Francisco *Examiner*, 207
San Francisco *Herald*, 2
San Francisco *Pacific News*, 26
San Francisco *Picayune*, 26
San Francisco *Real Estate Circular*, 171
Sargent, Senator Aaron, 124
Savage mine. *See* Mines, Comstock
Seals, protection improved, 182-183
Seligman, Abraham, 86
Seligman & Co., J. & W., 57, 93, 118-120, 128
Shafts, to aid digging of tunnel, 108, 115, 117, 132
Sharon, William, 46, 48, 59, 61-62, 66, 72-74, 137, 172; campaign for U. S. Senator, 124-127
Sheldon, Assistant Superintendent, 144, 153, 159
Ship disasters, 185-186
Sierra Buttes mine in California, 91-92
Silver City, Nev., 37

Silver Street Kindergarten, 177
Smith, Grant H., quoted, 55, 59
"Smoking Turk," Sutro's automaton, 31
Southern Pacific Railroad, 199-200, 203
Statue of Liberty, 187, 212
Stevens, Thaddeus, 68
Stewart, William M., 45, 48, 56, 66, 90
Stockton, Calif.: Sutro in, 27-29; fire of 1851, 27-28
Stonehill, E. J., 162
Street railways: Ferries and Cliff House, 182; Market Street Cable, 181; Park and Ocean, 181; Powell Street, 182; Sutro, 199-200, 202, 208; Telegraph Hill Cable, 181
Sunderland, Thomas, 97-102
Sutro (town): projected, 54-55; lots sold, 111-112; first child born, 118; sorrow, 129; booms, 156-159; declines, 159; General Grant's visit, 163-164
Sutro, Adolph: birthplace, 10; schooling, 10; childhood, 10-11; leaves school, 12; at Memel, 14-19; forced to go to U. S., 19; leaves New York for California, 20; journey via the Isthmus of Panama, 20-26; fire watcher in San Francisco, 26; joins cousin in Stockton, 27; sends for brothers, 27; establishes stores in San Francisco, 30; knifed, 32; votes and is married, 32; to Fraser River, 32; first trip to Washoe, 1-9; prepares for Washoe, 34; develops milling process with Randohr, 36-37; establishes

Sutro, Adolph (Continued)
mill at Dayton, 37; meets Samuel Clemens, 38; mill burns, 40; to first state legislature for tunnel franchise, 46; forms Nevada tunnel association, 48; to U. S. Congress for franchise (1866), 53; Nevada legislature expresses confidence and requests Federal loan, 57; Bank of California withdraws support (1867), 62; Adolph's sacred vow, 63; to Europe for money (1867), 65; return to Washington noted by Clemens, 65-66; publishes Mineral Resources of the U. S. (1868), 67; proposes National School of Mines (1869), 69; concern over disastrous Yellow Jacket fire, 72-74; miners unions agree to subscribe $50,000, 76; speech at Piper's Opera House, 77-80; "first pick" speech, 83; maintains medical facilities for workers, 85; forms Sutro Tunnel Co., a California corporation (1869), 87; receives five-twelfths interest in the company, 87; made General Superintendent, 87; defeats House Bill 1179 (1870), 90; obtains a Federal tunnel commission (1871), 92; on Comstock with the commission, 95; to London and then Washington (1872), 96; examines commissioners, 98-101; closing argument, 101-102; correspondence with Clemens on Riley, 105; gives illustrated lectures, 106; publishes Sutro Tunnel, 1872, 107; es-

Sutro, Adolph *(Continued)*
tablishes telegraph line, 108;
on mules, 109; plans Nevada
mansion, 110; establishes town
of Sutro, 112; maneuvers to
control mines, 113; acquires
frontage on Carson River (two
ranches), 114; enters politics,
114; returns to Washington
(1872), 115; visits mines and
tunnels in Europe (1873), 118;
Kendall recalls him to Washington (1874), 122; gets Senate Bill 16 postponed, 124;
sponsors newspaper, 125; runs
for U. S. Senator against Sharon, 125-126; to London (1874),
128; to Washington (1875),
131; to Nevada, 131; granted
salary, 133; to Washington
(1876), 136; to Pacific Coast,
then England (1876), 137;
contacts with family, 139-
141; seeks royalty agreements
(1878), 145-146, 152, 155-156;
enters Savage mine via tunnel
(1878), 151; "It Is Finished"
(1879), 160; scandal, 162; to
New York (1879), 163; tele-
graphs Ames re Aron, 165;
sells his tunnel stock (1880),
167-168; to San Francisco, 170;
to Nevada to obtain seat in U.
S. Senate (1880), 172-173; returns to California (1881), 173;
buys Tetlow cottage overlooking sea, 174; buys San Miguel
rancho, 174; writes will (1882),
174-176; takes world tour
(1882-1883), 176-177; writes
from Jerusalem (1884), 177;
buys books, 178-179; returns to

Sutro, Adolph *(Continued)*
San Francisco, 180; finances
street railways (1884), 181-
182; to Mexico (1889), 188; to
Europe and return, 189; religious views, 193-194; radical
economic ideas, 194; attacked
by Aron, 196; at home, 198;
fights Huntington on two
fronts, 200; mayoralty campaign, 203-204; Mayor of San
Francisco, 204-209; declared
mentally incompetent, 210;
death and funeral, 213. *See also*
Sutro Tunnel; Sutro Tunnel Co.
Sutro, Charles, cousin, 31
Sutro, Charles W., son, 52, 63,
140-141, 150, 170, 177, 188,
210-211
Sutro, Clara, daughter, 63, 140-
141, 155, 158, 170, 208, 210-
211
Sutro, Edgar, son, 52, 63, 140-
141, 150, 170, 177
Sutro, Emanuel, father, 9; just to
children, 10; takes Otto to see
Mendelssohn, 11; accident and
death, 12
Sutro, Emil, brother, 29, 212
Sutro, Emma Laura, daughter,
33, 52, 87, 140-141, 170, 173-
174, 208; obtains M.D. degree,
141; marries George W. Merritt, M.D., 177; father writes
from Jerusalem, 177; appointed
father's guardian, 210-212
Sutro, Gussie Emanuel, son, 34,
52
Sutro, Gustav, cousin, 31; to
Fraser River, 32; gets street
railway franchise, 182; death,
212

Sutro, Hugo, brother: to San Francisco, 29; to Nevada, 38; correspondence with Adolph, 139-140

Sutro, Kate, daughter, 52, 63, 140-141, 150-151, 170, 177, 208

Sutro, Laura, sister, 10, 17; death, 139

Sutro, Ludwig, brother, 17, 191

Sutro, Otto, brother: musical career encouraged, 11; remains in Brussels, 19; to San Francisco, 29; death, 212

Sutro, Rosa Victoria, daughter, 33, 140-141, 150-151, 170; married, 208

Sutro, Rosa Warendorf, mother: bears Adolph, 9; widowed, 12; takes children to U. S., 19; allows Adolph to go to California, 20; celebrates eightieth birthday, 177; death, 177

Sutro, S. & E., factory in Aachen, 9-13

Sutro, Sali, brother: helps run factory, 12; goes to U. S., 13; urges family to come, 17-18; described by Hugo, 139

Sutro, Simon, uncle: partner in woolen mill, 9, 11

Sutro, Theodore, brother: reorganizes Sutro Tunnel Co., 195-196

Sutro & Co., stock brokers, 31

Sutro & Frankenheimer: store in Stockton, 27-29

Sutro Baths, 189-190, 202, 208

Sutro Heights: purchased, 173-175; in will, 176; development, 180, 187; damaged by explosion of schooner, 186; prominent guests, 198; as a public park, 212

Sutro *Independent,* 138, 154, 156, 160

Sutro Library, 178-179, 187-189, 207-208, 213. *See also* Books

Sutro mansion, 110, 112, 158, 163-164

Sutro Mill, 37-38; burns, 40

Sutro Railroad Co., 200, 208. *See also* Street railways

Sutro Tunnel: conceived by Adolph Sutro, 5; Nevada franchise, 47; Nevada association formed, 48; Congress grants franchise, 53-54; "first pick," 82-83; in 52½ ft., 84; Sutro Tunnel Co., a California corp., formed, 87; on one shift, 92; on full shifts, 96; header in 2,792 ft., 109; eighteen men working, 115; expenses, 117; locomotives purchased, 117; Burleigh drills introduced, 121; progress, 128; casualty rate, 129; water problem, 131; bulkhead discussed, 131; progress, 131-132; header in 3,726 ft., 134; slow progress, 137; clay, 141; bulkhead nearly ready, 146; hot and humid, 146-147; break-through nears, 148; accomplished, 150; injunction incident, 153-154; flooded by Hale & Norcross, 155; laterals and drain begun, 156; tunnel finished, 160; visited by General Grant, 164; later history, 168. *See also* Sutro Tunnel Co.; Sutro, Adolph

[241]

Sutro Tunnel, 1872: book printed, 106-107

Sutro Tunnel Act (1866), 53-54

Sutro Tunnel Commission: created, 92; first meeting, 93; visits Comstock, 94; report of the commission, 96-97; commissioners examined before the House committee, 97-102; conclusions of the commission overruled, 102

Sutro Tunnel Co.: Nevada association formed, 48; contracts with mines, 48-49; California corporation formed, 86; shares authorized, 87; shares to Sutro, 87; Sutro's position, 103-104; rights of company, 126; first mortgage given on tunnel, 130; financial changes, 133; lack of royalty contracts, 145; new president, 146; projects, 152; injunction against, 153-154; royalty agreements signed, 155-156; active market for stock, 167-169; stockholders' equity saved by Theodore Sutro, 195-196. *See also* Sutro Tunnel; Sutro, Adolph

Telegraph, built via line of tunnel, 108

Tetlow, Samuel, 173-174

Toland Medical School, 141, 207, 213

Trees: Aachen, 11; Sutro, Nev., 112, 157; San Francisco, 184-185

Triumph of Light, statue, 187, 212

Trundle, Miss Hattie ("Mrs. George Allen"), 161-162, 175, 208

Union Mill and Mining Co., organized, 46

Union Pacific Railroad, 69, 116

U. S. Congress: passes Sutro Tunnel Act (1866), 53-54; loan for tunnel first proposed, 57; petition requesting loan, 64; House Bill 1179 secretly proposed, 89; defeated, 90; warned of "corruption fund," 122; Negley amendment proposed, 123, 131

U. S. Congress. House of Representatives. Committee on Mines and Mining, 68-69; hearings on report of Sutro Tunnel Commission, 97-102; recommends loan of $2 million, 102; passes Senate Bill 16, 123

U. S. Congress. House of Representatives. Committee on Ways and Means: visits Comstock, 74

U. S. Congress. Senate. Committee on the Judiciary: recommends postponement of action on Senate Bill 16, 124

U. S. Congress. Senate. Committee on Mines and Mining, 123

University of California, medical school, 207, 213

Unsworth, Archibald C., 188

Utah Territory, 2, 5

Vanderbilt, Commodore, 57

Vigilance, Committee of (San Francisco, 1851), 29

Virginia and Gold Hill Miners'
Unions: subscribe $50,000 to
tunnel, 76
Virginia and Truckee Railroad,
72-73
Virginia City, 61; naming, 4-5;
in 1860, 5; in 1861, 37; in 1864,
41-46; first train, 73; men out
of work, 118; fire of 1875, 133;
Sutro goes to by way of tunnel,
151
Virginia City *Chronicle*, 135, 151
Virginia City *Independent:* is
founded, 125; supplement, 127;
closes down, 130
Virginia City *Territorial Enterprise*, 38-40, 75-80, 83, 125

Washoe country, 2, 4; its appeal
to Sutro, 33-34
Washoe Stock and Exchange
Board, 41
Ways and Means Committee.
See U. S. Congress. House of
Rep.
Wiggin, Kate Douglas, 198
Wilde, Oscar, 198
Woodford's, 1, 6
Wright, Major General H. G., 93;
examined, 100

Yellow Jacket mine: fire, 70-72.
See also Mines, Comstock
Yosemite Valley, 142
Young, Frank S., 134, 172

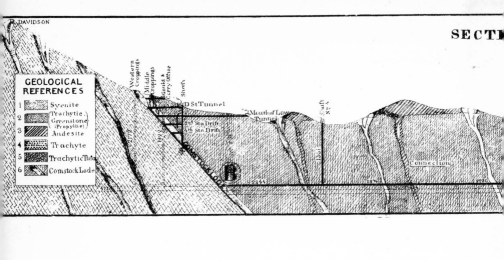

GEOLOGICAL REFERENCES

1	Syenite
2	Trachytic Greenstone (Propylite)
3	Andesite
4	Trachyte
5	Trachytic Tufa
6	Comstock Lode

DAVIDSON

Western Croppings
Middle Croppings
Gould & Curry Office
Shaft
D St Tunnel
3d Sta Drift
4th Sta Drift
Mouth of Lower Tunnel
South Sea
Connection

COMSTOCK LODE

B

LONGITUDINAL SEC

SHOWING THE WORKIN

SUT

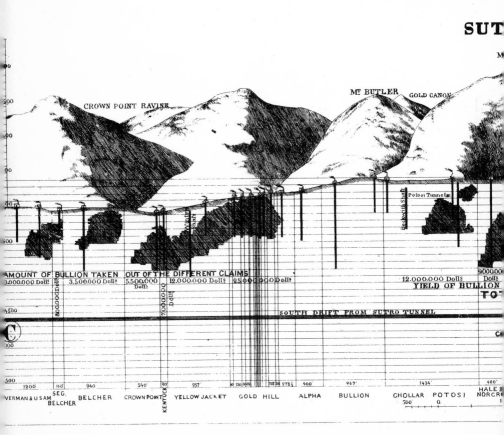

CROWN POINT RAVINE

Mt BUTLER   GOLD CANON

White Shaft
Beckwith Shaft
Potosi Tunnel

AMOUNT OF BULLION TAKEN OUT OF THE DIFFERENT CLAIMS

| 3,000,000 Dolls | 3,500,000 Dolls | 5,500,000 Dolls | 12,000,000 Dolls | 25,000,000 Dolls | 12,000,000 Dolls | 900,000 Dolls |

YIELD OF BULLION
TO

SOUTH DRIFT FROM SUTRO TUNNEL

C

1200	160	940	540	90	957	60 130 56	115 94 278½	400	967	1434	400

VERMAN & U S AM.   SEG. BELCHER   BELCHER   CROWN POINT   KENTUCK   YELLOW JACKET   GOLD HILL   ALPHA   BULLION   CHOLLAR POTOSI   HALE & NORCR

500   0